ENGLAND IN SHAKESPEARE'S DAY

BY

G. B. HARRISON, M.A.

LECTURER IN ENGLISH LITERATURE AT KING'S COLLEGE, UNIVERSITY OF LONDON

NEW YORK
HARCOURT, BRACE AND COMPANY

First Published in 1928

CONTENTS

			PAGE
INTRODUCTION			ix

SECTION I. THE COURT

I	OUR QUEEN	*Lyly*	1
II	QUEEN ELIZABETH ON PROGRESS	*Lyly*	3
III	A LAMENT FOR SIR PHILIP SIDNEY	*Spenser*	8
IV	SIR PHILIP SIDNEY	*Greville*	10
V	FULKE GREVILLE'S EPITAPH		11
VI	THE DEATH OF QUEEN ELIZABETH	*Carey*	11
VII	SIR ROBERT CAREY'S RIDE	*Carey*	13
VIII	THE CHARACTER OF KING JAMES	*Howard*	15
IX	THE OVERBURY MURDER	*Bacon*	18
X	THE MARRIAGE OF PRINCESS ELIZABETH	*Anon.*	23
XI	ON HIS MISTRESS, THE QUEEN OF BOHEMIA	*Wotton*	28
XII	THE RASCAL MULTITUDE	*Harrison*	29

SECTION II. THE SERVICE OF THE STATE

I	DEGREE	*Shakespeare*	31
II	MACHIAVEL	*Marlowe*	32
III	THE TROUBLES OF STATECRAFT	*R. Cecil*	33
IV	THE PRIVILEGES OF NOBLEMEN	*Peacham*	34
V	AN INNS OF COURT MAN	*Overbury*	36
VI	THE LAST FIGHT OF THE "REVENGE"	*Ralegh*	37
VII	AN AMBASSADOR'S LETTER	*Winwood*	42
VIII	RAISING RECRUITS	*Shakespeare*	45
IX	DRILLING THE TRAIN-BANDS	*Beaumont and Fletcher*	50
X	SEDITIONS AND TROUBLES	*Bacon*	52

v

			PAGE
XI	CANKERS OF THE COMMONWEALTH	Anon.	53
XII	A FALSE ALARM	Chamberlain	57
XIII	AN APPEAL FOR UNITY	Shakespeare	60

SECTION III. EDUCATION AND YOUTH

I	PARSON AND SCHOOLMASTER	Shakespeare	61
II	MUSIC IN THE SCHOOL CURRICULUM	Mulcaster	62
III	IN THE SCHOOLROOM	Marston	64
IV	A LESSON IN ACTING	Anon.	67
V	THE IDEAL STUDENT: RULES FOR BEHAVIOUR AT THE UNIVERSITY	Peacham	71
VI	REVELS AT GRAY'S INN	Anon.	73
VII	THE WOES OF A PRIVATE TUTOR	Anon.	74
VIII	ALCHEMIST'S JARGON	Jonson	76
IX	THE PATHWAY TO PREFERMENT	Powell	80

SECTION IV. TRAVEL AND TRADE

I	THE ENTHUSIASTIC TRAVELLER	Coryat	84
II	THE CHARACTER OF AN AFFECTATE TRAVELLER	Overbury	87
III	THE BOGUS TRAVELLER	Anon.	88
IV	CORYAT AND THE JEWS	Coryat	90
V	THE IDEAL WEAVER'S FACTORY	Deloney	92
VI	THE JOLLY SHOEMAKERS	Dekker	94
VII	IN PRAISE OF THE RED HERRING	Nashe	99
VIII	ADVICE TO YOUNG SAILORS	Smith	101
IX	TO THE VIRGINIAN VOYAGE	Drayton	103
X	THE RICHES OF VIRGINIA	Jonson, Chapman and Marston	105
XI	CAPTAIN BOBADILL ON TOBACCO	Jonson	107
XII	THE USURER'S WAYS	Lodge and Greene	108
XIII	THIS HEROIC AGE	Hakluyt	111

SECTION V. LONDON LIFE

I	PAUL'S WALK	Dekker	115
II	THE NIP AND THE FOIST	Greene	117
III	QUACKS	Chettle	119
IV	THE BARBER AND HIS WAYS	Lyly	121
V	THE WATCH	Dekker	124
VI	THE WICKEDNESS OF BALLAD SINGERS	Greene	126

CONTENTS

			PAGE
VII	BARTHOLOMEW FAIR	Stow	128
VIII	IN THE TAVERN	Heywood	129
IX	THE EIGHT KINDS OF DRUNKENNESS	Nashe	130
X	THE HORRORS OF PLAGUE . .	Dekker	131
XI	A MORALIST'S OBJECTION TO PLAYS	Gosson	132
XII	A SCHOLAR'S OBJECTION TO PLAYS	Sidney	134
XIII	A DEFENCE OF PLAYS . . .	Nashe	136
XIV	THE PLAYGOER	Marston	138
XV	A BOY ACTOR	Jonson	138
XVI	PUBLIUS, WHO LOVED BEAR-BAITING	Davies	139
XVII	AN EXECUTION	Anon.	140
XVIII	A BALLAD	Deloney	143

SECTION VI. COUNTRY LIFE

I	INNOVATIONS	Harrison	148
II	OF GARDENS	Bacon	150
III	SWEET ANKOR IN ARDEN . .	Drayton	154
IV	THE SCENT OF MOTHER EARTH.	Browne	155
V	POOR WAT	Shakespeare	156
VI	THE SIMPLE LIFE	Campion	157
VII	COURT LIFE AND COUNTRY LIFE .	Shakespeare	158
VIII	ENGLISH INNS	Moryson	160
IX	COUNTRY RECREATIONS . . .	Markham	163
X	THE PERFECT ANGLER . . .	Markham	165
XI	EATING AND DRINKING . . .	Harrison	168
XII	ENCLOSURES FOR SHEEP FARMING	Bastard	171

SECTION VII. MATTERS OF RELIGION

I	THE CHURCH OF ENGLAND . .	Harrison	172
II	SIMONY	Weever	173
III	THE CHARACTER OF A CHURCH PAPIST	Earle	173
IV	THE SPANISH INQUISITION . .	Hasleton	174
V	THE ENGLISH COLLEGE AT ROME	Munday	179
VI	A SEMINARY PRIEST	Dekker	183
VII	THE DANGERS OF THE PURITAN MOVEMENT	Hooker	183
VIII	THE PURITAN AT BARTHOLOMEW FAIR	Jonson	185
IX	HORROR OF HELL FIRE . . .	Greene	188

viii ENGLAND IN SHAKESPEARE'S DAY

			PAGE
X	HORROR OF HELL FIRE	Dekker	190
XI	"THE SPIRITS CALLED THE FAIRY"	King James	191
XII	A WISE WOMAN	Chettle	193
XIII	EVIL SPIRITS AVAUNT	Spenser	195

SECTION VIII. MEN OF LETTERS

I	A DEFENCE OF THE ENGLISH TONGUE	Mulcaster	196
II	THE PATRON AND THE POET	Anon.	198
III	THE POET AT WORK	Dekker	199
IV	LITERARY SOCIETY IN DUBLIN	Bryskett	200
V	THE MERMAID TAVERN	Beaumont	203
VI	A POT POET	Earle	206
VII	TO MY BOOKSELLER	Jonson	207
VIII	THE CHARACTER OF BEN JONSON	Drummond	207
IX	GABRIEL HARVEY ON ROBERT GREENE	Harvey	208
X	JONSON ON SHAKESPEARE	Jonson	210
XI	THE OLD POET REMEMBERS HIS YOUTH	Drayton	211
XII	THE POETS' ELYSIUM	Dekker	212

SECTION IX. MOODS AND MANNERS

I	THE ITALIANATE	Ascham	215
II	APING THE GREAT	Jonson	217
III	HOW TO BECOME A GENTLEMAN	Jonson	218
IV	THE GULL	Davies	222
V	THE MELANCHOLIC HUMOUR	Shakespeare	223
VI	THE DANCER	Marston	224
VII	DRESS	Harrison	225
VIII	FOLLIES AND FASHIONS	Lane	227
IX	THESE DEGENERATE DAYS	Riche	229
X	THESE DEGENERATE DAYS	Jonson	230
XI	THE NEEDY BORE	Donne	231

THE ENVOI	Shakespeare	235
INDEX		237

INTRODUCTION

IF a foreign historian wished to write the history of the English people during the first quarter of the twentieth century he would find ample material at hand. For statistics of trade, population, national income and the like he would turn to the Blue Books and other official compilations; for the administration of justice to the Law Reports; for legislation to Hansard; for a record of events, day by day or week by week, to *The Times* or the periodicals; and from these sources he would be able to compile an exact and detailed account of the things done by the English people. But much would be missing; the result would be a photograph and not a picture, giving the features only, and telling very little of the mind of the nation, especially as revealed in its everyday life; for newspapers, law courts and government departments are not much concerned with the commonplaces of humanity, nor with the ideals and problems of ordinary folk. The burning desire of the townsman to escape into the country finds no expression in the debates of Parliament until the charabanc becomes a nuisance to the Rural District Council.

To complete his picture the historian would needs leave the definite information of his Blue Books and to grope in the literature of the people of England for the inner life of those who read and wrote its books. And here he would perceive, without being able to define his feelings with any exactness, how, for instance, the romantic idealism of the 1880's, expressed by Lord Tennyson, merged into the national idealism of Mr. Rudyard Kipling in the Boer

War period, and was succeeded by the social idealisms of Mr. Bernard Shaw of the years before the War; and then how idealism for a time seemed to be blotted out altogether until it begins slowly to emerge in a new feeling towards co-operation between employer and worker.

With the period covered approximately by the life of Shakespeare, that is from about 1560 to 1625, the historian has much the same problem. Naturally there is less material; there are neither Blue Books nor newspapers; but detailed accounts of the business transacted in Parliament survive; the correspondence books of the Privy Council, which was an even more important body than the Cabinet to-day, are easily accessible; and by grouping together the records scattered in the collections of the State Papers, City Records, and Historical Manuscripts in private collections, a very complete account of Elizabethan England can be compiled.

In literature, however, the difficulties are greater. For the first two decades of this period, English literature is somewhat barren; the Muses were numb and torpid in those years, moving their stiff limbs slowly and laboriously.

The year 1579 is a landmark; Spenser published *The Shepherd's Calendar*, the greatest experiment in English poetry since the death of Chaucer; Lyly his *Euphues*; and Gosson did poets a good turn by attacking them in his *School of Abuse*, thereby rousing artists of all sorts to formulate their ideals in defence of their craft. The next twelve years were a time of experiment in technique; amongst the more important works in prose being Sidney's *Arcadia* and *The Apology for Poetry*, to be followed by the early euphuistic novels of Greene and Lodge; in verse by Spenser's *Complaints* and the first books of the *Fairy Queen*; in drama by Lyly's Court comedies, and, on the public stages, by Marlowe's *Tamburlane* and *Dr. Faustus*, Kyd's *Spanish Tragedy*, Greene's *Friar Bacon*, Peele's *Old Wives' Tale*. English writers were as yet more concerned with entertaining, apart from Sidney, Spenser and their group who were moved by a lofty idealism that poets

INTRODUCTION

"imitate both to delight and teach, and delight to move men to take that goodness in hand which without delight they would fly as from a stranger, and teach to make them know that goodness whereunto they are moved."

In the next decade (1590-1600) English writers passed beyond the stage of experimenting merely with form and now began to widen the range of their subjects. Marlowe's tragedies—*Dr. Faustus* and *The Jew of Malta*—are more than mere stage plays : they are concerned, though perhaps not very deeply, with psychological problems. Similarly in prose Greene ceased writing romantic love stories and in the winter of 1591 and spring of 1592 produced a series of pamphlets describing the tricks of the professional thieves and rascals about London. In poetry Spenser continued to allegorize his ideals in the *Fairy Queen*; but he was with the old and not the new generation, looking back to the Middle Ages for his models and not a little disgruntled at the apparent decadence of the younger poets and the lack of practical appreciation of his own work. The younger poets meanwhile were exploring many new tracts of knowledge and experience. From the sensuous romance of *Venus and Adonis* and *Hero and Leander* they passed to the subtle analyses or poems of ideas or sonneteering shown in Donne's earlier poems, Daniel's *Delia*, Chapman's *School of Night*, Davies' *Nosce teipsum*, Drayton's *Idea's Mirror*; or else to the castigation and delineation of the follies and vice of their contemporaries in satires of various grades of bitterness.

On the stage at the end of the century the simple stories of the older plays gave way to a new kind of drama wherein the characterization was of more importance than the plot ; in tragedy this can be seen in *Hamlet* and *Othello* ; in comedy the " Humour Plays " of Ben Jonson displayed rather the foolishnesses of ordinary types of Londoner than the romance of the Forest of Arden or the Woods near Athens. But so many and various are the subjects and themes of writers after the turn of the century that no brief summary can be made of the tendencies of these years. In the main the most noticeable trait is the air of melancholy and disillusion which creeps into literature. The causes were complex: bitter religious differences at home, unsuccessful and indecisive campaigns abroad; a general feeling of pessimism that when Queen Elizabeth died the country would once more be torn by civil wars; changes in social conditions felt but not understood—all these contributed to the general causes of pessimism.

New values were being created; money became more plentiful and men with money more powerful; at the same time the old ideals declined, and it is not surprising that to thinking men, as they saw all the things that they venerated most apparently falling into decay, the universe appeared "no other thing than a foul and pestilent congregation of vapours". Early in the sixteenth century the great humanists, such as More or Colet, had greeted the revival of learning as a new birth; after a hundred years' accumulation of new books, it was found that increase of knowledge had after all but increased man's realization of his own ignorance. All these feelings are expressed in the literature of the time; most of them, to go no farther, by Shakespeare.

At the same time it is always dangerous to generalize, and it needs very considerable study and skill to discern how far a writer is expressing the feelings of a nation or is simply writing for a small coterie of malcontents; for the Elizabethan reading public was divided into its own groups, and the more intellectual a writer, the less, usually, his public.

The task of selecting passages from Elizabethan writers which show English life in English literature is still further complicated by the fact that with certain exceptions most of the greatest writers are not much interested in the externals of ordinary existence. There are many books which describe or chronicle English life, but seldom are they of any great literary merit; these are such as the *Annals* which the antiquarian John Stow put together year by year: useful enough to the historian, but com-

INTRODUCTION xiii

piled in a tortuous style which reflects the heavy mind. Nor is Holinshed much better, though prefaced to his Chronicles (published in 1577 and 1587) is a most important account of contemporary England written by William Harrison, an Essex parson, who kept his eyes open and recorded what he saw. But in general it is true to say that the nearer an Elizabethan writer is to describing literally, the farther is he from being an artist. There are very few scenes in Shakespeare, apart from the Falstaff plays, which can in any way be claimed as true transcripts of English life; and even Ben Jonson's London types are caricatures, recognizable indeed, and valuable to the student of manners, but no nearer as portraits of living men than Cruikshank's illustrations to the *Pickwick Papers*.

Accordingly in this collection, though many of the passages describe Elizabethan life, most of them have been selected as much to catch the atmosphere as the moods of the period. They come therefore for the most part from the great writers, for only a great writer can preserve and transmit the subtle essence of his time; Jaques in Arden or Hamlet at Elsinore tell us more in a dozen lines of the "melancholick humour" than all Dr. Timothy Bright's *Treatise of Melancholy*.

This book, in short, is a gallery of Elizabethan pictures; it does not attempt to give a complete survey map of life in Shakespeare's day.

As it is not intended for the textual student, the spelling and punctuation of the original texts have been modernized throughout. To enable those who wish to read these extracts in their contexts, references are given to the most accessible editions.

G. B. HARRISON

KING'S COLLEGE
UNIVERSITY OF LONDON
July 1928

ENGLAND IN SHAKESPEARE'S DAY

SECTION ONE

THE COURT

I. OUR QUEEN

JOHN LYLY. Euphues' Glass for Europe, 1580 ; *vol. 2, page 206 in Bond's edition. The praise of Queen Elizabeth which occurs so constantly in Elizabethan literature is not merely the lip service of place-hunting courtiers, as can be seen by comparing the remarks passed on her successor.*

But being now placed in the seat royal, she first of all established religion, banished Popery, advanced the Word, that was before so much defaced, who having in her hand the sword to revenge, used rather bountifully to reward, being as far from rigour when she might have killed, as her enemies were from honesty when they could not, giving a general pardon when she had cause to use particular punishments, preferring the name of pity before the remembrance of perils, thinking no revenge more princely than to spare when she might spill, to stay when she might strike, to prefer to save with mercy when she might have destroyed with justice. Here is the clemency worthy commendation and admiration, nothing inferior to the gentle disposition of Aristides who after his exile did not so much as note them that had banished him, saying with Alexander that there can be nothing more noble than to do well to those that deserve ill.

This mighty and merciful Queen, having many bills of private persons, that sought before time to betray her, burnt them all, resembling Julius Caesar, who being presented with the like complaints of his commons, threw them into the fire, saying that he had rather not to know the names of the rebels than have occasion to revenge, thinking it better to be ignorant of those that hated him than to be angry with them.

This clemency did Her Majesty not only show at her coming to the crown but also throughout her whole government when she hath spared to shed their bloods that sought to spill hers, not racking the laws to extremity but mitigating the rigour with mercy insomuch as it may be said of that royal monarch as it was of Antoninus, surnamed the Godly Emperor, who reigned many years without the effusion of blood. What greater virtue can there be in a Prince than mercy, what greater praise than to abate the edge which she should whet, to pardon where she should punish, to reward where she should revenge?

I myself being in England when Her Majesty was for her recreation in her barge upon the Thames, heard of a gun that was shot off, though of the party unwittingly, yet to her noble person dangerously, which fact she most graciously pardoned, accepting a just excuse before a great amends, taking more grief for her poor bargeman that was a little hurt than care for herself that stood in greatest hazard. O rare example of pity! O singular spectacle of piety!

Divers besides have there been which by private conspiracies, open rebellions, close wiles, cruel witchcrafts, have sought to end her life, which saveth all their lives, whose practices by the Divine Providence of the Almighty have ever been disclosed, insomuch that He hath kept her safe in the whale's belly when her subjects went about to throw her into the sea, preserved her in the hot oven when her enemies increased the fire, not suffering a hair to fall from her, much less any harm to fasten upon her. These injuries and treasons of her subjects, these policies and undermining of foreign nations so little moved her, that she would often say, "Let them know that though it be not lawful for them to speak what they list, yet it is lawful for us to do with them what we list ", being always of that merciful mind, which was in Theodosius, who wished rather that he might call the dead to life than put the living to death, saying with Augustus, when she should set her hand to any condemnation, "I would to God we could not write." Infinite were the ensamples that might be alleged, and almost incredible, whereby she hath showed herself a lamb in meekness, when she had cause to be a lion in might, proved a dove in favour when she was provoked to be an eagle in fierceness, requiting injuries with benefits, revenging grudges with gifts, in highest majesty bearing the lowest mind, forgiving all that sued for mercy, and forgetting all that deserved justice.

O divine nature! O heavenly nobility! what thing can there more be required in a prince than in greatest power to show greatest patience, in chiefest glory to bring forth chiefest grace, in abundance of all earthly pomp to manifest abundance of all heavenly piety? O fortunate England that hath such a Queen; ungrateful if thou pray not for her, wicked if thou do not love her, miserable if thou lose her.

Here, ladies, is a glass for all princes to behold, that being called to dignity they use moderation, not might, tempering the severity of the laws with the mildness of love, not executing all they will, but showing what they may. Happy are they, and only they, that are under this glorious and gracious sovereignty, insomuch that I accompt all those abjects that be not her subjects.

II. QUEEN ELIZABETH ON PROGRESS

The Honourable Entertainment given to the Queen's Majesty in Progress, at Elvetham in Hampshire, by the Right Honourable the Earl of Hertford, 1591. Printed in Bond's edition of Lyly's Works, Vol. I, *pages 432 and 447.*

Elvetham House being situate in a park but of two miles in compass or thereabouts, and of no great receipt, as being none of the Earl's chief mansion houses, yet for the desire he had to show his unfeigned love and loyal duty to Her Most Gracious Highness, purposing to visit him in this her late progress, whereof he had to understand by the ordinary guess, as also by his honourable good friends in Court near to Her Majesty, his Honour with all expedition set artificers a work, to the number of three hundred, many days before Her Majesty's arrival to enlarge his house with new rooms and offices. Whereof I omit to speak how many were destined to the offices of the Queen's household, and will only make mention of other such buildings as were raised on the sudden, fourteen score off from the house on a hillside, within the said park, for entertainment of nobles, gentlemen and others whatsoever.

First there was made a room of estate for the nobles, and at the end thereof, a withdrawing place for Her Majesty. The outsides of the walls were all covered with boughs, and clusters of ripe hazel nuts, the insides with arras, the roof of the place with works of ivy leaves, the floor with sweet herbs and green rushes.

Near adjoining unto this, were many offices newly builded, as namely, spicery, lardery, chaundery,[1] wine-cellar, ewery [2] and pantry; all which were tiled. Not far off, was erected a large hall, for entertainment of knights, ladies and gentlemen of chief account.

There was also a several place for Her Majesty's footmen and their friends.

Then was there a long bower for Her Majesty's Guard.

An other for other officers of Her Majesty's house.

An other to entertain all comers, suitors and such-like.

An other for my Lord's Steward, to keep his table in.

An other for his gentleman that waited.

Most of these aforesaid rooms were furnished with tables, and the tables carried 23 yards in length.

Moreover on the same hill, there was raised a great common buttery.

A pitcher house.

[1] Candle store.   [2] Plate store.

THE COURT 5

A large pastery, with five ovens new built, some of them 14 foot deep.

A great kitchen, with four ranges and a boiling place for small boiled meats.

An other kitchen with a very long range, for the waste, to serve all commoners.

A boiling house for the great boiler.

A room for the scullery.

An other room for the cooks' lodgings.

Some of these were covered with canvas, and other some with boards.

Between my Lord's house and the aforesaid hill, where these rooms were raised, there had been made in the bottom, by handy labour, a goodly pond, cut to the perfect figure of a half-moon. In this pond were three notable grounds, where hence to prevent Her Majesty with sports and pastimes. The first was a Ship Isle of 100 foot in length, and 40 foot broad, bearing three trees orderly set for three masts. The second was a Fort 20 foot square every way, and overgrown with willows. The third and last was a Snail Mount, rising to four circles of green privy hedges, the whole in height 20 foot, and forty foot broad at the bottom. These three places were equally distant from the sides of the pond, and every one by a just measured proportion distant from other. In the said water were divers boats prepared for music, but especially there was a pinnace, full furnished with masts, yards, sails, anchors, cables and all other ordinary tackling; and with iron pieces, and lastly with flags, streamers and pendants, to the number of twelve, all painted with divers colours, and sundry devices. To what use these particulars served, it shall evidently appear by that which followeth. . . .

THE THIRD DAY'S ENTERTAINMENT

On Wednesday morning, about nine of the clock, as Her Majesty opened a casement of her gallery window, there were three excellent musicians, who, being disguised in ancient country attire, did greet her with a pleasant song of

Corydon and Phyllida, made in three parts of purpose. The song, as well for the worth of the ditty, as for the aptness of the note thereto applied, it pleased Her Majesty, after it had been once sung, to command it again, and highly to grace it with her cheerful acceptance and commendation.

The Plowman's Song

"In the merry month of May,
In a morn, by break of day,
Forth I walked by the wood side,
Where as May was in his pride.
There I spied, all alone
Phyllida and Corydon.
Much ado there was God wot,
He would love, and she would not.
She said, never man was true:
He said, none was false to you.
He said, he had loved her long:
She said, love should have no wrong
Corydon would kiss her then:
She said, maids must kiss no men,
Till they did for good and all.
Then she made the shepherd call
All the heavens to witness truth,
Never lov'd a truer youth.
Thus with many a pretty oath,
Yea and nay, and faith and troth,
Such as silly shepherds use,
When they will not love abuse,
Love, which had been long deluded,
Was with kisses sweet concluded;
And Phyllida with garlands gay,
Was made the Lady of the May."

The same day after dinner, about three of the clock, ten of my Lord of Hertford's servants, all Somersetshire men, in a square green court, before Her Majesty's window, did hang up lines, squaring out the form of a tennis-court, and making a cross line in the middle. In this square, they (being stripped out of their doublets) [1] played five to five with the hand ball, at board and cord (as they term it) to so great liking of Her Highness, that she graciously deigned to behold their pastime more than an hour and a half.

[1] Coats.

THE COURT

After supper there were two delights presented unto Her Majesty; curious fire-works, and a sumptuous banquet: the first from the three islands in the pond, the second in a low gallery in Her Majesty's privy [1] garden. But I first will briefly speak of the fire-works.

First there was a peal of a hundred chambers [2] discharged from the Snail Mount: in counter whereof, a like peal was discharged from the Ship Isle, and some great ordnance withal. Then was there a castle of fire-works of all sorts, which played in the Fort. Answerable to that, there was in the Snail Mount, a globe of all manner of fire-works, as big as a barrel. When these were spent on either side, there were many running rockets upon lines, which passed between the Snail Mount and the Castle in the Fort. On either side were many fire-wheels, pikes of pleasure, and balls of wild fire which burned in the water.

During the time of these fire-works in the water, there was a banquet served all in glass and silver, into the low gallery in the garden, from a hill-side fourteen score off, by two hundred of my Lord of Hertford's gentlemen, every one carrying so many dishes that the whole number amounted to a thousand, and there were to light them in their way a hundred torch-bearers. To satisfy the curious, I will here set down some particulars in the banquet:

Her Majesty's Arms in sugar-work.
The several Arms of all our nobility in sugar-work.
Many men and women in sugar-work, and some enforced [3] by hand.
Castles, forts, ordnance, drummers, trumpeters and soldiers of all sorts, in sugar-work.
Lions, unicorns, bears, horses, camels, bulls, rams, dogs, tigers, elephants, antelopes, dromedaries, apes, and all other beasts, in sugar-work.
Eagles, falcons, cranes, bustards, heronshawes, bitterns, pheasants, partridges, quails, larks, sparrows, pigeons, cocks, owls, and all that fly, in sugar-work.

[1] Private.   [2] Small cannon for firing salutes.
[3] Worked, not turned out of a mould.

8 ENGLAND IN SHAKESPEARE'S DAY

Snakes, adders, vipers, frogs, toads, and all kind of worms, in sugar-work.

Mermaids, whales, dolphins, congers, sturgeons, pikes, carps, breams, and all sorts of fishes, in sugar-work.

All these were standing dishes of sugar-work. The selfsame devices were also there all in flat-work. Moreover, these particulars following, and many such-like, were in flat sugar-work, and cinnamon:

Marchpanes, grapes, oysters, mussels, cockles, periwinkles, crabs, lobsters.

Apples, pears, and plums, of all sorts.

Preserves, suckets,[1] jellies, leaches, marmalades, pastes, comfits, of all sorts.

III. A LAMENT FOR SIR PHILIP SIDNEY

EDMUND SPENSER. A Pastoral Elegy upon the Death of the most Noble and Valorous Knight, Sir Philip Sidney. *Sir Philip Sidney was the Elizabethan ideal of a " verray parfit gentil knyght" and his extraordinary renown was due more to his general all-round excellence than to distinction in any particular field. He was a man of charming personality, and his devotion to the ideals of romantic chivalry was very real. Before setting out for the skirmish at Zutphen, he had donned his armour, but, seeing the Marshal of the Camp who went with him to be lightly armed, he put off his thigh-pieces so that they might share the danger equally. Soon after he received a mortal wound in the thigh.*

Spenser's tribute was one of many; seven are printed together in Astrophel: a Pastoral Elegie upon the Death of the most noble and Valorous Knight, Sir Philip Sidney.

Sidney died on October 16, 1586; his body was buried with great pomp in St. Paul's on February 16, 1587.

A gentle shepherd born in Arcady,
Of gentlest race that ever shepherd bore:
About the grassy banks of Hæmony,
Did keep his sheep, his little stock and store.
    Full carefully he kept them day and night.
    In fairest fields, and Astrophel[2] he hight. . . .

[1] Crystallized plums.

[2] The name which Sidney adopted in his Sonnets to " Stella" (the Lady Penelope Rich).

And many a Nymph both of the wood and brook,
Soon as his oaten pipe began to shrill;
Both crystal wells and shady groves forsook,
To hear the charms of his enchanting skill.
    And brought him presents, flowers if it were prime,
    Or mellow fruit if it were harvest time.

But he for none of them did care a whit,
Yet wood Gods for them often sighed sore:
Ne for their gifts unworthy of his wit,
Yet not unworthy of the countries store.
    For one alone he cared, for one he sigh'd,
    His life's desire, and his dear love's delight.

Stella the fair, the fairest star in sky,
As fair as Venus or the fairest fair:
A fairer star saw never living eye,
Shot her sharp pointed beams through purest air.
    Her he did love, her he alone did honour,
    His thoughts, his rhymes, his songs were all upon her.

To her he vowed the service of his days,
On her he spent the riches of his wit:
For her he made hymns of immortal praise,
Of only her he sung, he thought, he writ.
    Her, and but her, of love he worthy deemed,
    For all the rest but little he esteemed.

Ne her with idle words alone he wooed,
And verses vain (yet verses are not vain)
But with brave deeds to her sole service vowed,
And bold achievements her did entertain.
    For both in deeds and words he nurtured was,
    Both wise and hardy (too hardy, alas).

In wrestling nimble, and in running swift,
In shooting steady, and in swimming strong:
Well made to strike, to throw, to leap, to lift,
And all the sports that shepherds are among.
  In every one he vanquished every one,
  He vanquished all, and vanquished was of none.

IV. SIR PHILIP SIDNEY

FULKE GREVILLE, LORD BROOKE. The Life of the Renowned Sir Philip Sidney. 1652; *page* 33 *in Nowell Smith's edition.*

Indeed he was a true model of worth; a man fit for conquest, plantation,[1] reformation, or what action soever is greatest and hardest amongst men; withal such a lover of mankind and goodness that whosoever had any real parts in him he found comfort, participation, and protection to the uttermost of his power, like Zephyrus, he giving life where he blew. The Universities abroad and at home accompted him a general Mæcenas of Learning, dedicated their books to him, and communicated every invention or improvement of knowledge with him. Soldiers honoured him and were so honoured by him as no man thought he marched under the true banner of Mars that had not obtained Sir Philip Sidney's approbation. Men of affairs in most parts of Christendom entertained correspondency with him. But what speak I of these with whom his own ways and ends did concur? Since, to descend, his heart and capacity were so large, that there was not a cunning painter, a skilful engineer, an excellent musician, or any other artificer of extraordinary fame that made not himself known to this famous spirit and found him his true friend without hire, and the common rendezvous of worth in his time.

[1] Colonization.

V. FULKE GREVILLE'S EPITAPH

Fulke Grevil,
Servant to Queen Elizabeth,
Councellor to King James,
and Frend to Sr Philip Sidney.
Trophæum Peccati.[1]

VI. THE DEATH OF QUEEN ELIZABETH

Sir Robert Carey's Memoirs; *in the King's Classics, page* 70. *It was very generally believed that the death of Queen Elizabeth would be the signal for civil war. This accounts for the elaborate precautions taken to prevent the news from being known before the Privy Council was ready with its preparations for proclaiming King James.*

After that all things were quieted, and the Border in safety, towards the end of five years that I had been Warden there, having little to do, I resolved upon a journey to Court, to see my friends and renew my acquaintance there. I took my journey about the end of the year. When I came to Court I found the Queen ill disposed, and she kept her inner lodging; yet she, hearing of my arrival, sent for me. I found her in one of her withdrawing chambers, sitting low upon her cushions. She called me to her; I kissed her hand, and told her it was my chiefest happiness to see her in safety and in health, which I wished might long continue. She took me by the hand and wrung it hard, and said, "No, Robin, I am not well", and then discoursed with me of her indisposition, and that her heart had been sad and heavy for ten or twelve days, and in her discourse she fetched not so few as forty or fifty great sighs. I was grieved at the first to see her in this plight; for in all my lifetime before I never knew her fetch a sigh, but when the Queen of Scots was beheaded. Then upon my knowledge she shed many tears and sighs, manifesting her innocence that she never gave consent to the death of that Queen.

I used the best words I could to persuade her from this melancholy humour; but I found by her it was too deep rooted in her heart, and hardly to be removed. This

---

[1] The monument of a sinner.

was upon a Saturday night, and she gave command that the great closet should be prepared for her to go to chapel the next morning. The next day, all things being in a readiness, we long expected her coming. After eleven o'clock, one of the grooms came out and bade make ready for the private closet, she would not go to the great. There we stayed long for her coming, but at the last she had cushions laid for her in the privy chamber hard by the closet door, and there she heard service.

From that day forwards she grew worse and worse. She remained upon her cushions four days and nights at the least. All about her could not persuade her either to take any sustenance or go to bed.

I, hearing that neither the physicians nor none about her could persuade her to take any course for her safety, feared her death would soon after ensue. I could not but think in what a wretched estate I should be left, most of my livelihood depending on her life. And hereupon I bethought myself with what grace and favour I was ever received by the King of Scots, whensoever I was sent to him. I did assure myself it was neither unjust nor unhonest for me to do for myself, if God at that time should call her to His Mercy. Hereupon I wrote to the King of Scots (knowing him to be the right heir to the crown of England) and certified him in what state Her Majesty was. I desired him not to stir from Edinburgh; if of that sickness she should die, I would be the first man that should bring him news of it.

The Queen grew worse and worse, because she would be so, none about her being able to persuade her to go to bed. My Lord Admiral was sent for (who by reason of my sister's death, that was his wife, had absented himself some fortnight from Court); what by fair means, what by force, he got her to bed. There was no hope of her recovery, because she refused all remedies.

On Wednesday, the twenty-third of March, she grew speechless. That afternoon, by signs, she called for her Council, and by putting her hand to her head, when the

THE COURT

King of Scots was named to succeed her, they all knew he was the man she desired should reign after her.

About six at night she made signs for the Archbishop and her Chaplains to come to her, at which time I went in with them, and sat upon my knees full of tears to see that heavy sight. Her Majesty lay upon her back with one hand in the bed, and the other without. The Bishop kneeled down by her, and examined her first of her faith, and she so punctually answered all his several questions, by lifting up her eyes and holding up her hand, as it was a comfort to all the beholders. Then the good man told her plainly what she was, and what she was to come to; and though she had been long a great Queen here upon earth, yet shortly she was to yield an account of her stewardship to the King of kings. After this he began to pray, and all that were by did answer him. After he had continued long in prayer, till the old man's knees were weary, he blessed her, and meant to rise and leave her. The Queen made a sign with her hand. My sister Scroope, knowing her meaning, told the Bishop the Queen desired he would pray still. He did so for a long half-hour after, and then thought to leave her. The second time she made sign to have him continue in prayer. He did so for half an hour more, with earnest cries to God for her soul's health, which he uttered with that fervency of spirit as the Queen to all our sight much rejoiced thereat, and gave testimony to us all of her Christian and comfortable end. By this time it grew late and every one departed, all but her women that attended her.

VII. SIR ROBERT CAREY'S RIDE

SIR ROBERT CAREY's Memoirs; *page 76. Carey's anxiety to get to Scotland was due to the fact that he hoped, by being first with the news, to secure a lucrative post at Court. James did indeed make him a Gentleman of the Bedchamber, but later was obliged to cancel the appointment. On his side Carey covered almost 400 miles in three days.*

I got to horse, and rode to the Knight Marshal's [1] lodging by Charing Cross, and there stayed till the Lords

---
[1] The Knight Marshal was responsible for the domestic arrangements of the Court.

came to Whitehall Garden. I stayed there till it was nine o'clock in the morning, and hearing that all the lords were in the old orchard at Whitehall, I sent the Marshal to tell them that I had stayed all that while to know their pleasures, and that I would attend them if they would command me any service. They were very glad when they heard I was not gone, and desired the Marshal to send for me, and I should with all speed be dispatched for Scotland. The Marshal believed them, and sent Sir Arthur Savage for me. I made haste to them. One of the Council (my Lord of Banbury that now is) whispered the Marshal in the ear, and told him, if I came they would stay me, and send some other in my stead. The Marshal got from them, and met me coming to them between the two gates. He bade me be gone, for he had learned for certain that if I came to them they would betray me.

I returned and took horse between nine and ten o'clock, and that night rode to Doncaster. The Friday night I came to my own house at Witherington, and presently took order with my deputies to see the Borders kept in quiet, which they had much to do: and gave order the next morning the King of Scotland should be proclaimed King of England and at Morpeth and Alnwick. Very early on Saturday I took horse for Edinburgh, and came to Norham about twelve at noon, so that I might well have been with the King at supper time: but I got a great fall by the way, and my horse with one of his heels gave me a great blow on the head that made me shed much blood. It made me so weak that I was forced to ride a soft pace after, so that the King was newly gone to bed by the time that I knocked at the gate. I was quickly let in and carried up to the King's chamber. I kneeled by him, and saluted him by his title of England, Scotland, France, and Ireland. He gave me his hand to kiss, and bade me welcome. After he had long discoursed of the manner of the Queen's sickness and of her death, he asked what letters I had from the Council. I told him, none: and acquainted him how narrowly I escaped from them. And yet I had brought him a blue ring from a fair lady, that I hoped would give him assurance of the truth that I had reported. He took it and looked upon it, and said, "It is enough: I know by this you are a true messenger." Then he committed me to the charge of my Lord Hume, and gave straight command that I should want nothing. He sent for his chirurgeons to attend me, and when I kissed his hand at my departure he said to me these gracious words: "I know you have lost a near kinswoman, and a loving mistress; but take here my hand, I will be as good a master to you, and will requite this service with honour and reward."

So I left him that night, and went with my Lord Hume to my lodging, where I had all things fitting for so weary a man as I was. After my head was dressed, I took leave of my Lord and many others that attended me, and went to my rest.

VIII. THE CHARACTER OF KING JAMES

SIR JOHN HARINGTON. Nugæ Antiquæ. *A letter from Lord Thomas Howard to Sir John Harington. Harington had been one of Essex's Knights in the unfortunate Irish Campaign of* 1599–1600 *and since then had thought it wisest to avoid prominent notice at Court. On the accession of King James he hoped for a return of Court favour.*

MY GOOD AND TRUSTY KNIGHT,

If you have good will and good health to perform what I shall commend, you may set forward for Court whenever it suiteth your own conveniency: the King hath often inquired after you, and would readily see and converse again with the "merry blade", as he hath oft called you, since you was here. I will now premise certain things to be observed by you, toward well gaining our prince's good affection: He doth wondrously covet learned discourse, of which you can furnish out ample means; he doth admire good fashion in clothes, I pray you give good heed hereunto; strange devices oft come into man's conceit; some one regardeth the endowments of the inward sort, wit, valour, or virtue; another hath, perchance, special affection towards outward things, clothes, deportment and good countenance. I would wish you to be well trimmed; get a new jerkin, well bordered, and not too short; the King saith, he liketh a flowing garment; be sure it be not all of one sort, but diversely coloured, the collar falling somewhat down, and your ruff well stiffened and bushy. We have lately had many gallants who failed in their suits for want of due observance of these matters. The King is nicely heedful of such points, and dwelleth on good looks and handsome accoutrements. Eighteen servants were lately discharged, and many more will be discarded, who are not to his liking in these matters. I wish you to follow my directions, as I wish you to gain all you desire. Robert Carr is now most likely to win the Prince's affection, and doth it wondrously in a little time. The Prince leaneth on his arm, pinches his cheek, smoothes his ruffled garment, and, when he looketh at Carr, directeth discourse to divers others. This young man doth much study all art and device; he hath changed his tailors and tiremen many times, and all to please the Prince, who laugheth at the long grown fashion of our young courtiers, and wisheth for change every day. You must see Carr before you go to the King, as he was with him a boy in Scotland, and knoweth his taste and what pleaseth. In your discourse you must not dwell too long on any one subject, and touch but lightly on religion. Do not of yourself say, "This is good or bad"; but, "If it were your Majesty's good opinion, I myself should think so and so." Ask no more questions than what may serve to know the Prince's thought. In private discourse, the King seldom speaketh of any man's temper, discretion or good virtues; so meddle not at all, but find out a clue to guide you to the heart and most delightful subject of his mind. I will advise one thing—the roan jennet, whereon the King rideth every day, must not be forgotten to be praised; and the good furniture [1] above all, what lost a great man much notice the other day. A noble did come

---

[1] Harness, trappings.

in suit of a place, and saw the King mounting the roan; delivered his petition, which was heeded and read, but no answer was given. The noble departed, and came to Court the next day, and got no answer again. The Lord Treasurer was then pressed to move the King's pleasure touching the petition. When the King was asked for answer thereto, he said, in some wrath, "Shall a King give heed to a dirty paper, when a beggar noteth not his gilt stirrups?" Now it fell out that the King had new furniture when the noble saw him in the courtyard, but he was overcharged with confusion, and passed by admiring the dressing of the horse. Thus, good knight, our noble failed in his suit. I could relate and offer some other remarks on these matters, but Silence and Discretion should be linked together like dog and bitch, for of them is gendered Security: I am certain it proveth so at this place. You have lived to see the trim of old times, and what passed in the Queen's days. These things are no more the same. Your Queen did talk of her subjects' love and good affections, and in good truth she aimed well; our King talketh of his subjects' fear and subjection, and herein I think he doth well too, as long as it holdeth good. Carr hath all favours, as I told you before; the King teacheth him Latin every morning, and I think some one should teach him English too; for, as he is a Scottish lad, he hath much need of better language. The King doth much covet his presence; the ladies too are not behindhand in their admiration; for I tell you, good knight, this fellow is straight-limbed, well-favoured, strong-shouldered, and smooth-faced, with some sort of cunning and show of modesty; though God wot, he well knoweth when to show his impudence. You are not young, you are not handsome, you are not finely, and yet will you come to Court and think to be well favoured? Why, I say again, good knight, that your learning may somewhat prove worthy hereunto; your Latin and your Greek, your Italian, your Spanish tongues, your wit and discretion, may be well looked unto for a while, as strangers at such a place; but these are not the things men live by nowadays. Will you say the moon shineth all the summer? That the stars are bright jewels fit for Carr's ears? That the roan jennet surpasseth Bucephalus, and is worthy to be bestridden by Alexander? That his eyes are fire, his tail is Berenice's locks, and a few more such fancies worthy your noticing? Your lady is virtuous, and somewhat of a good housewife; has lived in a Court in her time, and I believe you may venture her forth again, but I know those would not quietly rest, were Carr to leer on their wives, as some do perceive, yea, and like it well too that they should be so noticed. If any mischance be to be wished, 'tis breaking a leg in the King's presence, for this fellow owes all his favour to that bout; I think he hath better reason to speak well of his own horse, than the King's roan jennet. We are almost worn out in our endeavours to keep pace with this fellow in his duty and labour to gain favour, but all in vain; where it endeth I cannot guess, but honours are talked of speedily for him. I trust this by my own son, that no danger may happen from our freedoms. If you come here, God speed your ploughing at the Court: I know you do it rarely at home. So adieu, my good knight, and I will always write me

Your truly loving old friend,
T. HOWARD.

IX. THE OVERBURY MURDER

From SIR FRANCIS BACON'S opening of the Case for the Crown against Robert Carr, Earl of Somerset (*in Bacon's complete works*). *The murder of Sir Thomas Overbury is one of the most sensational crimes in English criminal history. Robert Carr, Earl of Somerset, the King's favourite, fell in love with the Countess of Essex, who had been married, as was customary, to the Earl while still a child, some years before. Directly after the marriage the Earl went abroad to complete his education. On his return, the Countess refused to have anything to do with him. Eventually the marriage was annulled after a scandalous trial, and she married Carr. Overbury had originally been a favourite of Carr, but had become a nuisance. He was imprisoned in the Tower for a political offence and there poisoned. The extract is a good example of Bacon's skill as a barrister.*

For it fell out some twelve months before Overbury's imprisonment in the Tower, that my Lord of Somerset was entered into an unlawful love towards his unfortunate lady, then Countess of Essex, which went so far, as it was then secretly projected (chiefly between my Lord Privy Seal and my Lord of Somerset) to effect a nullity in the marriage with my Lord of Essex, and so to proceed to a marriage with Somerset. This marriage and purpose did Overbury mainly oppugn under pretence to do the true part of a friend (for that he counted her an unworthy woman); but the truth was, that Overbury, who (to speak plainly) had little that was solid for religion or moral virtue, but was a man possessed with ambition and vainglory, was loath to have any partners in the favour of my Lord of Somerset, and especially not the house of the Howards, against whom he had always professed hatred and opposition. So all was but miserable bargains of ambition. And, my lords, that this is no sinister construction, will well appear unto you when you shall hear that Overbury makes his brags to my Lord of Somerset that he had won him the love of the lady by his letters and industry, so far was he from cases of conscience in this matter. And certainly, my lords, howsoever the tragical misery of that poor gentleman Overbury ought somewhat to obliterate his faults, yet because we are not now upon point of civility but to discover the face of Truth to the face of Justice, and that it is material to the true understanding of the state of this cause, Overbury was naught and corrupt, the ballads [1] must be amended for that point. But to proceed: when Overbury saw that he was like to be dispossessed of my lord here whom he had possessed so long, and by whose greatness he had promised himself to do wonders, and being a man of unbounded and impetuous spirit, he began not only to dissuade, but to deter him from that love and marriage, and finding him fixed, thought to try stronger remedies, supposing that he had my lord's head under his girdle, in respect of communications of secrets of estate, or

---

[1] See page 143.

(as he calls them himself in his letters) secrets of all natures; and therefore dealt violently with him, to make him desist, with menaces of discovery of secrets and the like. Hereupon grew two streams of hatred upon Overbury; the one, from the lady, in respect that he crossed her love, and abused her name, which are furies to women; the other of a deeper and more mineral [1] nature, from my Lord of Somerset himself, who was afraid of Overbury's nature, and that if he did break from him and fly out, he would mine into him and trouble his whole fortunes. I might add a third stream from the Earl of Northampton's ambition, who desires to be first in favour with my Lord of Somerset, and knowing Overbury's malice to himself and his house, thought that man must be removed and cut off. So it was amongst them resolved and decreed that Overbury must die.

Hereupon they had variety of devices. To send him beyond sea upon occasion of employment, that was too weak; and they were so far from giving way to it, as they crossed [2] it. There rested but two ways, quarrel or assault, and poison. For that of assault, after some proposition and attempt, they passed from it; it was a thing too open and subject to more variety of chances. That of poison likewise was a hazardous thing and subject to many preventions and cautions, especially to such a jealous and working brain as Overbury had, except he were first fast in their hands. Therefore the way was first to get him into a trap and lay him up, and then they could not miss the mark. Therefore, in execution of this plot, it was devised that Overbury should be designed to some honourable employment in foreign parts,[3] and should underhand by the Lord of Somerset be encouraged to refuse it; and so upon that contempt he should be laid prisoner in the Tower, and then they would look he should be close enough, and death should be his bail. Yet were they not at their

---

[1] I.e. deep underground.   [2] Opposed.
[3] As ambassadors were underpaid "honourable employment in foreign parts" was very costly and usually unpopular.

THE COURT

end. For they considered, that if there was not a fit Lieutenant of the Tower for their purpose, and likewise a fit under-keeper of Overbury, first, they should meet with many impediments in the giving and exhibiting the poison, secondly, they should be exposed to note and observation that might discover them, and thirdly, Overbury in the meantime might write clamorous and furious letters to other his friends, and so all might be disappointed. And therefore the next link of the chain was to displace the then Lieutenant, Waade, and to place Helwisse a principal abetter in the empoisonment; again, to displace Cary, that was the under-keeper in Waade's time, and place Weston, who was the principal actor in the empoisonment: and this was done in such a while (that it may appear to be done, as it were, with one breath) as there were but fifteen days between the commitment of Overbury, the displacing of Waade, the placing of Helwisse, the displacing of Cary the under-keeper, the placing of Weston, and the first poison given two days after. Then, when they had this poor gentleman in the Tower, close prisoner, where he could not escape nor stir, where he could not feed but by their hands, where he could not speak nor write but through their trunks; then was the time to execute the last act of this tragedy. Then must Franklin be purveyor of the poisons, and procure five, six, seven several potions to be sure to hit his complexion. Then must Mrs. Turner [1] be the say-mistress [2] of the poisons, to try upon poor beasts what's present,[3] and what works at distance of time. Then must Weston be the tormenter and chase him with poison after poison; poison in salts, poison in meats, poison in sweetmeats, poison in medicines and vomits, until at last his body was almost come, by use of poisons, to the state that Mithridate's body was by the use of treacle and preservatives, that the force of the poisons were blunted upon him, Weston confessing when he was chid for not dispatching him, that he had given him

---

[1] Famous as the inventress of yellow starch.
[2] Tester. [3] Immediate.

enough to poison twenty men. Lastly, because all this asked time, courses were taken by Somerset, both to divert all means of Overbury's delivery and to entertain Overbury by continual letters, partly of hopes and projects for his delivery, and partly of other fables and negotiations ; somewhat like some kind of persons (which I will not name) which keep men in talk of fortune-telling, when they have a felonious meaning.

And this is the true narrative of this act of empoisonment which I have summarily recited.

[*Here Bacon addressed the accused.*] Now for the distribution of the proofs : there are four heads of proofs to prove you guilty, my Lord of Somerset, of this empoisonment, whereof two are precedent to the imprisonment, the third is present, the fourth is following or subsequent. For it is in proofs as it is in lights, there is a direct light, and there is a reflection of light, or back-light. The first head or proof thereof is that there was a root of bitterness, a mortal malice or hatred, mixed with deep and bottomless fears, that you had towards Sir Thomas Overbury. The second is that you were the principal actor, and had your hand in all those acts which did conduce to the empoisonment, and which gave opportunity and means to effect it ; and without which the empoisonment could never have been, and which could serve or tend to no other end but to the empoisonment. The third is that your hand was in the very empoisonment itself, which is more than needs to be proved ; that you did direct poison, that you did deliver poison, that you did continually hearken to the success of the empoisonment and that you spurred it on, and called for dispatch when you thought it lingered. And lastly, that you did all the things after the empoisonment which may detect a guilty conscience for the smothering of it, and avoiding punishment for it, which can be but of three kinds : That you suppressed, as much as in you was, testimony ; that you did deface and destroy, and clip and misdate, all writings that might give light to the empoisonment, and that you did fly to the altar of guilti-

THE COURT 23

ness, which is a pardon, and a pardon of murder, and a pardon for yourself and not for your lady. In this, my lord, I convert my speech to you, because I would have you attend the points of your charge, and so of your defence, the better. And two of these heads I have taken to myself, and left the other two to the King's two Sergeants.

X. THE MARRIAGE OF PRINCESS ELIZABETH

The Magnificent Marriage of the Two Great Princes, 1612 (printed in NICHOLS' Progresses of King James the First,1828); vol. 2, page 541. Princess Elizabeth, afterwards mother of Prince Rupert, was the last of the real fairy princesses. She had inherited the beauty of her grandmother, Mary, Queen of Scots, and possessed all the winning charm of the Stuarts. The marriage was not a success; the Elector Palatine lost his throne and died as a fugitive in his own kingdom. His Queen, after a long exile in Holland, returned to England after the Restoration, and died in 1662 in the house of the Earl of Craven, who had devoted his life and fortune to her service. The wedding was the most brilliant display of Court ceremonial during our period.

The Court being placed full of people of many estates, sorts and nations; and their eyes and hearts fixed to behold the pompous glory of this marriage in great royalty, between eleven and twelve of the clock, His Majesty, to make the procession more solemn, and in order that it might be seen by more people, proceeded from his Privy-chamber through the Presence and Guard-chamber, and through the new Banqueting House erected of purpose to solemnize this feast, and so down a pair of stairs at the upper end thereof by the Court-gate, and went along upon a stately scaffold to the Great-chamber stairs, and through the Great-chamber and Lobby to the Closet down the stairs to the Chapel, into which the entry was made in this manner:

First, the trumpets: then the Palsgrave from the new built Banqueting House, attired in a white suit, richly beset with pearls and gold, attended on by a number of young gallant courtiers, both English, and Scottish, and Dutch, all in rich manner, every one striving to exceed in sumptuous habiliments fit for the attendance of a princely bridegroom. After came (preceded by Lord Harington of Exton, her Tutor) the Lady Elizabeth, in her virgin robes, clothed in a gown of white satin, richly embroidered, led between her Royal brother Prince Charles and the Earl of Northampton (both bachelors); upon her head a crown of refined gold, made Imperial by the pearls and diamonds thereupon placed, which were so thick beset that they stood like shining pinnacles upon her amber-coloured hair, dependently hanging plaited down over her shoulders to her waist; between every plait a roll or list of gold spangles, pearls, rich stones and diamonds; and, withal, many diamonds of inestimable value, embroidered upon her sleeves, which even dazzled and amazed the eyes of the beholders; her train in most sumptuous manner carried up by fourteen or fifteen ladies, attired in white satin gowns, adorned with many rich jewels; then followed Lady Harington.

After went a train of noblemen's daughters in white vestments, gloriously set forth: which virgin Bridemaids attended upon the Princess, like a sky of celestial stars upon fair Phœbe. After them came another train of gallant young courtiers, flourishing in several suits, embroidered and pearled, who were knights and the sons of great courtiers; after them came four Heralds-at-Arms, in their rich coats of Heraldry; and then followed many Earls, Lords, and Barons, as well of Scotland as England, in most noble manner; then the King of Heralds, bearing upon his shoulder a mace of gold; and then followed the honourable Lords of his Highness' Privy Council, which passed along after the train towards the Chapel; and then came four reverend Bishops of the land in their Church-habiliments; after them four Sergeants of the Mace in great state, bearing upon their shoulders four rich enamelled maces. Then followed the right honourable the Earl of Arundel, carrying the King's sword; and then in great royalty the King's Majesty himself in a most sumptuous black suit, with a diamond in his hat of a wonderful great value; close unto him came the Queen,

THE COURT

attired in white satin, beautified with much embroidery and many diamonds; upon her attended a number of married ladies, the Countesses and wives of Earls and Barons, apparelled in most noble manner, which added glory unto this triumphant time and marriage. These were the passages of our States of England, accompanying the Princely Bride and Bridegroom to His Highness's Chapel.

The Chapel was in royal sort adorned; the upper end of it was hung with very rich hangings, containing part of the history of the Acts of the Apostles, and the Communion Table was furnished with rich plate. A stately stage or scaffold was raised in the midst of the Chapel, about five feet in height and about twenty feet in length, having six or seven stairs to ascend and descend at each end of it; the same was spread underneath with rich carpets, and railed on both sides; the rails being covered with cloth of tissue, but open at the top, that the whole assembly might the better see all the ceremonies. Upon the sides of the Chapel, from the stalls up to the Communion Table, there had been a double row of seats made for the Gentlemen of the Chapel, arrayed with tapestry. On the stage, in the chair upon the right hand, sat the King, most richly arrayed, his jewels being esteemed not to be less worth than six hundred thousand pounds; the Earl of Arundel, bearing the Sword, stood close by the chair. Next below the Sword sat the Bridegroom upon a stool; and after him Prince Charles upon another stool; and by him stood Prince Henry, who was brother to Count Maurice of Nassau, and uncle to the Palatine. On the opposite side sat the Queen in a chair, most gloriously attired; her jewels were valued at four hundred thousand pounds. Near unto her sat the Bride on a stool; the Lady Harington, her Governess, stood by her, bearing up her train; and no others ascended this place.

The Lord Chamberlain to the King stood at the end next the Altar, and the Queen's Lord Chamberlain at the other end. The Lord Privy Seal stood upon the stairs of the hautpas or stage, hard by the King. The Lords and Councillors of the King and the Lords and Councillors of the Palatine took their seats on the left hand of the Chapel. The Ladies of Honour took the other side of the seats. The young Lords and Gentlemen of Honour, and young Ladies and Bridewomen, with the necessary attendants upon the King and the Queen, stood all below upon the pavement. It is remarkable that by the extraordinary care of the Earl of Suffolk, Lord Chamberlain, the Chapel was so kept as not one person but of honour and great place came into it.

This royal assembly being in this sort settled in the Chapel, the organ ceased, and the Gentlemen of the Chapel sung a full anthem ; and then the Bishop of Bath and Wells, Dean of his Majesty's Chapel, went into the pulpit, which stood at the foot of the step before the Communion Table, and preached upon the second of St. John, the Marriage of Cana in Galilee ; and the sermon being ended (which continued not much above an half-hour), the choir began another anthem, which was the psalm, "Blessed art thou that fearest God." While the choir was singing the anthem, the Archbishop of Canterbury and Dean of the Chapel went into the vestry and put on their rich copes, and came to the Communion Table, where they stood till the anthem was ended.

They then ascended the hautpas,[1] where these two great Princes were married by the Archbishop of Canterbury, in all points according to the Book of Common Prayer : the Prince Palatine speaking the words of marriage in English after the Archbishop. The King's Majesty gave the Bride. When the Archbishop had ended the Benediction, " God the Father, God the Son ", &c., the choir sung the same benediction in an anthem made new for that purpose by Doctor Bull. The anthem ended, the Archbishop and the Dean descended from the hautpas ; the Bridegroom and Bride following them, kneeled before the Communion Table, while the versicles and prayers were

[1] Dais.

THE COURT

sung by the Archbishop and answered by the choir, which being ended, another psalm was sung.

Then Garter Principal King-of-Arms published the styles of the Prince and Princess to this effect: "All health, happiness, and honour be to the high and mighty Prince, Frederick the Fifth, by the grace of God, Count Palatine of the Rhine, &c.; and to Elizabeth his wife, only daughter of the high, mighty, and right-excellent James, by the grace of God, King of Great Britain", &c.

Then joy was given by the King and Queen, and seconded with the congratulations of the Lords there present, and then divers of these Lords brought out of the vestry bowls with wine, hippocras,[1] and wafers. After tasting the wafers, an health was begun to the prosperity of the marriage, out of a great gold bowl by the Prince Palatine, and answered by the Princess and others present in their order.

After the celebration of the marriage, contracted in the presence of the King, the Queen, Prince Charles, and the rest, aforesaid, they returned unto the Banqueting House with great joy. The Lady Elizabeth, being thus made a wife, was led back, not by two bachelors as before, but by the Duke of Lennox and the Earl of Nottingham, in a most reverent manner. Before the Palsgrave, at his return from the Chapel, went six of his own country gallants, clad in crimson velvet, laid exceedingly thick with gold lace, bearing in their hands six silver trumpets, who no sooner coming into the Banqueting House, but they presented him with a melodious sound of the same, flourishing so delightfully, that it greatly rejoiced the whole Court, and caused thousands to say at that instant time, "God give them joy, God give them joy!" Thus preparing for dinner, they passed away certain time.

[The King and Queen, leaving the Bride and Bridegroom in the Great-chamber, went to their Privy-lodgings; and the Bride and Bridegroom proceeded to dine in state in the new Banqueting House with the Prince, the Ambassadors

[1] Spiced wine, usually drunk at weddings.

of France, Venice, and the States, Count Henry, and all the Lords and Ladies who had been attendant on the Marriage.]

And then fell to dancing, masking, and revelling, according to the custom of such assemblies, which continued all the day and part of the night in great pleasure.

XI. ON HIS MISTRESS, THE QUEEN OF BOHEMIA

Princess Elizabeth became Queen of Bohemia in 1619.

Written by Sir HENRY WOTTON.

You meaner beauties of the night,
  That poorly satisfy our eyes
More by your number than your light,
  You common people of the skies;
  What are you when the Sun shall rise?

You curious chanters of the wood,
  That warble forth Dame Nature's lays,
Thinking your voices understood
  By your weak accents; what's your praise,
When Philomel her voice shall raise?

You violets that first appear,
  By your pure purple mantles known
Like the proud virgins of the year,
  As if the Spring were all your own;
  What are you when the rose is blown?

So, when my mistress shall be seen
  In form and beauty of her mind,
By virtue first, then choice, a Queen,
  Tell me if she were not designed
  The eclipse and glory of her kind?

XII. THE RASCAL·MULTITUDE

WILLIAM HARRISON. A Description of England; *page* 13 *in Furnivall's* Elizabethan England (*Scott Library*). *This passage explains why the doings of the poor find so little place in Elizabethan literature. This extract has been added by way of contrast.*

As for slaves and bondmen, we have none; nay, such is the privilege of our country by the especial grace of God and bounty of our princes, that if any come hither from other realms, so soon as they set foot on land they become so free of condition as their masters, whereby all note of servile bondage is utterly removed from them, wherein we resemble (not the Germans, who had slaves also, though such as in respect of the slaves of other countries, might well be reputed free, but) the old Indians and the Taprobanes, who supposed it a great injury to Nature to make or suffer them to be bond, whom she in her wonted course doth product and bring forth free.

This fourth and last sort of people, therefore, have neither voice nor authority in the commonwealth, but are to be ruled and not to rule other; yet they are not altogether neglected, for in cities and corporate towns, for default of yeomen, they are fain to make up their inquests of such manner of people. And in villages, they are commonly made churchwardens, sidesmen, aleconners, now and then constables, and many times enjoy the name of headboroughs.[1] Unto this sort, also, may our great swarms of idle serving-men be referred, of whom there runneth a proverb, "Young serving-men, old beggars", because service is none heritage. These men are profitable to none; for, if their condition be well perused, they are enemies to their masters, to their friends, and to themselves; for by them, oftentimes their masters are encouraged unto unlawful exactions of their tenants, their friends brought into poverty by their rents enhanced, and they themselves brought to confusion by their own prodigality and errors, as men that, having not wherewith of their own

[1] Deputy-constables.

to maintain their excesses, do search in highways, budgets,[1] coffers, mails and stables, which way to supply their wants. How divers of them also, coveting to bear an high sail, do insinuate themselves with young gentlemen and noblemen newly come to their lands, the case is too much apparent, whereby the good natures of the parties are not only a little impaired, but also their livelihoods and revenues so wasted and consumed, that, if at all, yet not in many years, they shall be able to recover themselves. It were very good therefore that the superfluous heaps of them were in part diminished. And since necessity enforceth to have some, yet let wisdom moderate their numbers, so shall their masters be rid of unnecessary charge, and the commonwealth of many thieves. No nation cherisheth such store of them as we do here in England, in hope of which maintenance many give themselves to idleness that otherwise would be brought to labour, and live in order like subjects.

[1] Bags.

SECTION TWO

THE SERVICE OF THE STATE

I. DEGREE

WM. SHAKESPEARE. Troilus and Cressida, c. 1604 ; *Act I, Scene 3.*
This speech of Ulysses on " Degree " sums up the political creed of most prosperous middle-class Englishmen.

The heavens themselves, the planets and this centre [1]
Observe degree, priority and place,
Insisture, course, proportion, season, form,
Office and custom, in all line of order :
And therefore is the glorious planet Sol,
In noble eminence enthron'd and spher'd
Amidst the other : whose medicinable eye
Corrects the ill aspects of planets evil,
And posts, like the commandment of a king,
Sans check, to good and bad : but when the planets
In evil mixture, to disorder wander,
What plagues, and what portents ! what mutiny !
What raging of the sea ! shaking of earth !
Commotion in the winds ! frights, changes, horrors,
Divert and crack, rend and deracinate
The unity and married calm of states
Quite from their fixture ! O, when degree is shak'd,
Which is the ladder of all high designs,
The enterprise is sick ! How could communities,
Degrees in schools, and brotherhoods in cities,
Peaceful commerce from dividable shores,
The primogenitive and due of birth,

[1] World, centre of the universe.

Prerogative of age, crowns, sceptres, laurels,
But by degree, stand in authentic place?
Take but degree away, untune that string,
And hark, what discord follows! each thing meets
In mere oppugnancy; the bounded waters
Should lift their bosoms higher than the shores,
And make a sop of all this solid globe:
Strength should be lord of imbecility,
And the rude son should strike his father dead:
Force should be right; or rather right and wrong,
Between whose endless jar justice resides,
Should lose their names, and so should justice too.
Then everything includes itself in power,
Power into will, will into appetite;
And appetite, an universal wolf,
So doubly seconded with will and power
Must make perforce an universal prey
And, last, eat up himself.

II. MACHIAVEL

CHRISTOPHER MARLOWE. The Jew of Malta, 1592; Prologue. *Machiavelli was the patron saint of the Italianate Englishman [see page 215], and nothing worse could be said of a statesman than to call him "Machiavellian." At the same time revolutionaries—of whom there were many, including Marlowe himself—accepted Machiavelli's* Prince *as a sound text-book for the unscrupulous, ambitious man.*

The Ghost of Machiavel speaks:

Albeit the world think Machiavel is dead,
Yet was his soul but flown beyond the Alps,
And now the Guise is dead, is come from France
To view this land and frolic with his friends.
To some perhaps my name is odious,
But such as love me, guard me from their tongues,
And let them know that I am Machiavel,
And weigh not men, and therefore not men's words:
Admir'd I am of those that hate me most.
Though some speak openly against my books,

THE SERVICE OF THE STATE

Yet will they read me, and thereby attain
To Peter's Chair: and when they cast me off,
Are poisoned by my climbing followers.
I count religion but a childish toy,
And hold there is no sin but ignorance.
Birds of the air will tell of murders past,
I am ashamed to hear such fooleries :
Many will talk of title to a crown ;
What right had Caesar to the Empire ?
Might first made kings, and laws were then most sure
When like the Draco's they were writ in blood.
Hence comes it, that a strong built citadel
Commands much more than letters can import :
Which maxim, had Phaleris observ'd,
H' had never bellowed in a brazen bull
Of great one's envy ; o' the poor petty wits,
Let me be envied and not pitied !
But whither am I bound ? I come not, I,
To read a lecture here in Britain,
But to present the Tragedy of a Jew,
Who smiles to see how full his bags are cramm'd,
Which money was not got without my means.
I crave but this ; grace him as he deserves,
And let him not be entertain'd the worse
Because he favours me.

III. THE TROUBLES OF STATECRAFT

A letter from Sir Robert Cecil to Sir John Harington, 1603 ; printed in Nugæ Antiquæ. This letter was written shortly after the accession of King James I. Compare page 15.

MY NOBLE KNIGHT,

My thanks come with your papers and wholesome statutes for your father's household. I shall, as far as in me lieth, pattern the same and give good heed for due observance thereof in my own state. Your father did much affect such prudence ; nor doth his son less follow his fair sample, of worth, learning and honour   I shall not fail to keep your grace and favour quick and lively in the King's breast as far as good discretion guideth me ; so as not to hazard my own reputation for humble suing, rather than bold and forward entreaties. You know all my former steps, good knight, rest content, and give heed to one that hath sorrowed in the bright lustre of a court and gone heavily even to the best seeming fair ground. 'Tis a great task to prove one's honesty, and yet not spoil one's fortune You have tasted a little hereof in our blessed Queen's time, who was more than a man, and (in troth) sometime less than a woman. I wish I waited now in her presence-chamber, with ease at my food, and rest in my bed. I am pushed from the shore of comfort and know not where the winds and waves of a court will bear me ; I know it bringeth little comfort on earth, and he is, I reckon, no wise man that looketh this way to Heaven. We have much stir about councils and more about honours. Many knights were made at Theobalds during the King's stay at mine house, and more to be made in the City. My father had much wisdom in directing the state, and I wish I could bear my part so discreetly as he did. Farewell, good knight ; but never come near London till I call you. Too much crowding doth not well for a cripple, and the King doth find scant room to sit himself, he hath so many friends, as they choose to be called, and Heaven prove they lie not in the end. In trouble, hurrying, feigning, suing and such-like matters, I now rest,

Your true friend,
R. CECIL.

29th May, 1603.

IV. THE PRIVILEGES OF NOBLEMEN

HENRY PEACHAM. The Compleat Gentleman, 1634 ; *page* 13 *in Gordon's edition.*

Noble or Gentleman ought to be preferred in fees, honours, offices, and other dignities of command and government, before the common people.

THE SERVICE OF THE STATE

They are to be admitted near and about the person of the Prince, to be of his Council in war, and to bear his Standard.

We ought to give credit to a Noble or Gentleman, before any of the inferior sort.

He must not be arrested, or pleaded against upon cosenage.[1]

We must attend him and come to his house, and not he to ours.

His punishment ought to be more favourable and honourable upon his trial, and that to be by his Peers of the same noble rank.

He ought in all sittings, meetings and salutations, to have the upper hand and greatest respect.

They must be cited by bill or writing to make their appearance.

In criminal causes, Noblemen may appear by their attorney or procurator.

They ought to take their recreations of hunting, hawking, &c., freely, without control in all places.

Their imprisonment ought not to be in base manner, or so strict as others.

They may eat the best and daintiest meat that the place affordeth; wear at their pleasure gold, jewels, the best apparel, and of what fashion they please, &c.

Beside, Nobility stirreth up emulation in great spirits, not only of equalling others, but excelling them; as in Cimon, the elder Scipio Africanus, Decius the son, Alexander, Edward our Black Prince, and many other.

It many times procureth a good marriage, as in Germany, where a fair coat and crest is often preferred before a good revenue.

It is a spur in brave and good spirits to bear in mind those things which their ancestors have nobly achieved.

It transferreth itself unto posterity: and as for the most part we see the children of noble personages to bear the lineaments and resemblance of their parents, so in like manner, for the most part, they possess their virtues and

---
[1] Fraud.

noble dispositions, which even in their tenderest years will bud forth and discover itself.

V. AN INNS OF COURT MAN

SIR THOMAS OVERBURY. Characters, 1616; *page 103 in Rimbault's edition. To the Inns of Court belonged most of the brilliant and wealthy young gentlemen who finished their education in London Society after a period at one of the Universities. The younger barristers were the keenest patrons of poets, dramatists and players, and, after the beginning of the seventeenth century, contributed most of the more learned poets.*

He is distinguished from a scholar by a pair of silk stockings and a beaver hat which makes him condemn a scholar as much as a scholar doth a schoolmaster. By that he hath heard one mooting and seen two plays, he thinks as basely of the University as a young sophister doth of the grammar school. He talks of the University with that state as if he were her Chancellor; finds fault with alterations and the fall of discipline with an " It was not so when I was a student "; although that was within this half-year. He will talk ends of Latin, though it be false, with as great confidence as ever Cicero could pronounce an oration, though his best authors for't be taverns and ordinaries. He is as far behind a courtier in his fashion as a scholar is behind him, and the best grace in his behaviour is to forget his acquaintance.

He laughs at every man whose band sits not well or that hath not a fair shoe-tie, and he is ashamed to be seen in any man's company that wears not his clothes well. His very essence he placeth in his outside and his chiefest prayer is that his revenues may hold out for taffeta cloaks in the summer and velvet in the winter. . . . To his acquaintance he offers two quarts of wine for one he gives. You shall never see him melancholy but when he wants a new suit or fears a sergeant; at which times only he betakes himself to Ploydon.[1] By that he hath read Littleton,[1] he can call

---

[1] Author of law text-books.

THE SERVICE OF THE STATE 37

Solon, Lycurgus and Justinian fools, and dares compare his law to a Lord Chief Justice's.

VI. THE LAST FIGHT OF THE *REVENGE*

SIR WALTER RALEGH. The Sea Fight about the Azores, 1591 ; *page* 148 *in Hadow's* Selections from Ralegh's Works.

The Spanish fleet, having shrouded their approach by reason of the land, were now so soon at hand as our ships had scarce time to weigh their anchors, but some of them were driven to let slip their cables and set sail. Sir Richard Grenville was the last weighed, to recover the men that were upon the land, which otherwise had been lost. The Lord Thomas with the rest very hardly recovered the wind, which Sir Richard Grenville not being able to do, was persuaded by the master and others to cut his main sail, and cast about, and to trust to the sailing of the ship; for the squadron of Seville were on his weather bow. But Sir Richard utterly refused to turn from the enemy, alleging that he would rather choose to die than to dishonour himself, his country, and Her Majesty's ship, persuading his company that he would pass through the two squadrons, in despite of them, and enforce those of Seville to give him way. Which he performed upon divers of the foremost, who as the mariners term it, sprang their luff, and fell under the lee of the *Revenge*. But the other course had been the better, and might right well have been answered in so great an impossibility of prevailing. Notwithstanding out of the greatness of his mind, he could not be persuaded. In the meanwhile as he attended those which were nearest him, the great *San Philip* being in the wind of him, and coming towards him, becalmed his sails in such sort, as the ship could neither weigh nor feel the helm ; so huge and high charged [1] was the Spanish ship, being of a thousand and five hundred tons ; who after laid the *Revenge* aboard. When he was thus bereft of his sails, the ships that were under his lee luffing up, also laid him aboard ; of which the

[1] Having a high poop.

next was the *Admiral of the Biscaines*, a very mighty and puissant ship commanded by Brittan Dona. The said *Philip* carried three tier of ordnance on a side, and eleven pieces on every tier. She shot eight forth right out of her chase, besides those of her stern ports.

After the *Revenge* was entangled with this *Philip*, four others boarded her; two on her larboard, and two on her starboard. The fight thus beginning at three of the clock in the afternoon, continued very terrible all that evening. But the great *San Philip* having received the lower tier of the *Revenge*, discharged with crossbar-shot, shifted herself with all diligence from her sides, utterly misliking her first entertainment.

Some say that the ship foundered, but we cannot report it for truth, unless we were assured. The Spanish ships were filled with companies of soldiers, in some two hundred besides the mariners; in some five, in others eight hundred. In ours there were none at all beside the mariners, but the servants of the commanders and some few voluntary gentlemen only. After many interchanged volleys of great ordnance and small shot, the Spaniards deliberated to enter the *Revenge*, and made divers attempts, hoping to force her by the multitudes of their armed soldiers and musketeers, but were still repulsed again and again, and at all times beaten back into their own ships, or into the seas. In the beginning of the fight, the *George Noble* of London, having received some shot through her by the armados fell under the lee of the *Revenge*, and asked Sir Richard what he would command him, being but one of the victuallers and of small force; Sir Richard bid him save himself and leave him to his fortune. After the fight had thus without intermission continued while the day lasted and some hours of the night, many of our men were slain and hurt, and one of the great galleons of the Armada, and the *Admiral of the Hulks* both sunk, and in many other of the Spanish ships great slaughter was made. Some write that Sir Richard was very dangerously hurt almost in the beginning of the fight, and lay speechless for a time ere

THE SERVICE OF THE STATE

he recovered. But two of the *Revenge's* own company, brought home in a ship of Lime from the Islands, examined by some of the lords and others, affirmed that he was never so wounded as that he forsook the upper deck, till an hour before midnight, and then being shot into the body with a musket as he was a-dressing, was again shot into the head, and withal his chirurgeon wounded to death. This agreeth also with an examination taken by Sir Francis Godolphin, of four other mariners of the same ship being returned, which examination, the said Sir Francis, sent unto Master William Killigrew, of Her Majesty's Privy Chamber.

But to return to the fight, the Spanish ships which attempted to board the *Revenge*, as they were wounded and beaten off, so always others came in their places, she having never less than two mighty galleons by her sides, and aboard her. So that ere the morning from three of the clock the day before, there had fifteen several armados assailed her, and all so ill approved their entertainment, as they were by the break of day far more willing to hearken to a composition, than hastily to make any more assaults or entries. But as the day increased, so our men decreased, and as the light grew more and more, by so much more grew our discomforts. For none appeared in sight but enemies, saving one small ship called the *Pilgrim*, commanded by Jacob Whiddon, who hovered all night to see the success, but in the morning bearing with the *Revenge*, was hunted like a hare amongst many ravenous hounds, but escaped.

All the powder of the *Revenge* to the last barrel was now spent, all her pikes broken, forty of her best men slain, and the most part of the rest hurt. In the beginning of the fight she had but one hundred free from sickness, and fourscore and ten sick laid in hold upon the ballast. A small troop to man such a ship, and a weak garrison to resist so mighty an army. By those hundred all was sustained, the volleys, boardings, and enterings of fifteen ships of war, besides those which beat her at large. On the contrary, the Spanish were always supplied with soldiers brought from every squadron; all manner of arms and powder at will. Unto ours there remained no comfort at all, no hope, no supply either of ships, men or weapons; the masts all beaten overboard, all her tackle cut asunder, her upper work altogether razed, and in effect evened she was with the water, but the very foundation or bottom of a ship, nothing being left overhead either for flight or defence.

Sir Richard finding himself in this distress, and unable any longer to make resistance, having endured in this fifteen hours' fight the assault of fifteen several armados, all by turns aboard him, and by estimation eight hundred shot of great artillery, besides many assaults and entries, and that himself and the ship must needs be possessed by the enemy, who were now all cast in a ring round about him, the *Revenge* not being able to move one way or other, but as she was moved with the waves and billows of the sea, commanded the master gunner, whom he knew to be a most resolute man to split and sink the ship, that thereby nothing might remain of glory or victory to the Spaniards. Seeing in so many hours' fight and with so great a navy they were not able to take her, having had fifteen hours time, fifteen thousand men, and fifty and three sail of men-of-war to perform it withal; and persuaded the company, or as many as he could induce, to yield themselves unto God, and to the mercy of none else; but as they had like valiant, resolute men repulsed so many enemies, they should not now shorten the honour of their nation by prolonging their own lives for a few hours, or a few days. The master gunner readily condescended and divers others, but the captain and the master were of another opinion, and besought Sir Richard to have care of them, alleging that the Spaniard would be as ready to entertain a composition as they were willing to offer the same and that there being divers sufficient and valiant men yet living, and whose wounds were not mortal, they might do their country and prince acceptable service hereafter; and that where Sir Richard had alleged that the Spaniards should never glory to have taken one ship of Her Majesty's, seeing that they had so long and so notably defended themselves, they answered that the ship had six foot of water in the hold, three shot under water, which were so weakly stopped, as with the first working of the sea she must needs sink, and was besides so crushed and bruised, as she could never be removed out of the place.

And as the matter was thus in dispute, and Sir Richard refusing to hearken to any of those reasons, the master of the *Revenge* (while the captain won unto him the greater party) was conveyed aboard the General Don Alfonso Bassan, who finding none over hasty to enter the *Revenge* again, doubting lest Sir Richard would have blown them up and himself, and perceiving by the report of the master of the *Revenge* his dangerous disposition, yielded that all their lives should be saved, the company sent for England, and the better sort to pay such reasonable ransom as their estate should bear, and in the mean season to be free from galley or imprisonment. To this he so much the rather condescended, as well as I have said, for fear of further loss and mischief to themselves, as also for the desire he had to recover Sir Richard Grenville, whom, for his notable valour, he seemed greatly to honour and admire.

When this answer was returned, and that safety of life was promised, the common sort being now at the end of their peril, the most drew back from Sir Richard and the master gunner, being no hard matter to dissuade men from death to life. The master gunner finding himself and Sir Richard thus prevented and mastered by the greater number, would have slain himself with a sword, had he not been by force withheld and locked into his cabin. Then the General sent many boats aboard the *Revenge*, and divers of our men fearing Sir Richard's disposition, stole away aboard the General and other ships. Sir Richard thus overmatched, was sent unto by Alfonso Bassan to remove out of the *Revenge*, the ship being marvellous unsavoury, filled with blood and bodies of dead and wounded men, like a slaughter-house. Sir Richard answered that he might do with his body what he list, for he esteemed it not, and as he was carried out of the ship he swooned, and reviving again, desired the company to pray for him. The General used Sir Richard with all humanity, and left nothing unattempted that tended to his recovery, highly commending his valour and worthiness, and greatly bewailed the danger wherein he was, being unto them a rare spectacle and a resolution seldom approved, to see one ship turn towards so many enemies, to endure the charge and boarding of so many huge armados, and to resist and repel the assaults and entries of so many soldiers; all of which and more is confirmed by a Spanish captain of the same Armada, and a present actor in the fight, who being severed from the rest in a storm was by the *Lion of London*, a small ship, taken and is now prisoner in London.

VII. AN AMBASSADOR'S LETTER

RALPH WINWOOD to SIR ROBERT CECIL, 1600; *Vol. I, page* 314 *in* Winwood's Memorials. *This letter is typical of many which the Cecils received from their correspondents abroad. The official letters of ambassadors were checked by the reports of regular Government spies and the information given by returned travellers or merchants.*

PARIS,
10*th April,* 1600.

RIGHT HONOURABLE,

The King departing from hence upon the last speech I had with him, to Fontainebleau, as I then advertised, and with him Monsieur de Villeroy (though he presently returned, and since hath been retired at his house at Conflans, this week being wholly consecrated to devotion) I have had no convenient means to procure answer of what I last negotiated; holding it better to attend until after the Feast than to importune in an unseasonable time their resolution in so unpleasing a subject. For nothing sounds so ill in the ears of this Court as the repayment of their debts and the return of those good offices which they have received from their allies and neighbour princes.

The King with the Queen doth keep his Easter at Orleans, whither in devotion he is gone to gain a Pardon, the Pope having thither transferred the Jubilee, which he promiseth in all points shall be available as that which the year past was observed at Rome. Before the holydays we look for his return to this town, whither his Guards are already come from Fontainebleau.

Here is a speech of one Monsieur Beaumont to succeed Monsieur de Boisisse; he is son to the premier President of the Parliament here, a man, Del Espee, and one that was sent to her Majesty from the King, at such time as he besieged Amiens. It is not yet resolved but he acknowledgeth he hath been solicited by his friends not to refuse so honourable a charge.

Though the King some time since hath been possessed of the country of Bresse, and of the Castle of Bourg, yet Monsieur Lesdiguieres maketh no haste to render the Fort of Montmelian to the Duke of Savoy, desiring first to be satisfied of the sum of 40,000 ducats, which since the last wars, for the ransom of certain prisoners which he delivered upon his word, the Duke doth owe him: which sum the King doth permit him to levy upon the country of Savoy, before the Duke shall re-enter into possession. They are likewise desirous to see what shall become of this great army, which the Duke of Savoy and the Count Fuentes doth still keep on foot in Lombardy. The Venetians have lately sent to Monsieur Vaudemont, the second son of Lorrain, who is their Lieutenant of their forces Oltromontaine, to be in a readiness whensoever they shall call him. Augustino di Hirrero, Chancellor of Gaunt, who passed this last week by this town into Flanders from Spain, doth confirm that the Queen there is with child. Whereupon some here discourse that the Archduke and Infanta, seeing themselves fallen from the hope of the succession of that crown, if the States would show themselves conformable to any honourable accord, they would easily be persuaded to chase the Spaniards from out their dominions, disunite themselves from the Crown of Spain, and renew the ancient alliances, which in former time the House of Burgundy so happily did hold. Neither would it be a matter of great difficulty to persuade the Duke of Savoy upon the same reason, his children being the next Pretenders, to undertake for the Duchy of Milan. In which cause he should find some good assistance from this realm, and perhaps might prevail, but that the other princes of Italy, who know the violence of his unquiet spirit, would oppose themselves to his designs, as both envying and fearing his greatness.

The King here hath assured the Agent of the States that the Treaty between her Majesty and Spain is dead, and not likely to be revived; partly because these troubles at home will not give leisure to attend to any foreign matters, partly because your honour will not further deal in it, to avoid the slander which the late Earl did affect to derive upon you. But they have been told that the reasons which induced her Majesty to hearken to the last motives were not founded upon so weak grounds; that when occasion should serve to follow them, you would not *ponere rumores ante salutem*.[1] Under your Honour's favour, I will presume to say thus much by the way, that there is no foundation to be made upon the amity of this nation, especially on the terms we now stand with them; witness both the small respect which is born to her Majesty for the reimbursement of her money, and the ill-treatment of her merchants, as well by the grievances of many heavy impositions, as by the rigour of those late edicts: which do not only abridge, but by consequence, banish out of their country, and utterly take away the free intercourse of our English commodities and trade. Your Honour may be pleased to consider whether it would not be convenient (at such time as her Majesty shall send her Ambassadors hither to congratulate this marriage, and to reside here) to have the Treaties which we hold with this Crown to be renewed, namely that of Bloys, whereby a universal *reglement* may be established for reviving of our trade, order taken for annual payment of her Majesty's debt until the debt be discharged, and provision made in all

[1] Place rumours before safety.

THE SERVICE OF THE STATE 45

cases maritime, and wrongs by sea that hereafter shall happen : for of those that are passed (most of them being of an ancient date), in my poor opinion, a general amnesty of both parts will be the surest and most sufficient remedy.

By letters from Spain it is advertised, that of the fleet which lately parted from Lisbon toward the Indies, 14 of the best ships are lost by tempest and 3,000 men, between mariners, merchants and passengers ; and from Flanders they say, that the Archduke hath contented all his mutineers, and paid all his garrisons so royally, that he hath advanced their pay for two months. Their rendezvous for the time was the 15th of this month by their style, and his purpose is to besiege Ostend.

Spinola, to those galleys which now he hath, doth attend eight more, which some say are by this time ready to set forward. Sir William Stanley is to return out of Spain, and hopes to have an employment in Ireland. Here is a bruit which closely and secretly passeth, that the Archduke either hath lately sent, or shortly is to send, certain sums of money to be distributed to the Catholics of England. I give the less credit to it, both because it is not probable that the Archduke hath such store, having so lately employed so much, and if he had, yet he knows how to bestow it to better purpose ; yet this report is here by some averred and believed. . . .

And so, &c.

Your Honour's, &c.
RALPH WINWOOD.

VIII. RAISING RECRUITS

WILLIAM SHAKESPEARE. *The Second Part of Henry IV*, 1600 ; *Act III, Scene* 2. *Shakespeare did not exaggerate the scandals of recruiting. Captains made a regular income by drawing the " dead pays " of soldiers who had died, and even faked their muster rolls with " shadows "—soldiers who were literally* nominis umbræ.

CAPTAIN SIR JOHN FALSTAFFE, *with* BARDOLPH, *his corporal, arrives at* JUSTICE SHALLOW'S *manor to choose his recruits.*

SHALLOW. Look, here comes good Sir John. Give me

your good hand, give me your worship's good hand: by my troth, you like [1] well and bear your years very well: welcome, good Sir John.

FALSTAFFE. I am glad to see you well, good Master Robert Shallow: [*saluting*] Master Surecard, as I think?

SHALLOW. No, Sir John; it is my cousin Silence, in commission with me.

FALSTAFFE. Good Master Silence, it well befits you should be of the peace.

SILENCE. Your good worship is welcome.

FALSTAFFE [*mopping his brow*]. Fie! this is hot weather, gentlemen. Have you provided me here half a dozen sufficient men?

SHALLOW. Marry, have we, sir. Will you sit? [FALSTAFFE *sits*.]

FALSTAFFE. Let me see them, I beseech you.

SHALLOW [*to his servants*]. Where's the roll? where's the roll? where's the roll? Let me see, let me see, let me see. [*Taking the roll and running his finger down it.*] So, so, so, so, so, so, so; yea, marry, sir; Ralph Mouldy! Let them appear as I call; let them do so, let them do so. Let me see: [*testily*] where is Mouldy?

MOULDY [*stepping forward*]. Here, an't please you.

SHALLOW What think you, Sir John? a good-limbed fellow; young, strong, and of good friends.

FALSTAFFE. Is thy name Mouldy?

MOULDY. Yea, an't please you.

FALSTAFFE. 'Tis the more time thou wert used.

SHALLOW. Ha, ha, ha! most excellent, i' faith! things that are mouldy lack use; very singular good! in faith, well said, Sir John, very well said.

FALSTAFFE [*to* SHALLOW]. Prick him.

MOULDY [*grumbling*]. I was pricked well enough before, an you could have let me alone: my old dame will be undone now for one to do her husbandry and her drudgery: you need not to have pricked me; there are other men fitter to go out than I.

[1] Look.

THE SERVICE OF THE STATE

FALSTAFFE. Go to: peace, Mouldy; you shall go Mouldy, it is time you were spent.

MOULDY. Spent!

SHALLOW. Peace, fellow, peace; stand aside: know you where you are? For the other, Sir John: let me see: Simon Shadow!

FALSTAFFE. Yea, marry, let me have him to sit under: he's like to be a cold soldier.

SHALLOW. Where's Shadow?

SHADOW [*stepping forward*]. Here, sir.

FALSTAFFE. Shadow, whose son art thou?

SHADOW. My mother's son, sir.

FALSTAFFE. Thy mother's son! like enough, and thy father's shadow: so the son of the female is the shadow of the male: it is often so, indeed; but much of the father's substance!

SHALLOW. Do you like him, Sir John?

FALSTAFFE. Shadow will serve for summer; prick him, for we have a number of shadows to fill up the muster-book.

SHALLOW. Thomas Wart!

FALSTAFFE. Where's he?

WART. Here, sir.

FALSTAFFE. Is thy name Wart?

WART. Yea, sir.

FALSTAFFE. Thou art a very ragged wart.

SHALLOW. Shall I prick him down, Sir John?

FALSTAFFE. It were superfluous; for his apparel is built upon his back and the whole frame stands upon pins: prick him no more.

SHALLOW. Ha, ha, ha! you can do it, sir; you can do it: I commend you well. Francis Feeble! [FEEBLE *steps forward.*]

FEEBLE. Here, sir.

FALSTAFFE. What trade art thou, Feeble?

FEEBLE. A woman's tailor, sir.

SHALLOW. Shall I prick him, sir?

FALSTAFFE. You may; but if he had been a man's

tailor, he'd ha' pricked you. Wilt thou make as many holes in an enemy's battle as thou hast done in a woman's petticoat?

FEEBLE [*valiantly*]. I will do my good will, sir; you can have no more.

FALSTAFFE. Well said, good woman's tailor! well said, courageous Feeble! thou wilt be as valiant as the wrathful dove or most magnanimous mouse. Prick the woman's tailor: well, Master Shallow; deep Master Shallow.

FEEBLE. I would Wart might have gone, sir.

FALSTAFFE. I would thou wert a man's tailor, that thou mightest mend him and make him fit to go. I cannot put him to a private soldier that is the leader of so many thousands: let that suffice, most forcible Feeble.

FEEBLE. It shall suffice, sir.

FALSTAFFE. I am bound to thee, reverend Feeble. Who is next?

SHALLOW. Peter Bullcalf o' the Green!

FALSTAFFE. Yea, marry, let's see Bullcalf.

BULLCALF. Here, sir.

FALSTAFFE. 'Fore God, a likely fellow. Come, prick me Bullcalf till he roar again.

BULLCALF. O Lord! good my lord captain——

FALSTAFFE. What, dost thou roar before thou art pricked?

BULLCALF [*huskily*]. O Lord, sir! I am a diseased man.

FALSTAFFE. What disease hast thou?

BULLCALF. A whoreson cold, sir, a cough, sir, which I caught with ringing in the King's affairs upon his Coronation Day, sir.

FALSTAFFE. Come, thou shalt go to the wars in a gown; we will have away thy cold; and I will take such order that thy friends shall ring for thee. Is here all?

SHALLOW. Here is two more called than your number; you must have but four here, sir: and so, I pray you, go in with me to dinner.

FALSTAFFE. Come, I will go drink with you, but I can-

THE SERVICE OF THE STATE 49

not tarry dinner. I am glad to see you, by my troth, Master Shallow.

SHALLOW. O, Sir John, do you remember since we lay all night in the windmill in Saint George's field?

FALSTAFFE. No more of that, good Master Shallow, no more of that.

SHALLOW. Ha! 'twas a merry night. And is Jane Nightwork alive?

FALSTAFFE. She lives, Master Shallow.

SHALLOW. She never could away with me.

FALSTAFFE. Never, never; she would always say she could not abide Master Shallow.

SHALLOW. By the mass, I could anger her to the heart. She was then a bona-roba. Doth she hold her own well?

FALSTAFFE. Old, old, Master Shallow.

SHALLOW. Nay, she must be old; she cannot choose but be old; certain she's old; and had Robin Nightwork by old Nightwork before I came to Clement's Inn

SILENCE. That's fifty-five years ago.

SHALLOW. Ha, cousin Silence, that thou hadst seen that that this knight and I have seen! Ha, Sir John, said I well?

FALSTAFFE. We have heard the chimes at midnight, Master Shallow.

SHALLOW. That we have, that we have, that we have; in faith, Sir John, we have: our watchword was "Hem boys!" Come, let's to dinner; come, let's to dinner: Jesus, the days that we have seen! Come, come.

[FALSTAFFE *and the* JUSTICES *withdraw*.]

BULLCALF [*quietly slipping some money into* BARDOLPH'S *hand*]. Good Master Corporate Bardolph, stand my friend; and here's four Harry ten shillings in French crowns for you. In very troth, sir, I had as lief be hanged, sir, as go: and, yet, for my own part, sir, I do not care; but rather because I am unwilling, and, for mine own part, have a desire to stay with my friends; else, sir, I did not care, for mine own part, so much.

BARDOLPH. Go to ; stand aside.
MOULDY [*piteously*]. And, good Master Corporal Captain, for my old dame's sake, stand my friend : she has nobody to do anything about her when I am gone ; and she is old, and cannot help herself : you shall have forty, sir.
BARDOLPH. Go to ; stand aside.
FEEBLE [*heroically*]. By my troth, I care not ; a man can die but once : we owe God a death : I'll ne'er bear a base mind : an't be my destiny, so ; an't be not, so ; no man is too good to serve's prince ; and let it go which way it will, he that dies this year is quit for the next.
BARDOLPH. Well said ; thou'rt a good fellow.
FEEBLE. Faith, I'll bear no base mind.

IX. DRILLING THE TRAIN-BANDS

FRANCIS BEAUMONT and JOHN FLETCHER. Knight of the Burning Pestle, 1611 ; *Act V, Scene* 11. *The train-bands of the City paraded annually at Mile-end.*

RALPH *marches in at the head of his company, with drums beating and colours flying.*

RALPH. March fair, my hearts ! Lieutenant, beat the rear up. Ancient, let your colours fly ; but have a great care of the butchers' hooks at Whitechapel ; they have been the death of many a fair ancient.[1] Open your files, that I may take a view both of your persons and munition. Sergeant, call a muster. [*He stands aside to watch his troops.*]
SERGEANT A stand ! [*The company halt ; the* SERGEANT *takes out his roll and proceeds to call it.*] William Hammerton, pewterer !
HAMMERTON. Here, captain !
RALPH [*critically examining his equipment*]. A corslet and a Spanish pike ! 'tis well. Can you shake it with a terror ?
HAMMERTON. I hope so, captain.

[1] Ancient (like its more modern form ensign) meant both standard and standard-bearer.

RALPH. Charge upon me. [*He levels his pike feebly at* RALPH.] 'Tis with the weakest: Put more strength, William Hammerton, more strength. As you were again. Proceed, Sergeant.

SERGEANT. George Greengoose, poulterer!

GREENGOOSE. Here!

RALPH. Let me see your piece, neighbour Greengoose; when was she shot in?

GREENGOOSE. An't like you, master captain, I made a shot even now, partly to scour her, and partly for audacity.

RALPH. It should seem so certainly; for her breath is yet inflamed. Get you a feather, neighbour, get you a feather, sweet oil, and paper, and your piece may do well enough yet. Where's your powder?

GREENGOOSE [*producing a paper bag from his pocket*] Here.

RALPH. What, in a paper? as I am a soldier and a gentleman, it craves a martial-court! You ought to die for't. Where's your horn? Answer me to that.

GREENGOOSE [*sheepishly*]. An't like you, sir, I was oblivious.

RALPH. It likes me not you should be so; 'tis a shame for you, and a scandal to all our neighbours, being a man of worth and estimation, to leave your horn behind you: I am afraid 'twill breed example. But let me tell you, no more on't. Stand, till I view you all. [*He passes down the ranks*]. What's become o' th' nose of your flask?

1ST SOLDIER. Indeed-la, captain, 'twas blown away with powder.

RALPH. Put on a new one at the City's charge. Where's the stone of this piece?

2ND SOLDIER. The dummer took it out to light tobacco.

RALPH. 'Tis a fault, my friend; put it in again. You want a nose, and you a stone. Sergeant, take a note on't, for I mean to stop it in the pay. [*He proceeds to drill the company.*] Remove and march! Soft and fair, gentlemen, soft and fair! Double your files. As you were! Faces about! Now, you with the sodden face, keep in there! Look to your match, sirrah, it will be in your fellow's flask anon. So; make a crescent now; advance your pikes; stand and give ear! [*He stands in front of his soldiers and addresses them.*] Gentlemen, countrymen, friends, and my fellow-soldiers, I have brought you this day from the shops of security, and the counters of content, to measure out in these furious fields, honour by the ell, and prowess by the pound. Let it not, oh, let it not, I say, be told hereafter, the noble issue of this City fainted; but bear yourselves in this fair action like men, valiant men, and free men! Fear not the face of the enemy, nor the noise of the guns; for, believe me, brethren, the rude rumbling of a brewer's cart is far more terrible, of which you have a daily experience: Neither let the stink of powder offend you, since a more valiant stink is nightly with you. To a resolved mind, his home is everywhere. I speak not this to take away the hope of your return; for you shall see (I do not doubt it) and that very shortly your loving wives again, and your sweet children, whose care doth bear you company in baskets. Remember then whose cause you have in hand, and, like a sort of true-born scavengers, scour me this famous realm of enemies. I have no more to say but this: Stand to your tacklings, lads, and show to the world, you can as well brandish a sword as shake an apron. Saint George, and on, hearts!

ALL [*valiantly*] Saint George, Saint George!

[*They shoulder their weapons and all march out.*]

X. SEDITIONS AND TROUBLES

FRANCIS BACON. Essays.

The causes and motives of seditions are: innovation in religion; taxes; alteration of laws and customs; breaking of privileges; general oppression; advancement of unworthy persons; strangers; dearths; disbanded soldiers; factions grown desperate; and whatsoever in

THE SERVICE OF THE STATE

offending people, joineth and knitteth them in a common cause.

For the remedies ; there may be some general preservatives, whereof we will speak ; as for the just cure, it must answer to the particular disease, and so be left to counsel rather than rule.

The first remedy or prevention is to remove by all means possible that material cause of sedition whereof we spake ; which is want and poverty in the estate. To which purpose serveth the opening and well-balancing of trade ; the cherishing of manufactures ; the banishing of idleness ; the repressing of waste and excess by sumptuary laws ; the improvement and husbanding of the soil ; the regulating of prices of things vendible ; the moderating of taxes and tributes ; and the like. Generally, it is to be foreseen that the population of a kingdom (especially if it be not mown down by wars) do not exceed the stock of the kingdom which should maintain them. Neither is the population to be reckoned only by number, for a smaller number, that spend more and earn less, do wear out an estate sooner than a greater number, that live lower and gather more. Therefore the multiplying nobility and other degrees of quality, in an over-proportion to the common people, doth speedily bring a State to necessity; and so doth likewise an overgrown clergy, for they bring nothing to the stock ; and in like manner, when more are bred scholars than preferments can take off.

XI. CANKERS OF THE COMMONWEALTH—A SCHOLAR AND A SOLDIER OUT OF EMPLOYMENT

The Puritan Widow, 1607 ; *Act I, Scene 2, printed in the* Shakespeare Apocrypha. *This passage illustrates the preceding one. The " scholar " without employment who was unwilling to turn his hand to manual labour was a perpetual nuisance ; yet from the overplus of scholars came the " University Wits " who made a precarious living by writing for the Press, and thence the real beginnings of English drama as literature.*

GEORGE PYEBORD, *a needy scholar, and a citizen enter;*
PETER SKIRMISH, *an old soldier, comes up to them.*

PYEBORD. What's to be done now, old Lad of War? thou that wert wont to be as hot as a turn-spit, as nimble as a fencer, and as lowsy as a schoolmaster; now thou art put to silence like a secretary. War sits now like a Justice of Peace, and does nothing. Where be your muskets, calivers [1] and hotshots? [2] In Long Lane, at pawn, at pawn. Now keys are your only guns, key-guns, key-guns, and bawds the gunners, who are your sentinels in peace, and stand ready charged to give warning, with hem, hums and pocky coughs; only your chambers are licensed to play upon you, and drabs enough to give fire to 'em.

SKIRMISH. Well, I cannot tell, but I am sure it goes wrong with me, for since the cessure of the wars, I have spent about a hundred crowns out a purse. I have been a soldier any time this forty years, and now I perceive an old soldier and an old courtier have both one destiny, and in the end, turn both into hobnails. [3]

PYEBORD. Pretty mystery for a beggar, for indeed, a hobnail is the true emblem of a beggar's shoe sole.

SKIRMISH. I will not say but that war is a blood-sucker, and so, but in my conscience, (as there is no soldier but has a piece of one, though it be full of holes like a shot ancient, no matter, 'twill serve to swear by) in my conscience, I think some kind of peace has more hidden oppressions, and violent heady sins (though looking of a gentle nature) than a professed war.

PYEBORD. Troth, and for mine own part, I am a poor gentleman and a scholar; I have been matriculated in the University, wore out six gowns there, seen some fools, and some scholars, some of the city, and some of the country, kept order, went bare-headed over the quadrangle, eat my commons with a good stomach, and battled [4] with discretion; at last, having done many sleights and tricks to

[1] A hand-gun lighter than a musket.
[2] Skirmishers. [3] I.e. take to the road.
[4] Battels are college accounts for board and provisions.

THE SERVICE OF THE STATE 55

maintain my wit in use (as my brain would never endure me to be idle) I was expelled the University, only for stealing a cheese out of Jesus College.[1]

SKIRMISH. Is't possible?

PYEBORD. Oh! there was one Welshman (God forgive him) pursued it hard; and never left, till I turned my staff toward London, where, when I came, all my friends were pit holed, gone to graves (as indeed there was but a few left before). Then was I turned to my wits, to shift in the world, to tour among sons and heirs, and fools and gulls, and ladies' eldest sons, to work upon nothing, to feed out of flint, and ever since has my belly been much beholding to my brain. But, now, to return to you, old Skirmish: I say as you say, and for my part wish a turbulency in the world, for I have nothing to lose but my wits, and I think they are as mad as they will be: and to strengthen your argument the more, I say, an honest war is better than a bawdy peace, as touching my profession. The multiplicity of scholars hatched and nourished in the idle calms of peace, makes 'em, like fishes, one devour another; and the community of learning has so played upon affections, and thereby almost religion is come about to fantasy, and discredited by being too much spoken of in so many and mean mouths, I myself, being a scholar and a graduate, have no other comfort by my learning, but the affection of my words,[2] to know how scholarlike to name what I want, and can call myself a beggar both in Greek and Latin; and therefore, not to cog[3] with peace, I'll not be afraid to say, 'tis a great breeder, but a barren nourisher; a great getter of children which must either be thieves or rich men, knaves or beggars.

SKIRMISH. Well, would I had been born a knave, than when I was born a beggar; for if the truth were known, I think I was begot when my father had never a penny in his purse.

PYEBORD. Puh, faint not, old Skirmish; let this war-

---

[1] Jesus College, Oxford, was much frequented by Welshmen.
[2] An affected vocabulary.   [3] Cheat.

rant thee, *facilis descensus Averni*,[1] 'tis an easy journey to a knave; thou may'st be a knave when thou wilt; and peace is a good madam to all other professions, and an arrant drab to us; let us handle her accordingly, and by our wits thrive in despite of her; for since the law lives by quarrels, the courtier by smooth God-morrows, and every profession makes itself greater by imperfections, why not we then by shifts, wiles and forgeries? and seeing our brains are our only patrimonies, let's spend with judgment, not like a desperate son and heir, but like a sober and discreet Templer—one that will never march beyond the bounds of his allowance. And for our thriving means, thus: I myself will put on the deceit of a Fortune-teller

SKIRMISH. A Fortune-teller? Very proper.

PYEBORD. And you of a figure-caster, or a conjurer

SKIRMISH. A conjurer?

PYEBORD. Let me alone; I'll instruct you, and teach you to deceive all eyes but the Devil's.

SKIRMISH. Oh ay, for I would not deceive him, and I could choose, of all others.

PYEBORD. Fear not, I warrant you; and so by those means we shall help one another to patients, as the condition of the age affords creatures enough for cunning to work upon.

SKIRMISH. Oh, wondrous! new fools and fresh asses.

PYEBORD. Oh, fit, fit! excellent.

SKIRMISH. What, in the name of conjuring?

PYEBORD. My memory greets me happily with an admirable subject to graze upon. The lady widow, who of late I saw weeping in her garden for the death of her husband; sure sh'as but a waterish soul and half on't by this time is dropped out of her eyes: deuce, well managed, may do good upon her. It stands firm, my first practice shall be there.

SKIRMISH. You have my voice, George.

PYEBORD. Sh'as a grey gull to her brother, a fool to her only son, and an ape to her youngest daughter. I

[1] " It's an easy journey to hell."

THE SERVICE OF THE STATE 57

overheard 'em severally, and from their words I'll derive my device; and thou, old Peter Skirmish, shalt be my second in all sleights.

SKIRMISH. Ne'er doubt me, George Pye-boord—only you must teach me to conjure.

PYEBORD. Puh, I'll perfect thee, Peter. [CAPTAIN IDLE, *with his arms pinioned, and surrounded by a guard, passes over the stage.*] How now, what's he?

SKIRMISH. Oh, George! this sight kills me. 'Tis my sworn brother, Captain Idle.

PYEBORD. Captain Idle!

SKIRMISH. Apprehended for some felonious act or other. He has started out, h'as made a night on't, lacked silver. I cannot but commend his resolution; he would not pawn his buff jerkin. I would either some of us were employed, or might pitch our tents at usurers' doors, to kill the slaves as they peep out at the wicket.

PYEBORD. Indeed, those are our ancient enemies; they keep our money in their hands, and make us to be hanged for robbing of 'em. But, come, let's follow after to the prison, and know the nature of his offence; and what we can stead him in, he shall be sure of; and I'll uphold it still, that a charitable knave is better than a soothing Puritan.

XII. A FALSE ALARM

A Letter from John Chamberlain to Dudley Carleton, 9th August, 1599; page 58 in the Camden Society's reprint, 1861. The defeat of the Spanish Armada in 1588 was by no means the end of the war with Spain; for fifteen years after the country was constantly disturbed by rumours of impending invasions and greater Armadas—a state of affairs which contributed not a little to the general feeling of unrest, social and intellectual, of the closing years of Elizabeth's reign.

Though here be little happened since I wrote last, but only scambling provisions and preparations for war, yet because I cannot tell when I shall write again if any sudden alarm call us away, I think it not amiss to let you understand what was and is intended to be done The news increasing daily of the Spaniards coming, and advertisements concurring from all parts, of their design for London, (whereof the Adelantado himself gave out proud speeches,) and the day of their departure from the Groin being said to be appointed at the uttermost as Sunday last, order was given for a camp to be raised, whereof the Lord Admiral to be General, the Lord Mountjoy Lieutenant, Sir Francis Vere Marshal, the Earl of Northumberland General of the Horse, the Earl of Sussex Colonel-General of the Infantry, Sir William Russell his Lieutenant (but he refused), Sir Thomas Wilford Sergeant-Major, Sir Edward Wotton a Treasurer, and Mr. Maynard Secretary. The rendezvous for Hertfordshire men was to be at Tottenham, the 12th of this month, and so forward to Tilbury, or somewhere else, as should be enjoined them. Your cousin Lytton hath the leading of 300 men, and came up to make his provisions, whom I mean to accompany, and (though I were never professed soldier) to offer myself in defence of my country, which is the best service I can do it. Twelve or thirteen of the Queen's ships are preparing in all haste, whereof the Lord Thomas Howard to be Admiral, Sir Walter Ralegh Vice-Admiral, Fulke Greville Rear Admiral. Sir Thomas Gerrard was appointed Colonel of the Londoners, but for an old grudge since the last Parliament, they would none of him, whereupon the Earl of Cumberland was given them, to have charge of them and the river, which he undertook with great confidence, meaning to make a bridge somewhat on this side Gravesend, after an apish imitation of that of Antwerp, and to that end, got together all the lighters, boats, Western barges, cables and anchors that were to be found, giving out that with 1,500 musketeers he would defend that bridge or lose his life upon it (but God forbid he should have been put to it); but whether upon trial they find it not feasible, as bearing another manner of breadth and billow than the river of Antwerp, or upon what other reason, I know not; yesterday, after much turmoil and great charges bestowed, it was quite given over, and now they have an imagination

THE SERVICE OF THE STATE 59

of sinking certain hulks in the channel, if need should be. Upon Monday, toward evening, came news (yet false) that the Spaniards were landed in the Isle of Wight, which bred such a fear and consternation in this town as I would little have looked for, with such a cry of women, chaining of streets and shutting of gates, as though the enemy had been at Blackwall. I am sorry and ashamed that this weakness and nakedness of ours on all sides should show itself so apparently as to be carried far and near, to our disgrace both with friends and foes. Great provision is made for horse, as being the best advantage we are like to have if the enemy come. And the noblemen about Court have rated themselves at round proportions, as the Lord Admiral 100, the Earl of Shrewsbury 100, the Earl of Pembroke 200, the Earl of Worcester 100, the Earl of Northumberland 100, Mr. Secretary 100, the Archbishop 100, Sir William Russell 50, and all the rest, both Court and country, according to their ability. But now, after all this noise and blustering, methinks the weather begins to clear somewhat, for our preparations begin to slack and go not on so headlong as they did, so that there may be hope all shall be well; and our rendezvous at Tottenham is put off for five days. Out of Ireland we have uncertain reports of divers feats done, as that the Lord Cromwell hath overthrown 6,000 of Tyrone's company, but I cannot learn when nor where; that the Earl of Essex hath likewise defeated 1,500 in Ofalie, laying 140 of them along and bringing away 1,000 cows and more; that Captain Masterson and Sir Francis Darcy should be slain; that there should be a new supply of eight or ten knights made. Sir Gelly Merricke, they say, is newly come over, by whom we shall understand some more certainty. The last that came, report that they left Sir Henry Norris in hard case, and make account his life will not long tarry after his leg. The world comes very fast upon Mr. Wallop, who going into Ireland to bury his father, within five days after his arrival his mother died also, so that he shall put them both into one account   The Lord Burleigh is made President of York,

and makes provision to go thither shortly. The Queen, at her being at Wimbledon, made two knights, Withipoole of Suffolk, and one Lassells, of Yorkshire. The Court continues at Nonesuch, where I wish it may tarry long. And so, commending myself to your good affections, I bid you farewell. From London, this 9th of August, 1599.
Yours most assuredly,
JOHN CHAMBERLAIN.

XIII. AN APPEAL FOR UNITY

WILLIAM SHAKESPEARE, King John, *c.* 1595, *Act V, Scene* 7, *line* 112. *This, and many other patriotic speeches pronounced on the stage, had, and was intended to have, a special meaning for the original audience, at a time when the country was threatened with invasion from abroad and civil war at home.*

This England never did, nor never shall,
Lie at the proud foot of a conqueror,
But when it first did help to wound itself.
Now these her princes are come home again,
Come the three corners of the world in arms,
And we shall shock them. Nought shall make us rue,
If England to itself do rest but true.

SECTION THREE
EDUCATION AND YOUTH

I. PARSON AND SCHOOLMASTER

WILLIAM SHAKESPEARE. Love's Labour's Lost, c. 1593; *Act V, Scene 1. There can be little doubt that Shakespeare was here caricaturing some well-known persons in this play. The pronunciation controversy was acute at the Universities at this time.*

[HOLOFERNES, *the Schoolmaster*, SIR NATHANIEL, *the Curate, and* DULL, *the Constable, after a hearty meal, enter together.*]

HOLOFERNES. *Satis quod sufficit.*

NATHANIEL. I praise God for you, sir: your reasons at dinner have been sharp and sententious: pleasant without scurrility, witty without affection,[1] audacious without impudency, learned without opinion, and strange without heresy. I did converse this quondam day with a companion of the King's, who is intituled, nominated, or called Don Adriano de Armado.

HOLOFERNES. *Novi hominem tanquam te:*[2] his humour is lofty, his discourse peremptory, his tongue filed, his eye ambitious, his gait majestical, and his general behaviour vain, ridiculous, and thrasonical. He is too picked, too spruce, too affected, too odd, as it were, too peregrinate,[3] as I may call it.

NATHANIEL [*jotting it down in his note-book*]. A most singular and choice epithet.

---

[1] Affectation.
[2] "I know the man as well as I know you."
[3] Has too many traveller's airs.

HOLOFERNES. He draweth out the thread of his verbosity finer than the staple of his argument. I abhor such fanatical phantasimes,[1] such insociable and point-devise companions; such rackers of orthography, as to speak "dout", fine, when he should say doubt; "det", when he should pronounce debt—d, e, b, t, not d, e, t; he clepeth [2] a calf, "cauf"; half, "hauf"; neighbour vocatur "nebour"; n e i g h abbreviated "ne". This is ab*h*ominable—which he would call "abbominable": it insinuateth me of insanie; *anne intelligis, domine?*[3] to make frantic, lunatic.

NATHANIEL. *Laus Deo, bene intelligo.*[4]

HOLOFERNES. Bon, bon, fort bon! Priscian a little scratched, 'twill serve.

NATHANIEL. *Videsne quis venit?*[5]

HOLOFERNES. *Video, et gaudeo.*[6]

II. MUSIC IN THE SCHOOL CURRICULUM

RICHARD MULCASTER, Elementary, 1582; *page 65 in Campagnac's edition. Mulcaster laid down as the five subjects, necessary to an Elementary education, reading, writing, drawing, music, and grammar. Until the overspreading of Puritanism the English were famous for their love of music and song.*

As for music, which I have divided into voice and instrument, I will keep this current. The training up in music, as in all other faculties, hath a special eye to these points: the child itself that is to learn; the matter itself which he is to learn; and the instrument whereon he is to learn. Wherein I will deal so for the first and last, that is for the child and the instrument, as neither of them shall lack whatsoever is needful either for framing of the child's voice or for the righting of his finger, or for the pricking of his lessons, or for the tuning of his instrument. For in the

---

[1] Fantastics.
[2] Calls.
[3] "Do you understand, master?"
[4] "Praise God, I understand well."
[5] "Do you see who is coming?"
[6] "I see and rejoice."

voice there is a right pitch, that it be neither over nor under strained, but delicately brought to her best ground, both to keep out long, and to rise or fall within due compass, and so to become tuneable with regard to health and pleasant to hear. And in the fingering also there is a regard to be had, both that the child strike so as he do not shuffle, neither spoil any sound, and that his finger run so both sure and sightly, as it cumber not itself with entangled delivery. Whereof the first commonly falleth out by too much haste in the young learner who is ever longing until he be a leaving ; the second fault comes of the master himself, who doth not consider the natural dexterity and sequel in the joints, which being used right and in a natural consequence procureth the finger a nimbleness with ease, and helpeth the delivery to readiness without pain, as the untoward fingering must needs bring in corruption, though corrupt use do not use to complain. For the matter of music which the child is to learn I will set it down how and by what degrees and in what lessons a boy that is to be brought up to sing, may and ought to proceed by ordinary ascent, from the first term of art, and the first note in sound, until he shall be able without any often or any great missing to sing his part in pricksong,[1] either himself alone, which is his first rudeness, or with some company, which is his best in practice. For I take so much to be enough for an elementary institution which saluteth but the faculty, though it perfect the principle, and I refer the residue for setting and discant, to increase of cunning, which daily will grow on, and to further years, when the holy body of music will come and crave place. And yet because the child must still mount somewhat that way, I will set him down some rules of setting and descant, which will make him better able to judge of singing being a setter himself, as in the tongue, he hath used to write, shall best judge of a writer. Concerning the virginals and the lute which two instruments I have therefore chosen because of the full music which is uttered by them and the variety of fingering, which is showed upon,

[1] Music sung from notes.

them, I will also set down so many chosen lessons for either of them as shall bring the young learner to play reasonable well on them both, though not at the first sight, whether by the ear or by the book, always provided that pricksong go before plain. All which lessons both for instrument and voice, I will not only name and set the learner over to get them where he can in the written song books set forth by music masters, but I will cause them all to be pricked and printed in the same principle of music, that both the reader may judge of them and the scholar learn by them. Which thing as well as all the rest that I have undertaken to perform in this *Elementary*, I hope by God's help to bring to such effect thorough conference with the best practitioners in our time and the counsel of the best learned writers in any time, in every of the principles, besides mine own travail, and some not negligent experience, as I shall discharge my promise, and content my good countrymen. What thing soever else besides this that I have named shall seem to be needful for the better opening of any particular point, I will see to it there, though I said nothing of it here. This is the sum of my elementary platform for the matter thereof.

III. IN THE SCHOOLROOM—A LESSON IN LATIN GRAMMAR

JOHN MARSTON. What You Will, 1601; *Act II, Scene 2.*

[*A schoolroom. The* PEDANT *draws the curtains, revealing* BATTUS, NOUS, SLIP, NATHANIEL *and* HOLOFERNES PIPPO, *his pupils, with books in their hands.*]

ALL. *Salve, magister!* [1]
PEDANT. *Salvete pueri, estote salvi, vos salvere exopto vobis salutem. Batte, mi fili, mi Batte!* [2]
BATTUS. *Quid vis?* [3]

---

[1] "Hail, master."
[2] "Good morning, my boys, I hope you are well. Battus, my boy, my Battus."
[3] "What is your wish?"

EDUCATION AND YOUTH

PEDANT. Stand forth: repeat your lesson without book.
BATTUS. A noun is the name of a thing that may be seen, felt, heard, or understood.
PEDANT. Good boy: on, on.
BATTUS. Of nouns, some be substantives and some be substantives.
PEDANT. Adjectives.
BATTUS. Adjectives. A noun substantive either is proper to the thing that it betokeneth——
PEDANT. Well, to numbers.
BATTUS. In nouns be two numbers, the singular and the plural: the singular number speaketh of one, as *lapis*, a stone; the plural speaketh of more than one, as *lapides*, stones.
PEDANT. Good child. Now thou art past *lapides*, stones, proceed to the cases. Nous, say you next, Nous. Where's your lesson, Nous?
NOUS. I am in a verb, forsooth.
PEDANT Say on, forsooth: say, say.
NOUS. A verb is a part of speech declined with mood and tense, and betokeneth doing, as *amo*, I love.
PEDANT. How many kinds of verbs are there?
NOUS. Two: personal and impersonal.
PEDANT. Of verbs personal, how many kinds?
NOUS. Five: active, passive, neuter, deponent, and common. A verb active endeth in *o*, and betokeneth to do, as *amo*, I love; and by putting to *r*, it may be a passive, as *amor*, I am loved.
PEDANT. Very good child. Now learn to know the deponent and common. Say you, Slip.
SLIP. *Cedant arma togæ, concedat laurea linguæ.*[1]
PEDANT. What part of speech is *lingua*? *Inflecte, inflecte.*
SLIP. *Singulariter, nominativo hæc lingua.*
PEDANT. Why is *lingua* the feminine gender?
SLIP. Forsooth because it is the feminine gender.

[1] "Let arms yield to the gown, the laurel give place to the tongue"—i.e. the arts and honours of peace take the place of war.

PEDANT. Ha, thou ass! thou dolt! *idem per idem;* mark it: *lingua* is declined with *hæc,* the feminine, because it is a household stuff, particularly belonging and most resident under the roof of women's mouths. Come on, you Nathaniel, say you, say you next; not too fast; say tretably [1]: say.

NATHANIEL. *Mascula dicuntur monosyllaba nomina quædam.* [2]

PEDANT. Faster! faster!

NATHANIEL. *Ut sal, sol, ren et splen: car, ser, vir, vas, vadis, as, mas,*
Bes, cres, pres et pes, glis, gliris habens genetivo,
Mos, flos, ros et tros, muns, dens, mons, pons——

PEDANT. *Rup, tup, snup, slup, bor, hor, cor, mor.* Holla! holla! holla! you Holofernes Pippo, put him down. Wipe your nose: fie, on your sleeve! where's your muckender [3] your grandmother gave you? Well, say on; say on.

HOLOFERNES. Pree, master, what word's this?

PEDANT. Ass! ass!

HOLOFERNES. ——*As in presenti perfectum format in, n, in*——

PEDANT. In what, sir?

HOLOFERNES [*confused*]. *Perfectum format* . . . In what, sir?

PEDANT. In what, sir?—*in avi.*

HOLOFERNES. In what, sir?—*in avi. Ut no, nas, navi: vocito, vocitas, voci . . . voci . . . voci*—— [4]

PEDANT. What's next?

HOLOFERNES. *Voci*—what's next?

PEDANT. Why, thou ungracious child! thou simple animal! thou barnacle! Nous, snare him; take him up: [5] and you were my father, you should up.

[1] With clear utterance.
[2] Certain monosyllabic nouns are called masculine.
[3] Handkerchief.
[4] "*-as* in the present forms its perfect in *-avi,* as *no, nas, navi; vocito, vocitas, vocitavi.*"
[5] Take up: mount, hoist on the back ready for a thrashing

EDUCATION AND YOUTH 67

HOLOFERNES. Indeed I am not your father. O Lord! now, for God sake let me go out. My mother told a thing: I shall bewray all else. Hark, you master: my grandmother entreats you to come to dinner to-morrow morning.

PEDANT [*his anger increasing*]. I say, untruss; take him up. Nous, dispatch! what, not perfect in an —*as in presenti*?

HOLOFERNES. In truth I'll be as perfect an *as in presenti* as any of this company, with the grace of God, law: this once—this once—and I do so any more——

PEDANT. I say, hold him up!

HOLOFERNES. Ha, let me say my prayers first. You know not what you ha' done now; all the syrup of my brain is run into my buttocks, and ye spill the juice of my wit well. Ha, sweet! ha, sweet! honey, Barbary sugar, sweet master.

PEDANT. Sans tricks, trifles, delays, demurrers,[1] procrastinations, or retardations, mount him, mount him.

IV. A LESSON IN ACTING

The Return from Parnassus. Part I, 1600; *Act IV, Scene* 3. The Pilgrimage to Parnassus *and its sequels the two parts of* The Return from Parnassus *were written for performances at St. John's College, Cambridge, in* 1597, 1600 *and* 1601. *They give a vivid picture of the seamy side of University life.* Philomusus *and* Studioso, *the two undergraduates, can find no employment after coming down from the University and in despair are forced to try acting. The University Wits were very jealous of the players for whom they wrote.*

[BURBAGE, *the tragedian, and* KEMPE, *the clown, wait for their prospective pupils.*]

BURBAGE. Now, Will Kempe, if we can entertain these scholars at a low rate, it will be well, they have oftentimes a good conceit in a part.

KEMPE. It's true indeed, honest Dick, but the slaves are somewhat proud, and, besides, it is a good sport in a part to see them never speak in their walk but at the end

[1] Legal objection.

of the stage ; just as though in walking with a fellow we should never speak but at a stile, a gate, or a ditch, where a man can go no farther. I was once at a comedy in Cambridge, and there I saw a parasite make faces and mouths of all sorts on this fashion. [*He makes a few.*]

BURBAGE. A little teaching will mend these faults, and it may be besides they will be able to pen a part.

KEMPE. Few of the University pen plays well, they smell too much of that writer Ovid, and that writer Metamorphosis, and talk too much of Proserpina and Jupiter. Why, here's our fellow Shakespeare puts them all down, aye, and Ben Jonson too. Oh, that Ben Jonson is a pestilent fellow ; he brought up Horace giving the poets a pill, but our fellow Shakespeare hath given him a purge that made him bewray his credit.[1]

BURBAGE. It's a shrewd fellow indeed. I wonder these scholars stay so long, they appointed to be here presently that we might try them ; oh, here they come.

[STUDIOSO *and* PHILOMUSUS, *the scholars, approach.*]

STUDIOSO. Take heart, these lets our clouded thoughts refine,
The sun shines brightest when it 'gins decline.

BURBAGE. Master Philomusus and Master Studioso, God save you.

KEMPE. Master Philomusus and Master Otioso, well met.

PHILOMUSUS. The same to you, good Master Burbage. What, Master Kempe, how doth the Emperor of Germany ?

STUDIOSO. God save you, Master Kempe : welcome Master Kempe from dancing the morris over the Alps.

KEMPE. Well, you merry knaves, you may come to the honour of it one day. Is it not better to make a fool of the world, as I have done, than to be fooled of the world,

---

[1] There is no satisfactory explanation of " Shakespeare's purge " ; it was presumably a play in which Jonson was brought on as a character. The incident was part of the stage war between Jonson with the Children of Blackfriars on one side, and Marston with the Children of Paul's and the professional players on the other.

EDUCATION AND YOUTH 69

as you scholars are ? But be merry, my lads, you have happened upon the most excellent vocation in the world for money ; they come North and South to bring it to our playhouse ; and for honours, who of more report than Dick Burbage and Will Kempe ? He is not counted a gentleman, that knows not Dick Burbage and Will Kempe. There's not a country wench that can dance Sellenger's Round but can talk of Dick Burbage and Will Kempe.

PHILOMUSUS. Indeed, Master Kempe, you are very famous, but that is as well for your works in print as your part in cue.

KEMPE. You are at Cambridge still with *size que*,[1] and be lusty humorous poets ; you must untruss ; I made this my last circuit purposely because I would be judge of your actions.

BURBAGE. Master Studioso, I pray you take some part in this book and act it, that I may see what will fit you best. I think your voice would serve for Hieronimo. Observe how I act it and then imitate me.

[BURBAGE *recites the speech,* " *Who calls Hieronimo from his waked bed ?* "[2] *Then* STUDIOSO *imitates him.*]

BURBAGE. You will do well after a while.

KEMPE. Now for you, Master Philomusus, methinks you should belong to my tuition, and your face methinks would be good for a foolish Mayor or a foolish Justice of Peace ; mark me : " Forasmuch as there be two states of a commonwealth, the one of peace, the other of tranquillity ; two states of war, the one of discord, the other of dissension ; two states of an incorporation, the one of the Aldermen, the other of the Brethren ; two states of magistrates, the one of governing, the other of bearing rule, now, as I said even now, for a good thing, thing cannot be said too often. Virtue is the shooing-horn of justice, that is, virtue is the shooing-horn of doing well, that is, virtue is the shooing-horn of doing justly, it behoveth me and is my part to

---

[1] Farthing allowances for food.
[2] From *The Spanish Tragedy.*

commend this shooing-horn unto you. I hope this word shooing-horn doth not offend any of you, my worshipful brethren, for you being the worshipful headsmen of the town, know well what the horn meaneth. Now, therefore, I am determined not only to teach but also to instruct, not only the ignorant, but also the simple, not only what is their duty towards their betters, but also what is their duty towards their superiors." Come, let me see how you can do, sit down in the chair.

[PHILOMUSUS *repeats the speech.*]

KEMPE. Thou wilt do well in time, if thou wilt be ruled by thy betters, that is, by myself, and such grave Aldermen of the playhouse as I am.

BURBAGE. I like your face and the proportion of your body for Richard the Third. I pray, Master Philomusus, let me see you act a little of it.

PHILOMUSUS. "Now is the winter of our discontent [1] Made glorious summer by the son of York . . ."

BURBAGE. Very well, I assure you; well, Master Philomusus and Master Studioso, we see what ability you are of; I pray walk with us to our fellows and we'll agree presently.

PHILOMUSUS. We will follow you straight, Master Burbage.

KEMPE. It's good manners to follow us, Master Philomusus and Master Otioso.

[*The two actors walk away.*]

PHILOMUSUS [*bitterly*]. And must the basest trade yield us relief?
Must we be practis'd to those leaden spouts,
That naught do vent but what they do receive?
Some fatal fire hath scorched our fortune's wing,
And still we fall, as we do upward spring;
As we strive upward to the vaulted sky,
We fall and feel our hateful destiny.

[1] From the prologue to Shakespeare's *Richard III.*

V. THE IDEAL STUDENT: RULES FOR BEHAVIOUR AT THE UNIVERSITY

HENRY PEACHAM. The Compleat Gentleman, 1632; *page 38 in Gordon's edition.*

Since the University whereunto you are embodied is not untruly called the Light and Eye of the Land, in regard from hence, as from the centre of the sun, the glorious beams of knowledge disperse themselves over all, without which a chaos of blindness would repossess us again; think now that you are in public view, and *nucibus relictis*,[1] with your gown you have put on the man, that from hence the reputation of your whole life taketh her first growth and beginning. For as no glory crowneth with more abundant praise than that which is here won by diligence and wit, so there is no infamy abaseth the value and esteem of a gentleman all his life after more than that procured by sloth and error in the Universities; yea, though in those years whose innocency have ever pleaded their pardon; whereat I have not a little marvelled, considering the freedom and privilege of greater places.

But as in a delicate garden kept by a cunning hand, and overlooked with a curious eye, the least disorder or rankness of any one flower putteth a beautiful bed or well-contrived knot out of square, when rudeness and deformity is born withal in rough and undressed places: so believe it, in this Paradise of the Muses, the least neglect and impression of error's foot is so much the more apparent and censured, by how much the sacred Arts have greater interest in the culture of the mind, and correction of manners.

Wherefore your first care, even with the pulling off your boots, let be the choice of your acquaintance and company. For as infection in cities in a time of sickness is taken by concourse and negligent running abroad, when those that keep within and are wary of themselves escape with more safety, so it falleth out here in the University; for this eye

[1] "Having put away childish things."

hath also her diseases as well as any other part of the body, (I will not say with the physicians, more) with those, whose private houses and studies being not able to contain them, are so cheap of themselves, and so pliable to good fellowship abroad, that in mind and manners (the tokens plainly appearing) they are past recovery ere any friend could hear they were sick.

Entertain therefore the acquaintance of men of the soundest reputation for religion, life and learning, whose conference and company may be unto you μουσεῖον ἔμψυχον, καὶ περιπατοῦν, a living and a moving library. "For conference and converse was the first mother of all arts and science," as being the greatest discovery of our ignorance and increaser of knowledge, teaching and making us wise by the judgments and examples of many: and you must learn herein of Plato, φιλομαθῆ, φιλήκοον, καὶ ζητητικὸν εἶναι that is, "To be a lover of knowledge; desirous to hear much, and lastly, to inquire and ask often."

For the companions of your recreation, comfort yourself with gentlemen of your own rank and quality, for that friendship is best contenting and lasting. To be over free and familiar with inferiors, argues a baseness of spirit, and begetteth contempt; for as one shall here at the first prize himself, so let him look at the same rate for ever after to be valued of others.

Carry yourself even and fairly, *Tanquam in statera*,[1] with that moderation in your speech and action (that you seem with Ulysses, to have Minerva always at your elbow :) which, should they be weighed by Envy herself, she might pass them for current; that you be thought rather leaving the University, than lately come thither. But hereto the regard of your worth, the dignity of the place, and abundance of so many fair precedents, will be sufficient motive to stir you up.

Husband your time to the best, for, "The greedy desire of gaining Time is a covetousness only honest." And if

[1] "As if on a balance."

you follow the advice of Erasmus, and the practice of Plinius secundus, *Diem in operas partiri*, to divide the day into several tasks of study, you shall find a great ease and furtherance hereby ; remembering ever to refer your most serious and important studies unto the morning, " which finisheth alone " (say the learned) " three parts of the work ". Julius Caesar having spent the whole day in the field about his military affairs, divided the night also, for three several uses : one part for his sleep, a second for the commonwealth and public business, the third for his book and studies. So careful and thrifty were they then of this precious treasure which we as prodigally lavish out, either vainly or viciously, by whole months and years, until we be called to an account by our great Creditor, who will not abate us the vain expense of a minute.

VI. REVELS AT GRAY'S INN

Gesta Grayorum, 1594 ; page 22 in the Malone Society Reprint. See page 36. These revels at Gray's Inn were held in 1594, when the members of Gray's Inn entertained the members of the Temple. Each Society pretended to be a kingdom, those of Gray's Inn electing their Prince with his officers.

When the Ambassador was placed, as aforesaid, and that there was something to be performed for the delight of the beholders, there arose such a disordered tumult and crowd upon the stage, that there was no opportunity to effect that which was intended ; there came so great a number of worshipful personages upon the stage that might not be displaced, and gentlewomen, whose sex did privilege them from violence, that when the Prince and his officers had in vain a good while expected and endeavoured a reformation, at length there was no hope of redress for that present. The Lord Ambassador and his train thought that they were not so kindly entertained as was before expected, and thereupon would not stay any longer at that time, but in a sort discontented and displeased. After their departure the throngs and tumults did somewhat cease, although so much of them continued as was able to disorder and confound any good inventions whatsoever. In regard whereof, as also for that the sports intended were especially for the gracing of the Templarians, it was thought good not to offer anything of account, saving dancing and revelling with gentlewomen, and after such sports, a *Comedy of Errors* (like to Plautus his *Menechmus*) was played by the players. So that night was begun, and continued to the end, in nothing but confusion and errors; whereupon it was ever afterwards called "The Night of Errors"

VII. THE WOES OF A PRIVATE TUTOR

The Return from Parnassus. Part I, 1600; *Act II, Scene* 1

[STUDIOSO *enters with his scholar, a spoilt child.*]

STUDIOSO. Ey, here's a true Pedantius, and yet no truculent Orsylius; one that can hear a boy speak false Latin without stamping of his feet, can look on a false verse without wrinkling of his brow, one that will give his scholar leave to prove as very a dunce as his father, and ne'er command the untrussing of his points.[1] My hands are bound to the peace, and his wit is bound to the good bearing, for it will not bear. I have in the bottom of my duty brought my young master a stool and a boss,[2] a boss for his worship's feet, and a stool for the young fool to speak false Latin on. Well, here comes the dandiprat!

BOY [*tossing up a coin*]. Schoolmaster, cross or pile now for 4 counters?[3]

STUDIOSO. Why cross, my wag! for things go cross with
    me,
Else would I whip this childish vanity.

BOY. Schoolmaster, it's pile.

---

[1] Laces, i.e. prepare himself for a beating.
[2] Footstool.   [3] Heads or tails.

EDUCATION AND YOUTH

STUDIOSO. Well may it pile in such a piled age,
When scholars serve in such base vassalage.
  BOY. I must have 4 counters of you.
  STUDIOSO. Full many a time Fortune encounters me;
More happy they that in the Counter [1] be.
  BOY. You'll pay them, I hope?
  STUDIOSO. Fortune hath paid me home, that I may pay;
And yet, sweet wag, I hope you'll give me day.
  BOY. What day will you take to pay them?
  STUDIOSO. That day I'll take when learning flourisheth,
When scholars are esteemed by country churls,
When ragged pedants have their passports sealed
To whip fond wags for all their knavery,
When scholars wear no baser livery
Nor spend their days in servile slavery.
  BOY. But when will this be, schoolmaster?
  STUDIOSO. When silly shrubs th' ambitious cedars beat,
Or when hard oaks soft honey 'gins to sweat.
But wilt please you to go to your book a little?
  BOY. What will you give me then?
  STUDIOSO. A rasin, or an apple; or a rod, if I had authority. Wilt please you, sir, to sit down and repeat your lecture?
  BOY [*repeating his lesson*]. *Quamquam te, Marce fili*; &c.
  STUDIOSO. *Quæ pars orationis,* " *Athenis* "?
  BOY. I'll speak English to-day.
  STUDIOSO. What part of speech is it then?
  BOY. A noun adjective.
  STUDIÓSO. No, it's a noun substantive.
  BOY. I say it's a noun adjective, and if I fetch my mother to you, I'll make you confess as much.
  STUDIOSO. I would thy mother could stand as well by herself as this word doth!
Then should thy sire have a more naked head,
And less shame waiting on his jaded bed.
  BOY. I am weary of learning; I'll go bowl awhile,
And then I will go to my book again.

[1] The City prison

VIII. ALCHEMIST'S JARGON

BEN JONSON. The Alchemist, 1610; *Act II, Scene 5*. *Jonson in this amusing play ridicules the " scientists " who were seeking to transmute base metals into gold. Many of them were quite serious experimenters, but there were not a few rascals such as Subtle. Any one who wishes to puzzle out the meaning of the alchemical terms should consult one of the annotated editions (e.g. that by F. E. Schelling in the " Belles Lettres Series "). The terms are taken from George Ripley's Compound of Alchemy, and other quite serious works.*

[ANANIAS, *the Puritan, pays a visit to* SUBTLE, *the supposed Alchemist.*]

SUBTLE. Where is my drudge?

[FACE *enters.*]

FACE. Sir!
SUBTLE. Take away the recipient,
And rectify your menstrue from the phlegma.
Then pour it on the Sol, in the cucurbite,
And let them macerate together.
FACE. Yes, sir.
And save the ground?
SUBTLE. No; *terra damnata*
Must not have entrance in the work.—Who are you?
ANANIAS. A faithful brother, if it please you.
SUBTLE. What's that?
A Lullianist? a Ripley?[1] *Filius artis?*
Can you sublime and dulcify? calcine?
Know you the sapor pontic? sapor stiptic?
Or what is homogene, or heterogene?
ANANIAS. I understand no heathen language, truly.
SUBTLE. Heathen! you Knipper-doling![2] is *Ars sacra*,
Or chrysopœia, or spagyrica,
Or the pamphysic, or panarchic knowledge,
A heathen language?
ANANIAS. Heathen Greek, I take it.

---
[1] Raymond Lully and George Ripley, two famous **alchemists**.
[2] An Anabaptist who led a revolt in Munster in 1533.

SUBTLE. How! heathen Greek?
ANANIAS. All's heathen but the Hebrew.
SUBTLE. Sirrah my varlet, stand you forth and speak to him,
Like a philosopher: answer in the language.
Name the vexations, and the martyrisations
Of metals in the work.
FACE. Sir, putrefaction,
Solu- on, ablution, sublimation,
Cohobation, calcination, ceration and
Fixation.
SUBTLE. This is heathen Greek, to you, now!—
And when comes vivification?
FACE. After mortification.
SUBTLE. What's cohobation?
FACE. 'Tis the pouring on
Your *aqua regis*, and then drawing him off,
To the trine circle of the seven spheres.
SUBTLE. What's the proper passion of metals?
FACE. Malleation.
SUBTLE. What's your *ultimum supplicium auri*?
FACE. Antimonium.
SUBTLE. This is heathen Greek to you!—
And what's your mercury?
FACE. A very fugitive, he will be gone, sir.
SUBTLE. How know you him?
FACE. By his viscosity,
His oleosity, and his suscitability.
SUBTLE. How do you sublime him?
FACE. With the calce of egg-shells,
White marble, talc.
SUBTLE. Your magisterium now,
What's that?
FACE. Shifting, sir, your elements,
Dry into cold, cold into moist, moist into hot,
Hot into dry.
SUBTLE. This is heathen Greek to you still!
Your *lapis philosophicus*?

FACE. 'Tis a stone,
And not a stone ; a spirit, a soul, and a body :
Which if you do dissolve, it is dissolved ;
If you coagulate, it is coagulated ;
If you make it to fly, it flieth.
SUBTLE. Enough.

[FACE *goes out.*]

This is heathen Greek to you ! What are you, sir ?
ANANIAS. Please you, a servant of the exiled brethren,
That deal with widows' and with orphans' goods,
And make a just account unto the saints :
A deacon.
SUBTLE. Oh, you are sent from Master Wholesome,
Your teacher ?
ANANIAS. From Tribulation Wholesome,
Our very zealous pastor.
SUBTLE. Good ! I have
Some orphans' goods to come here.
ANANIAS. Of what kind, sir ?
SUBTLE. Pewter and brass, andirons and kitchen ware,
Metals, that we must use our medicine on :
Wherein the brethren may have a pennyworth
For ready money.
ANANIAS. Were the orphans' parents
Sincere professors ?
SUBTLE. Why do you ask ?
ANANIAS. Because
We then are to deal justly, and give, in truth,
Their utmost value.
SUBTLE. 'Slid, you'd cozen else,
And if their parents were not of the faithful !—
I will not trust you, now I think on it,
Till I have talked with your pastor. Have you brought money
To buy more coals ?
ANANIAS. No, surely.
SUBTLE. No ! how so ?

ANANIAS. The brethren bid me say unto you, sir,
Surely, they will not venture any more
Till they may see projection.
  SUBTLE. How!
  ANANIAS. You have had,
For the instruments, as bricks, and loam, and glasses,
Already thirty pound; and for materials,
They say, some ninety more : and they have heard since,
That one, at Heidelberg, made it of an egg,
And a small paper of pin-dust.
  SUBTLE. What's your name?
  ANANIAS. My name is Ananias.
  SUBTLE. Out, the varlet.
That cozened the apostles! Hence, away!
Flee, mischief! had your holy consistory
No name to send me, of another sound,
Than wicked Ananias? send your elders
Hither, to make atonement for you, quickly,
And give me satisfaction; or out goes
The fire; and down th' alembics, and the furnace,
Piger Henricus, or what not. Thou wretch!
Both sericon and bufo shall be lost,
Tell them. All hope of rooting out the bishops,
Or the anti-Christian hierarchy [1] shall perish,
If they stay threescore minutes : the aqueity,
Terreity, and sulphureity
Shall run together again, and all be annulled,
Thou wicked Ananias!

[ANANIAS *hurries away.*]

This will fetch 'em,
And make them haste towards their gulling more.
A man must deal like a rough nurse, and fright
Those that are froward, to an appetite.

[1] The Puritan objected on conscientious grounds to bishops and wished to remodel the Church government on more Scriptural and democratic lines ; they proposed amongst other things to make the Sovereign subject to the supreme council of Elders. See page 183.

IX. THE PATHWAY TO PREFERMENT

WILLIAM POWELL. Tom of all Trades or the Plain Pathway to Preferment, 1631; *pages* 171 *and* 173 *in the New Shakespeare Society reprint.*

The Land Soldier.

If a land soldier think to thrive and rise by degrees of service, from a common soldier to a captain, in this age, alas, he is much deceived.

That custom is obsolete, and grown out of use. Do what he can do in land-service, he shall hardly rise by his single merit.

His happiness shall be but to fill his hungry belly, and satiate himself upon a pay-day.

But if he be of kin, or a favourite to some great officer, he may carry the colours the first day, be a lieutenant the second, and a captain before he knows how many days go to the week in their regiment.

The land-service, where a man may learn most experience of war discipline, is in the Low Countries, by reason of the long exercise of wars and variety of stratagems there.

Beyond that, northward, the service is both more unprofitable and more dangerous, and less experience is to be there learned.

The more your son turns his face to the south, the more profitable the land-service is.

Lastly, if he have no friend or kindred to raise him in the land-service, I assure you that there is no law against buying and selling of offices in the Low Countries, for aught that I have read; neither is it markable amongst them.

After the soldier returns home, it makes no matter what number of wounds he can reckon about him.

All the ways of relief for him that I can number are these:

A poor Knight's place of Windsor; if the Herald report him a gentleman and the Knights of the Honourable Order of the Garter will accept him.

A Brother of Sutton's Hospital; if the feoffees have not servants of their own to prefer before him.

EDUCATION AND YOUTH

Pensioner of the county; if the Justices find him worthy, and that he was pressed forth of the same county.

St. Thomas' in Southwark, and St. Bartholomew's, Smithfield, only till their wounds or diseases be cured, and no longer; and that, if the masters of the said Hospitals please to receive them.

For the Savoy, where soldiers had a foundation, I know none now.

And other houses appropriated for relief of soldiers now in use, I remember none.

For the chief are long since demolished, the Templarii are gone, the Knights of St. John of Jerusalem forgotten. That famous house upon Lincoln Green is razed to the ground, and many the like, now better known by the records than the remains of their ruins, with their revenue, are all diverted from the uses of their first foundation to private and peculiar inheritances, which I pity more than the dissolution of all the Monasteries that ever were.

Here, you see, is preferment enough for your six sons, though you bestow every one upon a several profession; only take this general rule for all, viz.:

To what course soever your sons shall betake them, be sure that they all have grammar learning at the least, so shall they be able to receive and retain the impression of any the said professions; and otherwise, shall scarce possibly become masters in the same, or any one of them; or if they do, it will be with more than ordinary pains and difficulty.

The Disposal of Daughters.

I would have their breeding like to the Dutch woman's clothing, tending to profit only and comeliness.

Though she never have a dancing-schoolmaster, a French tutor, nor a Scotch tailor to make her shoulders of the breadth of Bristow Cowsway, it makes no matter; for working in curious Italian purls or French borders, it is not worth the while. Let them learn plain works of all kind, so they take heed of too open seaming. Instead of song and music, let them learn cookery and laundry. And instead of reading Sir Philip Sidney's *Arcadia*, let them read the *Grounds of Good Housewifery*. I like not a female poetess at any hand. Let greater personages glory their skill in music, the posture of their bodies, their knowledge in languages, the greatness and freedom of their spirits, and their arts in arraigning of men's affections at their flattering faces. This is not the way to breed a private gentleman's daughter.

If the mother of them be a good housewife and religiously disposed, let her have the bringing up of one of them. Place the other two forth betimes, and before they can judge of a good manly leg. The one in the house of some good merchant, or citizen of civil and religious government; the other in the house of some lawyer, some judge, or well reported justice or gentleman of the country, where the serving man is not too predominant. In any of these she my learn what belongs to her improvement : for sempstry, for confectionery, and all requisites of housewifery. She shall be sure to be restrained of all rank company and unfitting liberty, which are the overthrow of too many of their sex. . . .

The merchant's factor and citizen's servant of the better sort cannot disparage your daughters with their society.

And the judges', lawyers', and justices' followers are not ordinary serving men, but men of good breed, and their education for the most part clerkly, whose service promiseth their farther and future advancement.

Your daughter at home will make a good wife for some good yeoman's eldest son, whose father will be glad to crown his sweating frugality with alliance to such a house of gentry.

The young man's fingers will itch to be handling of taffeta; and to be placed at the table, and to be carved unto by Mistress Dorothy, it will make him and the good plain old Joan, his mother, to pass over all respect of portion or patrimony.

EDUCATION AND YOUTH

For your daughter at the merchant's, and her sister, if they can carry it wittily, the City affords them variety.

The young factor, being fancy-caught in his days of innocency, and before he travels so far into experience as into foreign countries, may lay such a foundation of first love in her bosom as no alteration of climate can alter.

So likewise may Thomas, the foreman of the shop, when beard comes to him, as apprenticeship goes from him, be entangled and belimed with the like springs, for the better is as easily surprised as the worst.

Some of your clerkly men complain the moisture of their palms; others the sorpego in their wrists : both moving means.

With a little patience your daughter may light upon some Counsellor at Law who may be willing to take the young wench, in hope of favour with the old Judge. An attorney will be glad to give all his profits of a Michaelmas term, fees and all, but to woo her through a crevice. And the parson of the parish, being her Lady's chaplain, will forswear eating of tithe-pig for a whole year for such a parcel of glebe land at all times.

SECTION FOUR

TRAVEL AND TRADE

I. THE ENTHUSIASTIC TRAVELLER

THOMAS CORYAT. *Coryat's Crudities, 1611; Vol. I, page 8 in the Maclehose edition. The popular prejudice against travellers is constantly expressed in drama; but statesmen realized its value, and their views may be found in Bacon's essay* On Travel.

Since then I have thus far ventured with them, I will take occasion to speak a little of the thing which begat and produced these my observations, even of travel into foreign countries, whereby I may the better encourage gentlemen and lovers of travel to undertake journeys beyond the seas. Of all the pleasures in the world travel is, in my opinion, the sweetest and most delightful. For what can be more pleasant than to see passing variety of beautiful cities, Kings' and Princes' Courts, gorgeous palaces, impregnable castles and fortresses, towers piercing in a manner up to the clouds, fertile territories replenished with a very cornucopia of all manner of commodities as it were with the horn of Amalthea, tending both to pleasure and profit, that the heart of man can wish for; flourishing Universities (whereof only Germany yieldeth no less than three and twenty) furnished with store of learned men of all faculties, by whose conversation a learned traveller may much inform and augment his knowledge. What a singular and incomparable comfort is it to confer with those learned men in foreign Universities and noble cities, whose excellent works we read in our private studies at home, as with Isaac Casubonus the pearl of Paris; Paulus Aemylius in

TRAVEL AND TRADE

Padua; Rodolphus Hospinianus, Gasper Waserus, Henricus Bullingerus in Zurich; Amandus Polanus, Johannes Jacobus Gryneus in Basil; Janus Gruterus, David Pareus, Dionysius Gothofredus at Heidelberg; Johannes Piscator at Herborne; Bonaventura Vulcanius at Leyden. Most of whom it was my good hap not only to see in my travels, but also to my unspeakable solace to enjoy very copious and fruitful discourse with them. Again, what a contentment is it to a holy and religious Christian to visit the monuments and tombs of some of the ancient Saints and Fathers of the primitive Church; as of St. Augustin in Pavie, St. Ambrose in Milan, &c., also the ἐρείπια and ruins of the houses wherein those famous men lived as Cicero, Varro, Virgil, Livy, &c., that are to this day showed in sundry places of Italy, strike no small impression in the heart of an observative traveller. Likewise the places wherein divers famous battles have been fought, so much celebrated partly by the ancient Roman historiographers, and partly by other neoteric authors (many of which I exactly observed in my short voyage) when they are surveyed by a curious traveller, do seem to present to the eyes of his mind a certain idea of the bloody skirmishes themselves. Yea, such is the exuberancy and superfluity of these exotic pleasures that for my own part I will most truly affirm, I reaped more entire and sweet comfort in five months' travels of those seven countries mentioned in the front of my book, than I did all the days of my life before in England, which contained two and thirty years. Moreover, the knowledge of foreign languages (which the shortness of time did not afford me) acquired by industrious travel, yieldeth an ornament beyond all comparison the most precious and excellent that can be incident to a gentleman. For if the learning of two languages be commended by Ovid, who said:

Nec levis ingenuas pectus coluisse per artes
Cura sit, et linguas edidicisse duas,[1]

[1] "Take pains to cultivate your mind by the gentle arts, and to learn two languages."

much more praise doth he deserve that by travelling in France, Italy, Spain, Alemanny,[1] and the Netherlands, doth learn the five languages of those noble countries, which being added to his own mother tongue and the Latin, do answer the number of the seven liberal sciences. These certainly, and more, have been learned by famous travellers, as by Gulielmus Postellus, a Frenchman of excellent learning, who spake twelve languages; Julius Cæsar Scaliger, that incomparable scholar, nine; Joseph Scaliger that died not long since in Leyden, a University of Holland, spake ten. Gaspar Waserus that ornament of Zurich, my kind friend, speaketh eight. These are means that add much more grace and honour to an ingenious gentleman, than he can purchase unto himself by all the exterior gifts of fortune. For though gentility be of itself gracious, yet it is much more excellent when it is adorned with the experience of foreign countries. Even as a gold ring of itself is fair and beautiful, but much more resplendent when it is decked with a rich diamond or some other precious stone. I will also illustrate this matter by some famous examples that I have noted in my poor readings. . . .

But now I will descend to speak something of my own travels. It hath been oftentimes objected unto me since my coming home, by certain gentlemen of eminent note, and as it were laid in my dish as a choking pear, that for the short time that I was abroad I observed more solid matters than any Englishman did in the like space this long time. For I copied out more inscriptions and epitaphs (said a certain knight that shall pass nameless) that are written upon solid pieces of stone, than any judicious traveller would have done in many years. For which cause he branded me with the note of a tombstone traveller. Whereas it had been much more laudable, said he, to have observed the government of common-weals and affairs of state. I answer him that, because I am a private man and no statist, matters of policy are

[1] Germany.

impertinent unto me. For I observe that memorable distich:

Vive tibi, quantumque potes prælustria vita,
Sævum prælustri fulmen ab arce venit.[1]

Besides I have observed that in some places it is dangerous to pry very curiously into state matters, as divers travellers have observed by their dear experience: a most tragical example whereof I heard to have been showed in the city of Strasburg not long before my arrival there. Moreover, I hope that every gentle reader that shall with a mild censure peruse my observations, will say it was impossible for me in the space of five months to observe all these matters in descriptions of cities that I have handled, and politique affairs also. But because this objection shall not justly take hold upon me, that I am a tombstone traveller, if God shall grant me happy success in my next journey, I will so far wade into a few matters of politicy for the better satisfaction of the reader, as I may with security of my life attain unto.

II. THE CHARACTER OF AN AFFECTATE TRAVELLER

SIR THOMAS OVERBURY. Characters; *page 58 in Rimbault's edition.*

AN AFFECTATE TRAVELLER

Is a speaking fashion; he hath taken pains to be ridiculous, and hath seen more than he hath perceived. His attire speaks French or Italian, and his gait cries "Behold me". He censures all things by countenances, and shrugs and speaks his own language with shame and lisping: he will choke rather than confess beer good drink, and his toothpick is a main part of his behaviour. He chooseth rather to be counted a spy than not a politician; and

[1] "Live for yourself, and, as much as you can, avoid magnificence; the cruel thunderbolt comes from the magnificent sky," i.e. those who meddle with high matters run great risks.

maintains his reputation by naming great men familiarly. He chooseth rather to tell lies than not wonders, and talks with men singly. His discourse sounds big, but means nothing, and his boy is bound to admire him howsoever. He comes still from great personages, but goes with mean. He takes occasion to show jewels given him in regard of his virtue, that were bought in St. Martin's, and not long after having with a mountebank's method pronounced them worth thousands, impawneth them for a few shillings. Upon festival days he goes to Court, and salutes without re-saluting. At night in an ordinary he canvasseth the business in hand, and seems as conversant with all intents and plots as if he begot them. His extraordinary account of men is, first to tell them the ends of all matters of consequence, and then to borrow money of them; he offereth courtesies, to show them, rather than himself, humble. He disdains all things above his reach, and preferreth all countries before his own. He imputeth his want and poverty to the ignorance of the time, not his own unworthiness: and concludes his discourse with half a period, or a word, and leaves the rest to imagination. In a word, his religion is fashion, and both body and soul are governed by fame: he loves most voices above truth.

III. THE BOGUS TRAVELLER

"CUTHBERT CONNYCATCHER." The Defence of Conny Catching, 1592; *Vol. X, page* 33 *in the Bodley Head Quartos.*

There be in England, but especially about London, certain quaint, picked and neat companions [1] attired in their apparel, either *à la mode de France*, with a side cloak and a hat of a high block and a broad brim as if he could with his head cosmographize the world in a moment, or else *Allespanyole*, with a straight bombast sleeve like a quail pipe, his short cloak and his rapier hanging as if he were entering the list to a desperate combat, his beard squared with such art, either with his moustaches, after the lash of lions,

[1] Bad companions.

standing as stiff as if he wore a ruler in his mouth, or else nicked off with the Italian cut, as if he meant to profess one faith with the upper lip, and another with his nether lip, and then he must be marquisadoed with a side peak pendant, either sharp like the single of a deer, or curtold like the broad end of a mole spade. This gentleman, forsooth, haunteth tabling houses,[1] taverns, and such places, where young novices resort, and can fit his humour to all companies, and openly shadoweth his disguise with the name of a traveller, so that he will have a superficial insight into certain phrases of every language and pronounce them in such a grace as if he almost were that countryman born. Then shall you hear him vaunt of his travels, and tell what wonders he hath seen in strange countries ; how he hath been at Saint James of Compostella in Spain, at Madrid in the King's Court ; and then, drawing out his blade, he claps it on the board and swears he bought that in Toledo ; then will he rove to Venice, and with a sigh discover the situation of the city, how it is seated two leagues from Terrafrenia, in the sea, and speak of Rialto Treviso and Murano, where they make glasses ; and to set the young gentleman's teeth an edge, he will make a long tale of La Strado Courtizano, where the beautiful Courtesans dwell, describing their excellency, and what angelic creatures they be, and how amorously they will entertain strangers. Tush, he will discourse the state of Barbary, and there to Eschites and Alcaires, and from thence leap to France, Denmark and Germany ; after all, concluding thus :

"What is a gentleman", saith he, "without travel ? even as a man without one eye. The sight of sundry countries made Ulysses so famous. Bought wit is the sweetest and experience goeth beyond all patrimonies. Did young gentlemen, as well as I, know the pleasure and profit of travel, they would not keep them at home within their native continent but visit the world and win more wisdom in travelling two or three years, than all the wealth their ancestors left them to possess. Ah, the sweet sight

[1] Gambling dens.

of ladies, the strange wonders in cities, and the divers manners of men and their conditions were able to ravish a young gentleman's senses with the surfeit of content, and what is a thousand pounds spent to the obtaining of those pleasures ? "

All these novelties doth this pipned [1] bragout boast on, when his only travel hath been to look on a fair day from Dover cliffs to Calais, never having stepped a foot out of England, but surveyed the maps, and heard others talk what they knew by experience. Thus decking himself like the daw, with the fair feathers of other birds, and discoursing what he heard other men report, he grew so plausible among young gentlemen, that he got his ordinary at the least, and some gracious thanks for his labour.

IV. CORYAT AND THE JEWS IN VENICE

THOMAS CORYAT. *Coryat's Crudities*, 1611 ; *Vol. I, page* 374 *in the Maclehose edition.*

But now I will make relation of that which I promised in my treatise of Padua, I mean my discourse with the Jews about their religion. For when as walking in the court of the Ghetto, I casually met with a certain learned Jewish Rabbin that spake good Latin, I insinuated myself after some few terms of compliment into conference with him, and asked him his opinion of Christ, and why he did not receive Him for his Messias. He made me the same answer that the Turk did at Lyons, of whom I have before spoken, that Christ forsooth was a great Prophet, and in that respect as highly to be esteemed as any Prophet amongst the Jews that ever lived before Him, but derogated altogether from His divinity, and would not acknowledge Him for the Messias and Saviour of the world, because He came so contemptibly, and not with that pomp and majesty that beseemed the Redeemer of Mankind.

I replied that we Christians do, and will even to the effusion of our vital blood, confess Him to be the true and

[1] Probably for "picked", exquisite. See l. 2 of this extract.

TRAVEL AND TRADE 91

only Messias of the world, seeing He confirmed His doctrine while He was here on earth with such an innumerable multitude of divine miracles, which did most infallibly testify His divinity, and that they themselves, who are Christ's irreconcilable enemies, could not produce any authority either out of Moses, the Prophets, or any other authentic author to strengthen their opinion concerning the temporal kingdom of the Messias, seeing it was foretold to be spiritual : and told him that Christ did as a spiritual king reign over His subjects in conquering their spiritual enemies, the flesh, the world and the devil. Withal I added that the predictions and sacred oracles both of Moses, and all the holy Prophets of God, aimed altogether at Christ as their only mark, in regard He was the full consummation of the Law and the Prophets, and I urged a place of Esay unto him concerning the name Emanuel, and a virgin's conceiving and bearing of a son ; and at last descended to the persuasion of him to abandon and renounce his Jewish religion and to undertake the Christian Faith, without the which he should be eternally damned.

He again replied that we Christians do misinterpret the Prophets, and very perversely wrest them to our own sense, and for his own part, he had confidently resolved to live and die in his Jewish faith, hoping to be saved by the observations of Moses' Law. In the end he seemed to be somewhat exasperated against me, because I sharply taxed their superstitious ceremonies. For many of them are such refractory people that they cannot endure to hear any reconciliation to the Church of Christ, in regard they esteem Him but for a carpenter's son, and a silly poor wretch that once rode upon an ass, and most unworthy to be the Messias whom they expect to come with most pompous magnificence and imperial royalty, like a peerless monarch, guarded with many legions of the gallantest worthies, and most eminent personages of the whole world, to conquer not only their old country Judea and all those opulent and flourishing kingdoms, which heretofore belonged to the four ancient monarchies (such is their insupportable pride), but also all the nations generally under the cope of heaven, and make the King of Guiane, and all other Princes whatsoever dwelling in the remotest parts of the habitable world, His tributary vassals. Thus hath God justly infatuated their understandings, and given them the spirit of slumber (as St. Paul speaketh out of the Prophet Esay), "eyes that they should not see, and ears that they should not hear," unto this day.

But to shut up this narration of my conflict with the Jewish Rabbin, after there had passed many vehement speeches to and fro betwixt us, it happened that some forty or fifty Jews more flocked about me, and some of them began very insolently to swagger with me, because I durst reprehend their religion. Whereupon, fearing lest they would have offered me some violence, I withdrew myself by little and little, towards the bridge at the entrance into the Ghetto, with an intent to fly from them, but by good fortune, our noble Ambassador, Sir Henry Wotton, passing under the bridge in his gondola at that very time, espied me somewhat earnestly bickering with them, and so incontinently sent unto me out of his boat one of his principal gentlemen, Master Belford, his secretary, who conveyed me safely from these unchristian miscreants, which perhaps would have given me just occasion to forswear any more coming to the Ghetto. Thus much for the Jewish Ghetto, their service, and my discourse with one of their Rabbins.

V. THE IDEAL WEAVER'S FACTORY

THOMAS DELONEY. *The Pleasant History of Jack of Newbury,* 1596; *page* 20 *in Mann's edition of Deloney's Works. Deloney wrote for the trading middle-class reader. Jack of Newbury, the weaver, is an early specimen of the "financial magnate" of modern times.*

> Within one room being large and long,
> There stood two hundred looms full strong:
> Two hundred men the truth is so,
> Wrought in these looms all in a row.

By every one a pretty boy,
Sat making quills with mickle joy.
And in another place hard by,
An hundred women merrily,
Were carding hard with joyful cheer,
Who singing sat with voices clear.
And in a chamber close beside,
Two hundred maidens did abide
In petticoats of stammell red,
And milk-white kerchers on their head:
Their smock-sleeves like to winter snow,
That on the Western mountains flow,
And each sleeve with a silken band,
Was featly tied at the hand.
These pretty maids did never lin,
But in that place all day did spin:
And spinning so with voices meet,
Like nightingales they sung full sweet.
Then to another room came they,
Where children were in poor array:
And every one sat picking wool,
The finest from the coarse to cull:
The number was seven score and ten,
The children of poor silly [1] men;
And these their labours to requite,
Had every one a penny at night,
Beside their meat and drink all day,
Which was to them a wondrous stay.
Within another place likewise,
Full fifty proper men he spies,
And these were shearmen every one,
Whose skill and cunning there was shown:
And hard by them there did remain,
Full fourscore rowers taking pain.
A dye-house likewise had he then,
Wherein he kept full forty men;

[1] Simple.

And likewise in his fulling mill,
Full twenty persons kept he still.
Each week ten good fat oxen he
Spent in his house for certainty:
Beside good butter, cheese, and fish,
And many another wholesome dish.
He kept a butcher all the year,
A brewer eke for ale and beer;
A baker for to bake his bread,
Which stood his household in good stead.
Five cooks within his kitchen great,
Were all the year to dress his meat.
Six scullion boys unto their hands,
To make clean dishes, pots and pans,
Beside poor children that did stay,
To turn the broachs [1] every day.
The old man that did see this sight,
Was much amazed, as well he might:
This was a gallant clothier sure,
Whose fame for ever shall endure.

VI. THE JOLLY SHOEMAKERS

THOMAS DEKKER. The Shoemaker's Holiday, 1599; *Act II, Scene* 3.

Early in the morning, SIMON EYRE, *having risen before the rest of his household, enters his shop, full of enthusiasm for the day's work.*

EYRE. Where be these boys, these girls, these drabs, these scoundrels? They wallow in the fat brewis of my bounty, and lick up the crumbs of my table, yet will not rise to see my walks cleansed. [*Calling at the women's room.*] Come out, you powder-beef queans! What, Nan! What, Madge Mumble-crust! Come out, you fat midriff-swag-belly-whores, and sweep me these kennels that the noisesome stench offend not the noses of my neighbours. [*At the door of the journeymen's room.*] What,

[1] Spits.

TRAVEL AND TRADE

Firk, I say; what, Hodge! Open my shop-windows!
What, Firk, I say!

[FIRK *shuffles in.*]

FIRK. Oh, master, is't you that speak bandog and Bedlam this morning? I was in a dream, and mused what madman was got into the street so early; have you drunk this morning that your throat is so clear?

EYRE. Ah, well said, Firk; well said, Firk. To work, my fine knave, to work! Wash thy face, and thou'lt be more blest.

FIRK. Let them wash my face that will eat it. Good master, send for a souse-wife,[1] if you will have my face cleaner.

[HODGE *joins them.*]

EYRE. Away, sloven! Avaunt, scoundrel! Good-morrow, Hodge; good-morrow, my fine foreman.

HODGE [*yawning*]. Oh, master, good-morrow; y' are an early stirrer. Here's a fair morning. Good-morrow, Firk, I could have slept this hour. Here's a brave day towards.

EYRE. Oh, haste to work, my fine foreman, haste to work.

FIRK. Master, I am dry as dust to hear my fellow Roger talk of fair weather; let us pray for good leather, and let clowns and ploughboys and those that work in the fields pray for brave days. We work in a dry shop; what care I if it rain?

[MRS. EYRE *enters, in ill-humour.*]

EYRE. How now, Dame Margery, can you see to rise? Trip and go, call up the drabs, your maids.

MRS. EYRE. See to rise? I hope 'tis time enough; 'tis early enough for any woman to be seen abroad. I marvel how many wives in Tower Street are up so soon. Gods me, 'tis not noon—here's a yawling!

---

[1] One who pickles pork.

EYRE. Peace, Margery, peace! Where's Cicely Bumtrinket, your maid? Call the quean up; if my men want shoe-thread, I'll swinge her in a stirrup.

FIRK. Yet that's but a dry beating; here's still a sign of drought.

[*They settle down at their benches and begin work.* ROWLAND LACY (*disguised as* HANS, *a Dutch shoemaker*), *carrying his shoemaker's tools, passes by.*]

HANS [*singing*]. Der was een bore van Gelderland
   Frolick sie byen;
  He was als dronck he cold nyet stand
   Upsolce sie byen.
  Tap eens de canneken,
  Drincke, schone mannekin.

[*He halts, looking inquiringly at the shoemakers in the shop.*]

FIRK. Master, for my life, yonder's a brother of the Gentle Craft; if he bear not Saint Hugh's bones, I'll forfeit my bones; he's some uplandish workman. Hire him, good master, that I may learn some gibble-gabble; 'twill make us work the faster.

EYRE. Peace, Firk! A hard world! Let him pass, let him vanish; we have journeyman enow. Peace, my fine Firk!

MRS. EYRE [*sarcastically*]. Nay, nay, y' are best follow your man's counsel; you shall see what will come on't. We have not men enow, but we must entertain every butter-box; but let that pass.

HODGE. Dame, 'fore God, if my master follow your counsel, he'll consume little beef He shall be glad of men, an he can catch them.

FIRK. Ay, that he shall.

HODGE [*throwing down his tools*]. 'Fore God, a proper man, and I warrant a fine workman. Master, farewell; dame, adieu; if such a man as he cannot find work, Hodge is not for you.

EYRE. Stay, my fine Hodge!

TRAVEL AND TRADE 97

FIRK [*also dropping his tools*]. Faith, an your foreman go, dame, you must take a journey to seek a new journeyman; if Roger remove, Firk follows. If Saint Hugh's bones shall not be set a-work, I may prick mine awl in the wall, and go play. Fare ye well, master; good-bye, dame.

[*As they make their way out,* EYRE *stands in the doorway.*]

EYRE. Tarry, my fine Hodge, my brisk foreman! Stay, Firk! [*To his wife.*] Peace, pudding-broth! By the Lord of Ludgate, I love my men as my life. Peace, you gallimaufry! Hodge, if he want work, I'll hire him. One of you to him; stay—he comes to us.

[HANS *comes into the shop.*]

HANS. Goeden dach, meester, ende u vro oak.

FIRK. Nails, if I should speak after him without drinking, I should choke. And you, friend Oake, are you of the Gentle Craft?

HANS. Yaw, yaw, ik bin den skomawker.

FIRK. Den skomaker, quoth a! And hark you, skomaker, have you all your tools, a good rubbing-pin, a good stopper, a good dresser, your four sorts of awls, and your two balls of wax, your paring knife, your hand- and thumb-leathers, and good St. Hugh's bones to smooth up your work?

HANS. Yaw, yaw; be niet vorveard. Ik hab all de dingen voour mack skooes groot and cleane.

FIRK. Ha, ha! Good master, hire him; he'll make me laugh so that I shall work more in mirth than I can in earnest.

EYRE [*on his dignity*]. Hear ye, friend, have ye any skill in the Mystery of Cordwainers?

HANS. Ik weet niet wat yow seg; ich verstaw you niet.

FIRK. Why, thus, man: [*going through the motions*] "Ich verste u niet," quoth a.

HANS. Yaw, yaw, yaw; ick can dat wel doen.

FIRK. Yaw, yaw! He speaks yawing like a jackdaw that gapes to be fed with cheese-curds. Oh, he'll give a villainous pull at a can of double-beer; but Hodge and I have the vantage, we must drink first, because we are the eldest journeymen.

EYRE. What is thy name?

HANS. Hans—Hans Meulter.

EYRE. Give me thy hand; th' art welcome. Hodge, entertain him; Firk, bid him welcome; come, Hans. Run, wife, bid your maids, your trullibubs, make ready my fine men's breakfasts. To him, Hodge!

HODGE. Hans, th' art welcome; use thyself friendly, for we are good fellows; if not, thou shalt be fought with, wert thou bigger than a giant.

FIRK. Yea, and drunk with, wert thou Gargantua. My master keeps no cowards, I tell thee. [*Calling.*] Ho, boy, bring him an heel-block, here's a new journeyman.

[*The boy enters.*]

HANS. Oh, ich wersto you; ich moet een halve dossen cans betaelen; [*giving the boy a shilling*] here, boy, nempt dis skilling, tap eens freelicke.

[*The boy runs out.*]

EYRE. Quick, snipper-snapper, away! Firk, scour thy throat, thou shalt wash it with Castilian liquor.

[*The boy returns with the drink.*]

Come, my last of the fives,[1] give me a can. Have to thee, Hans; here, Hodge; here, Firk; drink, you mad Greeks, and work like true Trojans, and pray for Simon Eyre, the shoemaker. Here, Hans, and th' art welcome.

FIRK [*as he drinks*]. Lo, dame, you would have lost a good fellow that will teach us to laugh. This beer came hopping in well.

MRS. EYRE. Simon, it is almost seven.

EYRE. Is 't so, Dame Clapper-dudgeon? Is 't seven a clock, and my men's breakfast not ready? Trip and go, you soused conger, away! Come, you mad hyperboreans;

---

[1] Size 5 last.

follow me, Hodge; follow me, Hans; come after, my fine Firk; to work, to work a while, and then to breakfast!

[*He goes into the house.*]

FIRK. Soft! Yaw, yaw, good Hans, though my master have no more wit but to call you afore me, I am not so foolish to go behind you, I being the elder journeyman.

[HODGE, FIRK, HANS *and the boy follow in order of seniority.*]

VII. IN PRAISE OF THE RED HERRING

THOMAS NASHE. Lenten Stuff, 1599; *Vol. III, page 222 in McKerrow's edition of Nashe's Works.*

Every year about Lent tide, the sheriffs of Norwich bake certain herring pies (four and twenty, as I take it) and send them as a homage to the Lord of Caster hard by there, for lands that they hold of him; who, presently upon the like tenure, in bouncing hampers covered over with his cloth of arms, sees them conveyed to the court in the best equipage. At court, when they are arrived, his man rudely enters not at first, but knocketh very civilly, and then officers come and fetch him in with torchlight, where having disfraughted and unloaded his luggage, to supper he sets him down like a lord, with his wax lights before him, and hath his mess of meat allowed him with the largest, and his horses (*quatenus*[1] horses) are provendered as epicurely. After this, some four mark[2] fee towards his charges is tendered him, and he jogs home again merrily.

A white pickled herring? why, it is meat for a Prince! Haunce Vandervecke of Rotterdam (as a Dutch post informed me) in bare pickled herring laid out twenty thousand pound the last fishing; he had lost his drinking belike, and thought to store himself of medicines enough to recover it. Noble Caesarean Charlemaine herring, Pliny and Gesner were to blame they slubbered thee over

[1] "Seeing they are."   [2] 13s. 4d.

so negligently. I do not see why any man should envy thee, since thou art none of these lurcones [1] or epulones,[2] gluttons or fleshpots of Egypt (as one that writes of the Christians' captivity under the Turk enstyleth us Englishmen), nor livest thou by the unliving or eviscerating of others, as most fishes do, or by any extraordinary filth whatsoever, but, as the chameleon liveth by the air, and the salamander by the fire, so only by the water art thou nourished, and naught else, and must swim as well dead as alive.

Be of good cheer, my weary readers, for I have espied land, as Diogenes said to his weary scholars when he had read to a waste leaf. Fisherman, I hope, will not find fault with me for fishing before the net, or making all fish that comes to the net in this history, since, as the Athenians bragged they were the first that invented wrestling, and one Ericthonius amongst them that he was the first that joined horses in collar couples for drawing, so I am the first that ever set quill to paper in praise of any fish or fishermen. . . . But let none of these scum of the suburbs be too vinegar tart with me; for if they be, I'll take mine oath upon a red herring and eat it, to prove that their fathers, their grandfathers, and their great-grandfathers, or any other of their kin, were scullions' dishwash and dirty draff and swill, set against a red herring. The puissant red herring, the golden Hesperides red herring, the Mæonian red herring, the red herring of Red Herrings Hall, every pregnant peculiar of whose resplendent laud and honour to delineate and adumbrate to the ample life were a work that would drink dry four score and eighteen Castalian fountains of eloquence, consume another Athens of fecundity, and abate the haughtiest poetical fury twixt this and the burning zone and the tropic of Cancer. My conceit is cast into a sweating sickness, with ascending these few steps of his renown; into what a hot broiling Saint Lawrence fever would it relapse then, should I spend the whole bag of my wind in climbing up to the lofty mountain crest of

---

[1] Gluttons.   [2] Carousers.

his trophies? But no more wind will I spend on it but this; Saint Dennis for France, Saint James for Spain, Saint Patrick for Ireland, Saint George for England, and the Red Herring for Yarmouth.

VIII. ADVICE TO YOUNG SAILORS

JOHN SMITH. An Accidence for Young Seamen, 1626; *Vol. II, page 803 in Arber and Bradley's edition.*

Young gentlemen that desires command ought well to consider the condition of his ship, victual and company; for if there be more learners than sailors, how slightly soever many esteem sailors, all the work to save ship, goods and lives must lie upon them, especially in foul weather; the labour, hazard, wet and cold is so incredible I cannot express it. It is not then the number of them that here will say at home, what I cannot do I can quickly learn, and what a great matter it is to sail a ship or go to sea. Surely those for a good time will do most trouble than good. I confess it is more necessary such should go, but not too many in one ship; for if the labour of sixty should lie upon thirty, as many times it doth, they are so overcharged with labour, bruises and overstraining themselves (for there is no dallying nor excuses with storms, gusts, overgrown seas and lee shores), they fall sick of one disease or other, and then if their victuals be putrefied, it endangers all.

Men of all other professions, in lightning, thunder, storms and tempests, with rain and snow, may shelter themselves in dry houses, by good fires and good cheer; but those are the chief times that seamen must stand to their tacklings, and attend with all diligence their greatest labour upon the decks. Many supposeth anything is good enough to serve men at sea and yet nothing sufficient for them ashore, either for their healths, for their ease, or estates, or state. A commander at sea should do well to think the contrary, and provide for himself and company in like manner : also seriously to consider what will be his charge to furnish himself at sea with bedding, linen, arms and apparel ; how to keep his table aboard, his expenses on shore, and his petty tally, which is a competent proportion according to your number, of these particulars following :

Fine wheat flour, close and well packed, rice, currants, sugar, prunes, cinnamon, ginger, pepper, cloves, green-ginger, oil, butter, old cheese, or holland, wine, vinegar, canary sack, aqua vitæ, the best wines, the best waters, the juice of lemons for the scurvy, white biscuit, oatmeal, gammons of bacon, dried neats' tongues, roasted beef packed up in vinegar, legs of mutton minced and stewed, and close packed up with butter in earthen pots. To entertain strangers, marmalet, suckets, almonds, comfits and such-like.

Some it may be will say I would have men rather to feast than fight. But I say the want of those necessaries occasions the loss of more men than in any English fleet hath been slain in any fight since 1588 : for when a man is ill sick, or at the point of death, I would know whether a dish of buttered rice, with a little cinnamon and sugar, a little minced meat, or roast beef, a few stewed prunes, a race of green-ginger, a flap-jack,[1] a can of fresh water brewed with a little cinnamon, ginger and sugar, be not better than a little poor John,[2] or salt fish with oil and mustard, or biscuit, butter, cheese or oatmeal pottage on fish days, salt beef, pork and pease, and six shillings' beer. This is your ordinary ship's allowance and good for them are well, if well conditioned, which is not always, as seamen can too well witness ; and after a storm, when poor men are all wet and some not so much a cloth to shift him, shaking with cold, few of those but will tell you a little sack or aqua vitæ is much better to keep them in health than a little small beer or cold water, although it be sweet. Now that everyone should provide those things for himself, few of them have either that providence or means. And there is

[1] Pancake.   [2] Salt cod.

TRAVEL AND TRADE

neither alehouse, tavern nor inn to burn a faggot in; neither grocer, poulterery, apothecary, nor butcher's shop; and therefore the use of this petty tally is necessary, and thus to be employed as there is occasion to entertain strangers, as they are in quality, every commander should show himself as like himself as he can, as well for the credit of the ship and his setters forth as himself. But, in that, herein every one may moderate themselves according to their own pleasures, therefore I leave it to their own discretions. And this brief discourse and myself, to their friendly construction and good opinion.

JOHN SMITH writ with his own hand.

IX. TO THE VIRGINIAN VOYAGE

MICHAEL DRAYTON. Odes, 1619; *page 70 in Brett's edition.*

You brave heroic minds,
Worthy your country's name,
   That honour still pursue
   Go, and subdue,
Whilst loitering hinds
Lurk here at home, with shame.

Britons you stay too long,
Quickly aboard bestow you,
   And with a merry gale
   Swell your stretched sail,
With vows as strong,
As the winds that blow you.

Your course securely steer,
West and south forth keep,
   Rocks, lee shores, nor shoals,
   When Eolus scowls,
You need not fear,
So absolute the deep.

And cheerfully at sea
Success you still entice
    To get the pearl and gold
    And ours to hold,
VIRGINIA,
Earth's only paradise.

Where Nature hath in store
Fowl, venison, and fish,
    And the fruitfull'st soil
    Without your toil,
Three harvests more,
All greater than your wish.

And the ambitious vine
Crowns with his purple mass,
    Cedar reaching high
    To kiss the sky,
Cypress, pine,
And useful sassafras.

To whom the Golden Age
Still Nature's laws doth give,
    No other cares that tend,
    But them to defend
From winter's rage
That long there doth not live.

When as the luscious smell
Of that delicious land,
    Above the seas, that flows,
    The clear wind throws,
Your hearts to swell
Approaching the dear strand.

In kenning of the shore
(Thanks to God first given)
　O you the happiest men,
　Be frolic then,
Let cannons roar,
Frighting the wide heaven.

And in regions far
Such heroes bring ye forth,
　As those from whom we came,
　And plant our name
Under that star
Not known unto our North.

And as there plenty grows
Of laurel everywhere,
　Apollo's sacred tree,
　You may it see,
A poet's brows
To crown, that may sing there.

Thy voyages attend,
Industrious Hakluyt
　Whose reading shall inflame
　Men to seek fame,
And much commend
To after times thy wit.

X. THE RICHES OF VIRGINIA

BEN JONSON, GEORGE CHAPMAN and JOHN MARSTON. Eastward Ho, 1605; *Act III, Scene 3. Many of the first colonists in Virginia were " Spendalls " and " Scapethrifts " who were attracted to the West by tales of easily won gold ; as a result the early history of the colony makes most harrowing reading. The settlers knew no trade, were idle and mutinous, and soon died of disease or starvation.*

SEAGULL. Come, boys, Virginia longs till we share the rest of her maidenhead.

SPENDALL. Why, is she inhabited already with any English ?

SEAGULL. A whole country of English is there, man, bred of those that were left there in '79. They have married with the Indians, and make 'em bring forth as beautiful faces as any we have in England; and therefore the Indians are so in love with them that all the treasure they have they lay at their feet.

SCAPETHRIFT. But is there such treasure there, captain, as I have heard?

SEAGULL. I tell thee, gold is more plentiful there than copper is with us; and for as much red copper as I can bring, I'll have thrice the weight in gold. Why, man, all their dripping-pans and their chamber-pots are pure gold; and all the chains with which they chain up their streets are massy gold; all the prisoners they take are fettered in gold; and for rubies and diamonds, they go forth on holidays and gather 'em by the sea-shore to hang on their children's coats and stick in their caps, as commonly as our children wear saffron-gilt brooches and groats with holes in 'em.

SCAPETHRIFT. And is it a pleasant country withal?

SEAGULL. As ever the sun shined on; temperate and full of all sorts of excellent viands: wild boar is as common there as our tamest bacon is here; venison as mutton. And then you shall live freely there, without sergeants, or courtiers, or lawyers, or intelligencers, only a few industrious Scots, perhaps, who, indeed, are dispersed over the face of the whole earth. But as for them, there are no greater friends to Englishmen and England, when they are out on't, in the world, than they are. And for my own part, I would a hundred thousand of 'em were there, for we are all one countrymen now, ye know, and we should find ten times more comfort of them there than we do here. Then for your means to advancement there, it is simple, and not preposterously mixed. You may be an alderman there, and never be a scavenger: you may be a nobleman, and never be a slave. You may come to preferment enough, and never be a pander; to riches and fortune enough, and have never the more villainy nor the less wit.

TRAVEL AND TRADE

SPENDALL. God's me! And how far is it thither?
SEAGULL. Some six weeks' sail, no more, with any indifferent good wind. And if I get to any part of the coast of Africa, I'll sail thither with any wind; or when I come to Cape Finisterre, there's a foreright wind continual wafts us till we come at Virginia.

XI. CAPTAIN BOBADILL ON TOBACCO

BEN JONSON. Every Man in His Humour, 1598; *Act III, Scene 2.*

BOBADILL. Body o' me! here's the remainder of seven pound since yesterday was seven-night. 'Tis your right Trinidado; did you never take any, Master Stephen?

STEPHEN. No, truly, sir; but I'll learn to take it now, since you commend it so.

BOBADILL. Sir, believe me, upon my relation, for what I tell you, the world shall not reprove. I have been in the Indies, where this herb grows, where neither myself nor a dozen gentlemen more of my knowledge have received the taste of any other nutriment in the world for the space of one and twenty weeks but the fume of this simple only; therefore it cannot be, but 'tis most divine. Further, take it in the nature, in the true kind; so, it makes an antidote, that had you taken the most deadly poisonous plant in all Italy, it should expel it and clarify you with as much ease as I speak. And for your green wound—your Balsamum and your St. John's wort are all mere gulleries and trash to it, especially your Trinidado; your Nicotian is good too. I could say what I know of the virtue of it, for the expulsion of rheums, raw humours, crudities, obstructions, with a thousand of this kind, but I profess myself no quacksalver. Only thus much: by Hercules I do hold it, and will affirm it before any Prince in Europe, to be the most sovereign and precious weed that ever the earth tendered to the use of man.

EDWARD KNOWELL. This speech would have done decently in a tobacco trader's mouth.

XII. THE USURER'S WAYS

THOMAS LODGE and ROBERT GREENE. A Looking Glasse for London and England, 1590; *Act I, Scene* 3. *Usury was illegal; but the law was evaded by such methods as are here shown.*

[*The* USURER, *followed by* THRASIBULUS, *a young gentleman, and* ALCON, *a poor man, enters.*]

USURER. Come on, I am every day troubled with these needy companions : what news with you ? what wind brings you hither ?

THRASIBULUS. Sir, I hope, how far soever you make it off, you remember too well for me, that this is the day therein I should pay you money that I took up of you alate in a commodity.

ALCON. And, sir, sir reverence of your manhood and gentry, I have brought home such money as you lent me.

USURER. You, young gentleman, is my money ready ?

THRASIBULUS. Truly, sir, this time was so short, the commodity so bad, and the promise of friends so broken, that I could not provide it against the day; wherefore I am come to entreat you to stand my friend and to favour me with a longer time, and I will make you sufficient consideration.

USURER. Is the wind in that door ? If thou hast my money, so it is, I will not defer a day, an hour, a minute, but take the forfeit of the bond.

THRASIBULUS. I pray you, sir, consider that my loss was great by the commodity I took up ; you know, sir, I borrowed of you forty pounds, whereof I had ten pounds in money, and thirty pounds in lute strings, which when I came to sell again, I could get but five pounds for them, so had I, sir, but fifteen pounds for my forty. In consideration of this ill bargain, I pray you, sir, give me a month longer.

USURER. I answered thee afore, not a minute ; what have I to do how thy bargain proved : I have thy hand set to my book that thou receivedst forty pounds of me in money.

THRASIBULUS. Ay, sir, it was your device that, to colour the statute, but your conscience knows what I had

ALCON. Friend, thou speakest Hebrew to him when thou talkest to him of conscience, for he hath as much conscience about the forfeit of an obligation as my blind mare, God bless her, hath over a manger of oats.

THRASIBULUS. Then there is no favour, sir?

USURER. Come to-morrow to me, and see how I will use thee.

THRASIBULUS [*suddenly producing a bag from under his cloak*]. No, covetous caterpillar, know that I have made extreme shift rather than I would fall into the hands of such a ravening panther, and therefore here is thy money and deliver me the recognisance of my lands.

USURER. What a spite is this? hath sped of his crowns! If he had missed but one half-hour, what a goodly farm had I got for forty pounds! Well, 'tis my cursed fortune. Oh! have I no shift to make him forfeit his recognisance?

THRASIBULUS. Come, sir, will you dispatch and tell your money?

[*The clock strikes four.*]

USURER. Stay, what is this a clock? four; let me see: [*perusing the bond*] " to be paid between the hours of three and four in the afternoon." This goes right for me; you, sir, hear you not the clock, and have you not a counterpain of your obligation? The hour is past, it was to be paid between three and four, and now the clock hath struck four, I will receive none; I'll stand to the forfeit of the recognisance.

THRASIBULUS [*taken aback*]. Why, sir, I hope you do but jest; why, 'tis but four, and will you for a minute take forfeit of my bond? If it were so, sir, I was here before four.

USURER. Why didst thou not tender thy money then? If I offer thee injury, take the law of me; complain to the judge, I will receive no money.

ALCON. Well, sir, I hope you will stand my good master for my cow. I borrowed thirty shillings on her, and for that I have paid you eighteenpence a week, and for her meat you have had her milk, and I tell you, sir, she gives a goodly sup; now, sir, here is your money.

USURER. Hang, beggarly knave, comest to me for a cow? Did I not bind her bought and sold for a penny, and was not thy day to have paid yesterday? Thou getst no cow at my hand.

ALCON. No cow, sir! alas that word, "no cow," goes as cold to my heart as a draught of small drink in a frosty morning. No cow, sir, why, alas, alas, Master Usurer what shall become of me, my wife and my poor child?

USURER. Thou getst no cow of me, knave! I cannot stand prating with you, I must be gone.

ALCON. Nay, but hear you, Master Usurer: "no cow," why, sir, here's your thirty shillings; I have paid you eighteenpence a week, and therefore there is reason I should have my cow.

USURER. Why pratest thou? Have I not answered thee, thy day is broken?

ALCON. Why, sir, alas, my cow is a commonwealth to me; for first, sir, she allows me, my wife and son, for to blanket ourselves withal, butter, cheese, whey, curds, cream, sod milk, raw milk, sour milk, sweet milk and butter milk; besides, sir, she saved me every year a penny in almanacs, for she was as good to me as a prognostication; if she had but set up her tail and have galloped about the mead, my little boy was able to say, "Oh, father, there will be a storm"; her very tail was a calendar to me; and now to lose my cow! alas, Master Usurer, take pity upon me.

USURER. I have other matters to talk on; farewell, fellows.

THRASIBULUS. Why, but, thou covetous churl, wilt thou not receive thy money and deliver me my recognisances?

USURER. I'll deliver thee none; if I have wronged thee, seek thy mends at the law.

XIII. THIS HEROIC AGE

RICHARD HAKLUYT, Principal Voyages of the English Nation, 1589. *The Epistle dedicatory to Sir Francis Walsingham ; vol. i, page 1 in the Everyman edition.*

Right honourable, I do remember that being a youth, and one of her Majesty's scholars at Westminster, that fruitful nursery, it was my hap to visit the chamber of M. Richard Hakluyt, my cousin, a gentleman of the Middle Temple, well known unto you, at a time when I found lying open upon his board certain books of cosmography, with a universal map. He seeing me somewhat curious in the view thereof, began to instruct my ignorance, by showing me the division of the earth into three parts after the old account, and then according to the latter and better distribution into more. He pointed with his wand to all the known seas, gulfs, bays, straits, capes, rivers, empires, kingdoms, dukedoms and territories of each part, the declaration of their special commodities and particular wants which by the benefit of traffic and intercourse of merchants are plentifully supplied. From the map he brought me to the Bible, and turning to the 117th Psalm directed me to the 23rd and 24th verses, where I read that they which go down to the sea in ships, and occupy by the great waters, they see the works of the Lord, and His wonders in the deep, etc. Which words of the prophet together with my cousin's discourse (things of high and rare delight to my young nature) took in me so deep an impression that I constantly resolved, if ever I were preferred to the University where better time, and more convenient place might be ministered to these studies, I would by God's assistance prosecute that knowledge and kind of literature, the doors whereof, after a sort, were so happily opened before me.

According to which my resolution when not long after I was removed to Christchurch in Oxford, my exercises of duty first performed, I feel to my intended course, and by degrees read over whatsoever printed or written discoveries and voyages I found extant either in the Greek, Latin,

Italian, Spanish, Portugal, French, or English languages, and in my public lectures was the first that produced and showed both the old imperfectly composed and the new lately reformed maps, globes, spheres, and other instruments of this art for demonstration in the common schools, to the singular pleasure and general contentment of my auditories. In continuance of time and by reason principally of my insight in this study, I grew familiarly acquainted with the chiefest captains at sea, the greatest merchants, and the best mariners of our nation ; by which means having gotten somewhat more than common knowledge, I passed at length the Narrow Seas into France with Sir Edward Stafford, her Majesty's careful and discreet ligier,[1] where during my five years abroad with him in his dangerous and chargeable residency in her Highness' service, I both heard in speech and read in books other nations miraculously extolled for their discoveries and notable enterprises by sea, but the English of all others for their security and continual neglect of the like attempts, especially in so long and happy time of peace, either ignominiously reported or exceedingly condemned : which singular opportunity, if some other people our neighbours had been blessed with, their protestations are often and vehement, they would far otherwise have used. And that the truth and elegance thereof may better appear, these are the very words of Popiliniere in his book called *L'Amiral de France* and printed at Paris. . . .

Thus both hearing and reading the obloquy of our nation and finding few or none of our men able to reply herein : and further not seeing any man to have care to recommend to the world the industrious labours and painful travels of our countrymen : for stopping the mouths of the reproachers, myself being the last winter returned from France with the honourable the Lady Sheffield, for her passing good behaviour highly esteemed in all the French court, determined, notwithstanding all difficulty, to undertake the burden of that work wherein all others pretended either ignorance, or lack of leisure, or want of sufficient argu-

[1] Ambassador.

TRAVEL AND TRADE

ment, whereas, to speak truly, the huge toil and the small profit to ensue were the chief causes of the refusal. I call the work a burden in consideration that these voyages lay so dispersed, scattered, and hidden in several hucksters' hands, that I now wonder at myself, to see how I was able to endure the delays, curiosity, and backwardness of many from whom I was to receive my originals ; so that I have just cause to make that complaint of the maliciousness of divers in our times, which Pliny made of the men of his age : *At nos elaborata iis abscondere atque supprimere cupimus, et fraudare vitam etiam alienis bonis*,[1] *etc.*

To harp no longer upon this string and to speak a word of that just commendation which our nation do indeed deserve ; it cannot be denied, but as in all former ages they have been men full of activity, stirrers abroad and searchers of the remote parts of the world, so in this most famous and fearless government of her Most Excellent Majesty, through the special assistance and blessing of God, in search of the most opposite corners and quarters of the world, and to speak plainly in compassing the vast globe of the earth more than once have excelled all the nations and people of the earth. For which of the kings of this land before her Majesty had their banners ever seen in the Caspian Sea ? Which of them hath ever dealt with the Emperor of Persia, as her Majesty hath done, and obtained for her merchant large and loving privileges ? Whoever saw before this regiment an English ligier in the stately porch of the Grand Signior at Constantinople ? Whoever found English consuls and agents at Tripolis in Syria, at Aleppo, at Babylon, at Balsara, and, which is more, whoever heard of Englishmen at Goa before now ? What English ships did heretofore ever anchor in the mighty river of Plate ? Pass and repass the unpassable (in former opinion) Strait of Magellan, range along the coast of Chile, Peru, and all the backside of Nova Hispania, further than any Christian ever passed,

[1] "But we desire to hide and suppress what others have laboured at, and to cheat humanity even of the services that others [seek to] render."

traverse the mighty breadth of the South Sea, land upon the Luzones in despite of the enemy, enter into alliance, amity, and traffic with the Princes of the Moluccaes and the Isle of Java, double the famous Cape of Bona Speranza, arrive at the Isle of Santa Helena, and, last of all, return most richly laden with the commodities of China, as the subjects of this now flourishing monarchy have done?

SECTION FIVE

LONDON LIFE

I. PAUL'S WALK

THOMAS DEKKER. The Dead Term. 1608 ; *in Grosart's edition, vol. iii, page* 49. *" Paul's Walk," the central aisle of the Cathedral, was the general rendezvous for business men, servants looking for masters, needy idlers wanting a free meal, and rogues of all sorts. The " Paul's man " was a recognized type of hanger-on, the best example in literature being Captain Bobadill in* Every Man in His Humour. *See page* 53.

The Steeple on St. Paul's is speaking :

For whereas I was at first consecrated to a mystical and religious purpose (the ceremonies of which are daily observed in the better part of me, for my heart is even to this hour an altar upon which are offered the sacrifices of holy prayers for men's sins), yet are some limbs of my venerable body abused and put to profane, horrid and servile customs : no marvel though my head rots,[1] when the body is so full of diseases ; no marvel if the Divine Executioner cut me off by the shoulders, when in my bosom is so much horrible and close treason practised against the King of the whole world.

For albeit I never yet came down all my stairs, to be an ocular witness-bearer of what I speak, and what is (sometimes spoke openly and sometimes spoke in private) committed in my walks, yet doth the daily sound and echo of much knavish villainy strike up into mine ear. What

[1] The steeple on Old St. Paul's collapsed in 1561, and had not been rebuilt.

whispering is there in Term times how by some sleight to cheat the poor country client of his full purse that is stuck under his girdle ? What plots are laid to furnish young gallants with ready money (which is shared afterwards at a tavern) thereby to disfurnish him of his patrimony ? What buying up of oaths out of the hands of Knights of the Post,[1] who for a few shillings do daily sell their souls ? What laying of heads is there together and sifting of the brain, still and anon, as it grows towards eleven of the clock (even amongst those that wear gilt rapiers by their sides) where for that noon they may shift from Duke Humphrey [2] and be furnished with a dinner at some meaner man's table ? What damnable bargains of unmerciful brokery and of unmeasurable usury are there clapped up ? What swearing is there, yea, what swaggering, what facing and out-facing ? What shuffling, what shouldering, what jostling, what jeering, what biting of thumbs to beget quarrels,[3] what holding up of fingers to remember drunken meetings, what braving with feathers, what bearding with moustaches, what casting open of cloaks to publish new clothes, what muffling in cloaks to hide broken elbows, so that when I hear such trampling up and down, such spitting, such hawking and such humming (every man's lips making a noise, yet not a word to be understood) I verily believe that I am the Tower of Babel newly to be builded up, but presently despair of ever being finished, because there is in me such a confusion of languages.

For at one time, in one and the same rank, yea, foot by foot and elbow by elbow, shall you see walking, the knight, the gull, the gallant, the upstart, the gentleman, the clown, the captain, the apple-squire,[4] the lawyer, the usurer, the

---

[1] Professional perjurers who hired themselves out as " witnesses " in lawsuits.

[2] The supposed tomb of Duke Humphrey was a notable monument in Old St. Paul's; "to dine with Duke Humphrey" meant to go hungry.

[3] As in the opening scene of *Romeo and Juliet*.

[4] Pimp.

citizen, the bankerout,[1] the scholar, the beggar, the doctor, the idiot, the ruffian, the cheater, the puritan, the cut-throat, the high-man, the low-man, the true-man, and the thief; of all trades and professions some, of all countries some; and thus doth my middle aisle show like the Mediterranean Sea, in which as well the merchant hoists up sails to purchase wealth honestly, as the rover to light upon prize unjustly. Thus am I like a common mart where all commodities (both the good and the bad) are to be bought and sold. Thus whilst devotion kneels at her prayers, doth profanation walk under her nose in contempt of religion. But my lamentations are scattered with the winds, my sighs are lost in the air, and I myself not thought worthy to stand high in the love of those that are born and nourished by me. An end therefore do I make here of this my mourning.

II. THE NIP AND THE FOIST

ROBERT GREENE. The Second Part of Connycatching. 1592; *vol. 1, pages 30, 33, in the Bodley Head Quartos. Greene's Connycatching Pamphlets are most valuable accounts of the professional rascals who infested London. Greene knew his subject intimately and at first-hand, and wrote five pamphlets to expose their practices. He also promised to produce a " Black Book " giving the names, addresses and haunts of the most important members of the profession, but died before it was finished.*

The nip and the foist, although their subject is one which they work on, that is, a well-lined purse, yet their manner is different, for the nip useth his knife, and the foist his hand : the one cutting the purse, the other drawing the pocket. But of these two scurvy trades, the foist holdeth himself of the highest degree, and therefore they term themselves " gentlemen foists ", and so much disdain to be called " cutpurses ", as the honest man that lives by his hand or occupation,[2] in so much that the foist refuseth even to wear a knife about him to cut his meat withal, lest he might be suspected to grow into the nature of a nip.

[1] Bankrupt. [2] Handicraft.

Yet, as I said before, is their subject and haunt both alike; for their gains lie by all places of resort and assemblies; therefore their chief walk is Paul's, Westminster, the Exchange, plays, Bear Garden, running at tilt, the Lord Mayor's Day, any festival meetings, frays, shootings, or great fairs, to be short, wheresoever is any extraordinary resort of people, there the nip and the foist have fittest opportunity to show their juggling agility. . . .

In Paul's, especially in the term time, between ten and eleven, then is their hours, and there they walk, and perhaps if there be a great press, strike a stroke [1] in the middle walk; but that is upon some plain man that stands gazing about, having never seen the church before. But their chiefest time is at divine service, when men, devoutly given, do go up to hear either a sermon or else the harmony of the choir and the organs. There the nip and the foist, as devoutly as if he were some zealous person, standeth soberly with his eyes elevated to heaven, when his hand is either on the purse or in the pocket, surveying every corner of it for coin. Then when the service is done, and the people press away, he thrusteth amidst the throng, and there worketh his villainy. . . .

So likewise at plays the nip standeth there leaning like some mannerly gentleman against the door as men go in, and there finding talk with some of his companions, spieth what every man hath in his purse, and where, in what place, and in which sleeve or pocket, he puts the bung,[2] and according to that so he worketh, either where the thrust is great within, or else as they come out at the doors. But suppose that the foist is smoked[3] and the man misseth his purse and apprehendeth him for it. Then straight he either conveyeth to his stall,[4] or else droppeth the bung and with a great brave he defieth his accuser; and though the purse be found at his feet, yet because he hath it not about him, he comes not within the compass of life. . . .

Therefore let all men take this caveat,[5] that when they

---

[1] In thieves' language, to take a purse.   [2] Purse.
[3] Caught out.   [4] Accomplice.   [5] Warning.

walk abroad amid any of the forenamed places or like assemblies, that they take great care for their purse, how they place it, and not leave it careless in their pockets or hose, for the foist is so nimble-handed that he exceeds the juggler for agility and hath his *leger de main* as perfectly. Therefore an exquisite foist must have three properties that a good surgeon should have, and that is, an eagle's eye, a lady's hand, and a lion's heart. An eagle's eye to spy out a purchase,[1] to have a quick insight where the bung lies; and then a lion's heart not to fear what the end will be; and then a lady's hand, to be little and nimble, the better and the more easy to dive into any man's pocket.

III. QUACKS

HENRY CHETTLE. Kind-heart's Dream. 1592; *vol. iv, pages 26, 27, 32 in the Bodley Head Quartos.*

For the dead palsy, there is a woman hath a desperate drink that either helps in a year, or kills in an hour. Beside, she hath a charm that mumbled thrice over the ear, together with oil of suamone (as she terms it) will make them that can hear but a little, hear in short time never a whit. But above all, her medicine for the quartine ague is admirable, viz. a pint of exceeding strong March beer, wherein is diffused one drop of *aqua mirabilis*; this, taken at a draught before the fit, is intolerable good, and for a precedent, let this serve.

A gentlewoman about London, whose husband is heir of a right worshipful house, was induced to take this drench from this wise woman; for every drop of that strong water she must have twelve pence. A spoonful at the least was prized at forty shillings. Thus, daily for almost a month, she ministered, the gentlewoman, having still good hope, at last was put by her husband quite out of comfort for any good at this woman's hands; for he, by chance getting the deceiver's glass, would needs pour out a spoonful whatever he paid; she cried out she could not spare it; all helped

[1] Plunder.

not, he took it and tasted, and found it to be no other than fountain water. . . .

Besides these runagates, there are some of good experience, that giving themselves to inordinate excess, when they are writ unto by learned physicians to minister for the patient's health, according to their advised prescription, negligently mistake. As for example, a doctor directs to his apothecary a bill to minister to a man having an ulcerous sore, certain pills for the preparing of his body, withal, a receipt for the making a corrosive to apply to the sore; he (either witless, which is too bad, or wilful, which is worse) prepares the corrosive in pills, and forms the receipt for the pills in manner of a plaster. The party receives the corrosive inward, his maw is fretted, death follows. If there be such an apothecary that hath so done, let him repent his dealings, lest the blood of that man light on his head. . . .

A Charm. First, he must know your name, then your age, which in a little paper he sets down. On the top are these words, *In verbis, et in herbis, et in lapidibus sunt virtutes,*[1] underneath he writes in capital letters *A AB ILLA, HURS GIBELLA*, which he swears is pure Chaldee, and the names of three spirits that enter into the blood and cause rheums,[2] and so consequently the toothache. This paper must be likewise three times blessed,[3] and at last with a little frankincense burned, which being thrice used, is of power to expel the spirits, purify the blood, and ease the pain, or else he lies, for he hath practised it long, but shall approve it never.

Another sort get hot wires, and with them they burn out the worm that so torments the grieved. These fellows are fit to visit curst[4] wives, and might by their practice do a number of honest men ease, if they would miss the tooth and worm the tongue.

[1] " In words, and in herbs, and in stones are there powers."
[2] Moistures. The humour or rheum in the body was considered responsible for most diseases of body and mind.
[3] Signed with cross.   [4] Shrewish.

Others there are that persuade the pained to hold their mouths open over a basin of water by the fireside, and to cast into the fire a handful of henbane seed, the which naturally hath in every seed a little worm ; the seeds breaking in the fire, use a kind of cracking, and out of them it is hard among so many, if no worm fly into the water : which worms the deceivers affirm to have fallen from the teeth of the diseased. This rare secret is much used, and not smally liked. Sundry other could I set down practised by our banner-bearers,[1] but all is foppery, for this I find to be the only remedy for the tooth pain, either to have patience, or to pull them out.

IV. THE BARBER AND HIS WAYS

JOHN LYLY. Midas. 1592 ; *Act III, Scene 2.*

King Midas, according to the old fable, asked that everything he touched should be turned to gold. The petition was granted, with most embarrassing results. His barber has accordingly benefited by the golden hairs of Midas' beard, but has been robbed of them by Petulus. But Petulus now suffers from the toothache and is obliged to seek the barber's professional services. He waits with his friend Licio. Motto, the barber, enters with Dello, his boy.

MOTTO. Dello, thou knowest Midas touched his beard, and 'twas gold.
DELLO. Well.
MOTTO. That the pages cozened[2] me of it.
DELLO. No lie.
MOTTO. That I must be revenged.
DELLO. In good time.
MOTTO. Thou knowest I have taught thee the knacking[3] of the hands, the tickling on a man's hairs, like the tuning of a cittern.[4]
DELLO. True.
MOTTO. Besides, I instructed thee in the phrases of our

---
[1] Quacks, who proclaimed their skill by displaying placards.
[2] Cheated.   [3] Massage.
[4] Guitar, kept in the shop to amuse waiting customers.

eloquent occupation, as "How, sir, will you be trimmed? will you have your beard like a spade, or a bodkin? a penthouse on your upper lip, or an ally on your chin?[1] a low curl on your head like a bull, or dangling lock like a spaniel? your moustaches sharp at the ends like shoemakers' awls, or hanging down to your mouth like goats' flakes? your love-locks wreathed with a silken twist, or shaggy to fall on your shoulders?"

DELLO. I confess you have taught me Tully *De Oratore*, the very art of trimming.

MOTTO. Well, for all this I desire no more at thy hands than to keep secret the revenge I have prepared for the pages.

DELLO. O sir, you know I am a barber, and cannot tittle-tattle. I am one of those whose tongues are swelled with silence.

MOTTO. Indeed thou shouldst be no blab because a barber, therefore be secret. Was it not a good cure, Dello, to ease the toothache and never touch the tooth?

DELLO. O master, he that is your patient for the toothache, I warrant is patient of all aches.

MOTTO. I did but rub his gums, and presently the rheum evaporated.

LICIO. *Deus bone*, is that word come into the barber's basin?

DELLO. Ay, sir, and why not? My master is a barber and a surgeon.

LICIO. In good time.

PETULUS. O Motto, I am almost dead with the toothache, all my gums are swollen, and my teeth stand in my head like thorns.

MOTTO. It may be that it is only the breeding of a beard, and being the first beard, you shall have a hard travail.

PETULUS. Old fool, dost thou think hairs will breed in my teeth?

MOTTO. As likely, sir, for anything I know, as on your chin.

[1] Forked beard.

PETULUS [*in agony*]. O teeth! O torments!—O torments! O teeth!

MOTTO [*to the boy*]. May I but touch them, Dello, I'll teach his tongue to tell a tale, what villainy it is to cozen one of a beard; but stand not thou nigh, for it is odds when he spits but that all his teeth fly in thy face.

LICIO. Good Motto, give some ease, for at thy coming in I overheard of a cure thou hadst done.

PETULUS. My teeth! I will not have this pain, that's certain!

MOTTO. Ay, so did you overhear me when you cozened me of a beard; but I forget all.

DELLO. My master is mild and merciful; and merciful because a barber, for when he hath the throat at command, you know he taketh revenge but on a silly hair.

MOTTO. How now, Petulus, do they still ache?

PETULUS. Ay, Motto.

MOTTO. Let me rub your gums with this leaf.

PETULUS. Do, Motto, and for thy labour I will requite thee. [*Motto rubs his gums hard.*] Out, rascal! what hast thou done? All my nether teeth are loose, and wag like the keys of a pair of virginals.[1]

DELLO. O sir, if you will, I will sing to them, your mouth being the instrument.

PETULUS. Do, Dello.

DELLO. Out, villain, thou bitest. I cannot tune these virginal keys.

PETULUS. They were the jacks above; the keys beneath were easy.

DELLO. A bots on your jacks and jaws too!

LICIO. They were virginals of your master's making.

PETULUS. O my teeth! Good Motto, what will ease my pain?

MOTTO. Nothing in the world but to let me lay a golden beard to your chin.

PETULUS. It is at pawn.

[1] An early form of pianoforte.

MOTTO. You are like to fetch it out with your teeth, or go without your teeth.

PETULUS. Motto, withdraw thyself, it may be thou shalt draw my teeth; attend my resolution. [MOTTO *and* DELLO *retire into the background.*] A doubtful dispute, whether I were best to lose my golden beard or my bone tooth? Help me, Licio, to determine.

LICIO. Your teeth ache, Petulus, your beard doth not.

PETULUS. Ay, but Licio, if I part from my beard, my heart will ache.

LICIO. If your tooth be hollow it must be stopped, or pulled out; and stop it the barber will not, without the beard.

PETULUS. My heart is hollow too, and nothing can stop it but gold.

LICIO. Thou canst not eat meat without teeth.

PETULUS. Nor buy it without money.

LICIO. Thou mayst get more gold; if thou lose these, more teeth thou canst not.

V. THE WATCH

THOMAS DEKKER. *The Gull's Hornbook, 1609; page 77 in the King's Classics edition. With this passage compare Dogberry's charge to the Watch in Much Ado About Nothing, Act III, Scene 3. Dekker advises the Gallant how to behave himself passing through the City at all hours of the night; and how to pass by any Watch.*

After the sound of pottle-pots [1] is out of your ears, and that the spirit of wine and tobacco walks in your brain; the tavern door being shut upon your back, cast about to pass through the widest and goodliest streets in the City. And if your means cannot reach to the keeping of a boy, hire one of the drawers to be as a lanthorn unto your feet, and to light you home; and, still as you approach near any nightwalker that is up as late as yourself, curse and swear, like one that speaks high Dutch, in a lofty voice, because your men have used you so like a rascal in not waiting upon you, and vow the next morning to pull their

[1] Two quart pots.

blue cases [1] over their ears; though, if your chamber were well searched, you give only sixpence a week to some old woman to make your bed, and that she is all the serving-creatures you give wages to. If you smell a watch, and that you may easily do, for commonly they eat onions to keep them in sleeping, which they account a medicine against cold; or, if you come within danger of their brown bills [2]; let him that is your candlestick, and holds up your torch from dropping, for to march after a link [3] is shoemaker-like; let *ignis fatuus*, I say, being within the reach of the constable's staff, asked aloud, "Sir Giles,"—or "Sir Abram,"—"will you turn this way, or down that street?" It skills not, though there be none dubbed in your bunch; the watch will wink at you, only for the love they bear to arms and knighthood. Marry, if the sentinel and his court of guard stand strictly upon his martial law, and cry "Stand!", commanding you to give the word and to show reason why your ghost walks so late; do it in some jest: for that will show you have a desperate wit, and perhaps make him and his halberdiers afraid to lay foul hands upon you; or, if you read a *mittimus* [4] in the constable's book, counterfeit to be a Frenchman, a Dutchman, or any other nation whose country is in peace with your own, and you may pass the pikes; for, being not able to understand you, they cannot by the customs of the City take your examination, and so by consequence they have nothing to say to you. . . .

All the way as you pass, especially being approached near some of the gates, talk of none but lords, and such ladies with whom you have played at primero,[5] or danced in the presence,[6] the very same day; it is a chance to lock up the lips of an inquisitive bellman: and, being arrived at your lodging door, which I would counsel you to choose in some rich citizen's house, salute at parting no man but by the name of "Sir", as though you had supped with

[1] Liveries.
[2] The regular weapon of a watch.
[3] Torch.
[4] Order to commit.
[5] A card game.
[6] At Court.

knights; albeit you had none in your company but your perinado [1] or your ingle.[2]

Happily it will be blown abroad, that you and your shoal of gallants swam through such an ocean of wine, that you danced so much money out at heels, and that in wild-fowl [3] there flew away thus much; and I assure you, to have the bill of your reckoning lost of purpose, so that it may be published, will make you to be held in dear estimation: only the danger is, if you owe money, and that your revealing gets your creditors by the ears; for then, look to have a peal of ordnance thundering at your chamber-door the next morning. But if either your tailor, mercer, haberdasher, silkman, cutter, linen-draper, or sempster, stand like a guard of Switzers about your lodging, watching your uprising, or, if they miss of that, your downlying in one of the Counters,[4] you have no means to avoid the galling of their small-shot than by sending out a light horseman to call your poticary to your aid, who, encountering this desperate band of your creditors only with two or three glasses in his hand, as though that day you purged, is able to drive them all to their holes like so many foxes; for the name of taking physic [5] is a sufficient *quietus est* [6] to any endangered gentleman, and gives an acquittance,[6] for the time, to them all; though the twelve companies [7] stand with their hoods to attend your coming forth, and their officers with them.

VI. THE WICKEDNESS OF BALLAD SINGERS

ROBERT GREENE. The Third Part of Connycatching, 1592; *in Vol. III, page 26, of the Bodley Head Quartos. With this, compare the adventures of Autolycus at the sheepshearing feast in the* Winter's Tale, *Act IV, Scene 4.*

This trade, or rather unsufferable loitering quality, in singing of ballets and songs at the doors of such houses

[1] Hanger-on.   [2] Crony.   [3] Wild company.
[4] One of the City prisons.
[5] I.e. as if suffering from the plague.
[6] Release, receipt.   [7] The City companies.

where plays are used, as also in open markets and other places of this city where is most resort, which is nothing else but a sly fetch [1] to draw many together, who, listening unto a harmless ditty, afterward walk home to their houses with heavy hearts: from such as are hereof true witnesses to their cost, do I deliver this example. A subtle fellow, belike emboldened by acquaintance with the former deceit, or else, being but a beginner to practise the same, calling certain of his companions together, would try whether he could attain to be master of his art or no, by taking a great many of fools with one train. But let his intent and what else beside remain to abide the censure after the matter is heard, and come to Gracious Street, where this villainous prank was performed. A roguing mate and such another with him, were there got upon a stall singing of ballets, which belike was some pretty toy,[2] for very many gathered about to hear it, and divers buying, as their affections served, drew to their purses and paid the singers for them. The sly mate and his fellows, who were dispersed among them that stood to hear the songs, well noted where every man that bought put up his purse again, and to such as would not buy, counterfeit warning was sundry times given by the rogue and his associate, to beware of the cut-purse, and look to their purses, which made them often feel where their purses were, either in sleeve, hose, or at girdle, to know whether they were safe or no. Thus the crafty copesmates [3] were acquainted with what they most desired, and as they were scattered, by shouldering, thrusting, feigning to let fall something, and other wily tricks fit for their purpose, here one lost his purse, there another had his pocket picked, and to say all in brief, at one instant, upon the complaint of one or two that saw their purses were gone, eight more in the same company found themselves in like predicament. Some angry, others sorrowful and all greatly discontented, looking about them, knew not who to suspect or challenge, in that the villains themselves that had thus beguiled

[1] Trick.   [2] Trifle.   [3] Companions.

them, made show that they had sustained like loss. But one angry fellow, more impatient than all the rest, he falls upon the ballad singer, and beating him with his fists well favouredly, says, if he had not listened his singing, he had not lost his purse, and therefore would not be otherwise persuaded but that they two and the cut-purses were compacted together. The rest that had lost their purses likewise and saw that so many complain together, they jump in opinion with the other fellow, and begin to tug and hail the ballad singers, when one after one, the false knaves began to shrink away with the purses. By means of some officer then being there present, the two rogues were had before a Justice, and upon his discreet examination made, it was found that they and the cut-purses were compacted together, and that by this unsuspected villainy, they had deceived many. The fine fool-taker himself, with one or two more of that company, was not long after apprehended, when I doubt not but they had their reward answerable to their deserving, for I hear of their journey westward,[1] but not of their return. Let this forewarn those that listen to singing in the streets.

VII. BARTHOLOMEW FAIR

JOHN STOW. Survey of London, 1603; *Vol. I, page* 104 *in C. L. Kingsford's edition.*

In the month of August, about the feast of St. Bartholomew the Apostle, before the Lord Mayor, Aldermen and Sheriffs of London, placed in a large tent near unto Clerkenwell, of old time were divers days spent in the pastime of wrestling, where the officers of the City, namely the Sheriffs, Sergeants and Yeomen, the Porters of the King's Beam or Weigh House, now no such men, and other of the City, were challengers of all men in the suburbs, to wrestle for games appointed. And on other days, before the said Mayor, Aldermen and Sheriffs, in Finsbury Field, to shoot

[1] To Tyburn where the gallows stood: the site is near the Marble Arch.

the Standard, Broad Arrow, and Flight, for games; but now of late years, the wrestling is only practised on Bartholomew Day [1] in the afternoon, and the shooting some three or four days after, in one afternoon and no more. What should I speak of the ancient daily exercises in the long bow by citizens of this City, now almost clean left off and forsaken ? I overpass it ; for by the mean of closing in the common grounds, our archers, for want of room to shoot abroad, creep into bowling alleys and ordinary dicing houses nearer home, where they have room enough to hazard their money at unlawful games ; and there I leave them to take their pleasures.

VIII. IN THE TAVERN

THOMAS HEYWOOD. The Fair Maid of the West, 1617; *Act III, Scene* 4.

CLEM, *the vintner's prentice, enters to wait on* CAPTAIN GOODLACK.

CLEM. You are welcome, gentleman. What wine will you drink ? Claret, metheglin,[2] or muscadine ? Cider, or perry, to make you merry ? Aragoosa, or peter-see-me ? Canary, or charnico ? But, by your nose, sir, you should love a cup of malmsey : you shall have a cup of the best in Cornwall.

GOODLACK. Here's a brave drawer will quarrel with his wine.

CLEM. But if you prefer the Frenchman before the Spaniard, you shall have either here of the deep red grape, or the pallid white. You are a pretty tall gentleman ; you should love high country wine : none but clerks and sextons love Graves wine. Or, are you a married man, I'll furnish you with bastard, white or brown, according to the complexion of your bedfellow.

GOODLACK. You rogue, how many years of your prenticeship have you spent in studying this set speech ?

[1] August 24.   [2] A rich wine, smelling of musk.

CLEM. The first line of my part was "Anon, anon, sir "; [1] and the first question I answered to, was loggerhead, or blockhead—I know not whether.

GOODLACK. Speak: where's your mistress?

CLEM. Gone up to her chamber.

GOODLACK. Set a pottle of sack in the fire, and carry it into the next room.

[*He goes out.*]

CLEM. Score a pottle of sack in the Crown,[2] and see at the bar for some rotten eggs, to burn it: we must have one trick or other, to vent away our bad commodities.

IX. THE EIGHT KINDS OF DRUNKENNESS

THOMAS NASHE. Piers Penniless, his Supplication to the Devil, 1592; *Vol. I, page 207, in McKerrow's edition. Compare* Twelfth Night, *Act I, Scene 5, l. 139.*

Nor have we one or two kind of drunkards only, but eight kinds. The first is ape drunk, and he leaps and sings and hollows and danceth for the heavens; the second is lion drunk, and he flings the pots about the house, calls his hostess whore, breaks the glass windows with his dagger, and is apt to quarrel with any man that speaks to him; the third is swine drunk, heavy, lumpish and sleepy, and cries for a little more drink and a few more clothes; the fourth is sheep drunk, wise in his own conceit, when he cannot bring forth a right word; the fifth is maudlin drunk, when a fellow will weep for kindness in the midst of his ale, and kiss you, saying, "By God, Captain, I love thee; go thy ways, thou dost not think so often of me as I do of thee, I would (if it please God) I could not love thee so well as I do ", and then he puts his finger in his eye and cries; the sixth is martin [3] drunk, when a man is drunk

---

[1] "Coming, sir": the drawer's regular answer.
[2] The separate rooms in a tavern were named.
[3] Like a scurrilous Puritan pamphleteer.

and drinks himself sober ere he stir; the seventh is goat drunk, when in his drunkenness he hath no mind but on lechery; the eighth is fox drunk, when he is crafty drunk, as many of the Dutchmen be, that will never bargain but when they are drunk. All these species and more I have seen practised in one company at one sitting, when I have been permitted to remain sober amongst them, only to note their several humours. He that plies any one of them hard, it will make him to write admirable verses and to have a deep casting [1] head, though he were never so very a dunce before.

X. THE HORRORS OF PLAGUE

THOMAS DEKKER. The Wonderful Year, 1603; *Vol. VIII, page 38, in the Bodley Head Quartos. Plague broke out in London frequently, especially in a hot and rainless summer, because the garbage bred f which spread any contagious sickness. There were particularly bad outbreaks in 1593 and again in 1603, shortly after the death of Queen Elizabeth.*

What an unmatchable torment were it for a man to be barred up every night in a vast silent charnel house, hung (to make it more hideous) with lamps dimly and slowly burning in hollow and glimmering corners: where all the pavement should, instead of green rushes, be strewed with blasted rosemary,[2] withered hyacinths, fatal cypress and yew, thickly mingled with heaps of dead men's bones: the bare ribs of a father that begat him lying there; here the chapless, hollow skull of a mother that bore him; round about him a thousand corpses, some standing bolt upright in their knotted winding-sheets, others half mouldered in rotten coffins that should suddenly yawn wide open, filling his nostrils with noisome stench and his eyes with the sight of nothing but crawling worms. And to keep such a poor wretch waking, he should hear no noise

[1] Calculating.
[2] Rosemary was believed to be a disinfectant and was much used in houses at plague time. In this passage, however, Dekker refers to the funeral wreaths.

but of toads croaking, screech-owls howling, mandrakes shrieking: were not this an infernal prison? Would not the strongest hearted man beset with such a ghastly horror look wild and run mad and die? And even such a formidable shape did the diseased City appear in; for he that durst in the dead hour of gloomy midnight have been so valiant as to have walked through the still and melancholy streets, what think you should have been his music? Surely the loud groans of raving, sick men, the struggling pangs of souls departing; in every house grief striking up an alarum; servants crying out for masters, wives for husbands, parents for children, children for their mothers; here he should have met with some frantically running to knock up sextons; there, others fearfully sweating with coffins to steal forth dead bodies lest the fatal handwriting of death should seal up their doors. And to make this dismal consort [1] more full, round about him bells heavily tolling in one place and ringing out in another. The dreadfulness of such an hour is unutterable.

XI. A MORALIST'S OBJECTION TO PLAYS

STEPHEN GOSSON. *The School of Abuse, 1579; page 34 in Arber's reprint. Gosson objects to plays mainly on moral grounds, but he was not exaggerating. The City authorities were equally emphatic in their denunciation of plays which attracted crowds, and with them loose characters of all sorts. They were a convenient meeting-place for rioters; above all, they increased the dangers of infection in time of plague.*

Consider with thyself, gentle reader, the old discipline of England; mark what we were before and what we are now. . . . Oh, what a wonderful change is this! Our wrestling at arms is turned to wallowing in ladies' laps; our courage to cowardice; our running to riot, our bows to bowls, and our darts to dishes. We have robbed Greece of gluttony; Italy of wantonness; Spain of pride; France of deceit, and Dutchland of quaffing. Compare London to Rome, and England to Italy: you shall find the theatre

[1] Concert.

of the one, and the abuses of the other, to be rife among us. *Experto crede*,[1] I have seen somewhat, and therefore I think may say the more. In Rome, when plays or pageants are shown, Ovid chargeth his pilgrims to creep close to the Saints whom they serve, and show their double diligence to lift the gentlewomen's robes from the ground, for soiling in the dust; to sweep motes from their kirtles, to keep their fingers in ure;[2] to lay their hands at their backs for an easy stay; to look upon those whom they behold; to praise that which they commend; to like everything that pleaseth them; to present them pomegranates to pick as they sit; and when all is done, to wait on them mannerly to their houses. In our assemblies at plays in London you shall see such heaving and shoving, such itching and shouldering to sit by women; such care for their garments that they be not trod on; such eyes to their laps, that no chips light in them; such pillows to their backs, that they take no hurt; such masking in their ears, I know not what; such giving them pippins to pass the time; such playing at foot-saunt[3] without cards; such tickling, such toying, such smiling, such winking and such manning them home when the sports are ended, that it is a right comedy to mark their behaviour, to watch their conceits, as the cat for the mouse, and as good as a course at the game itself, to dog them a little, or follow aloof by the print of their feet and so discover by slot where the deer taketh soil. If this were as well noted as ill seen, or as openly punished as secretly practised, I have no doubt but the cause would be feared to dry up the effect and these pretty rabbits very cunningly ferreted from their burrows. For they that lack customers all the week, either because their haunt is unknown or the constables and officers of their parish watch them so narrowly that they dare not queach;[4] to celebrate the Sabbath, flock to the theatres and there keep a general market of bawdry. Not that any filthiness indeed is committed within the compass of that ground, as

---

[1] "Believe one who has tried it."   [2] Use.
[3] Or "cent", a card game like piquet.   [4] Stir.

was done in Rome, but that every wanton and his paramour, every man and his mistress, every John and his Joan, every knave and his quean, are there first acquainted and cheapen the merchandise in that place, which they pay for elsewhere as they can agree.

XII. A SCHOLAR'S OBJECTION TO PLAYS

SIR PHILIP SIDNEY. Apology for Poetry, c. 1580 ; *pages 51 and 54 in J. C. Collins' edition. Sidney was obsessed with the Classical rules which had been evolved by the Italian critics of the early sixteenth century from the Poetics of Aristotle ; but even so no plays had yet been produced which could be compared with the classical dramas. Marlowe, Kyd, Lyly, and the other University Wits did not begin to write for the stage for another six years.*

Our tragedies and comedies (not without cause cried out against), observing rules neither of honest civility nor of skilful poetry, excepting *Gorboduc* [1] (again, I say, of those that I have seen), which notwithstanding, as it is full of stately speeches and well-sounding phrases, climbing to the height of Seneca his style, and as full of notable morality, which it doth most delightfully teach and so obtain the very end of poesy, yet in truth it is very defectious in the circumstances, which grieveth me, because it might not remain as an exact model of all tragedies. For it is faulty both in place and time, the two necessary companions of all corporal actions. For where the stage should always represent but one place, and the uttermost time presupposed in it should be, both by Aristotle's precept and common reason, but one day, there is both many days and many places inartificially imagined. But if it be so in *Gorboduc*, how much more in all the rest, where you shall have Asia of the one side, and Afric of the other, and so many other under-kingdoms, that the player, when he cometh in, must ever begin with telling where he is, or else the tale will not be conceived. Now ye shall have three ladies walk to gather flowers, and then we must believe the stage to be a garden.

[1] Written by Thomas Sackville and Thomas Norton about 1560, the earliest extant English tragedy.

By and by we hear news of shipwreck in the same place, and then we are to blame if we accept it not for a rock. Upon the back of that comes out a hideous monster, with fire and smoke, and then the miserable beholders are bound to take it for a cave ; while in the meantime, two armies fly in, represented with four swords and bucklers, and then what hard heart will not receive it for a pitched field ?

Now, of time they are much more liberal, for ordinary it is that two young princes fall in love. After many traverses, she is got with child, delivered of a fair boy ; he is lost, groweth a man, falls in love, and is ready to get another child ; and all this in two hours space, which how absurd it is in sense, even sense may imagine, and Art hath taught, and all the ancient examples justified, and, at this day, the ordinary players in Italy will not err in. Yet will some bring in an example of *Eunuchus* in Terence, that containeth matter of two days, yet far short of twenty years. True it is, and so was it to be played in two days, and so fitted to the time it set forth. And though Plautus hath in one place done amiss, let us hit with him, and not miss with him. . . .

And besides these gross absurdities, how all their plays be neither right tragedies, nor right comedies, mingling kings and clowns, not because the matter so carrieth it, but thrust in clowns by head and shoulders, to play a part in majestical matters, with neither decency nor discretion, so as neither the admiration and commiseration, nor the right sportfulness, is by their mongrel tragi-comedy obtained. I know Apuleius did somewhat so, but that is a thing recounted with space of time, not represented in one moment ; and I know the Ancients have one or two examples of tragi-comedies, as Plautus hath *Amphitruo*. But, if we mark them well, we shall find that they never, or very daintily, match hornpipes and funerals. So falleth it out, that having indeed no right comedy in that comical part of our tragedy, we have nothing but scurrility, unworthy of any chaste ears, or some extreme show of doltishness, indeed fit to lift up a loud laughter, and nothing else, where the whole tract of a comedy should be full of delight, as the tragedy should be still maintained in a well-raised admiration.

XIII. A DEFENCE OF PLAYS

THOMAS NASHE. Piers Penniless; *Vol. I, page* 211 *in McKerrow's edition.*

That state or kingdom that is in league with all the world and hath no foreign sword to vex it, is not half so strong or confirmed to endure as that which lives every hour in fear of invasion. There is a certain waste of the people for whom there is no use but war; and these men must have some employment still to cut them off: *Nam si foras hostem non habent, domi invenient*;[1] if they have no service abroad, they will make mutinies at home. Or, if the affairs of the State be such as cannot exhale all these corrupt excrements, it is very expedient they have some light toys to busy their heads withal cast before them as bones to gnaw upon, which may keep them from having leisure to intermeddle with higher matters. To this effect, the policy of plays is very necessary, howsoever some shallow-brained censurers (not the deepest searchers into the secrets of government) mightily oppugn them. For, whereas the afternoon being the idlest time of the day, wherein men that are their own masters (as gentlemen of the Court, the Inns of the Court, and the number of captains and soldiers about London) do wholly bestow themselves upon pleasure, and that pleasure they divide (how virtuously it skills now) either into gaming, following of harlots, drinking, or seeing a play. Is it not then better (since of four extremes all the world cannot keep them, but they will choose one) that they should betake them to the least, which is plays? Nay, what if I prove plays to be no extreme, but a rare exercise of virtue? First, for the subject of them (for the most part) it is borrowed out of our English Chronicles,

[1] "If they have no enemy abroad, they will find one at home."

wherein our forefathers' valiant acts (that have lain long buried in rusty brass and worm-eaten books) are revived, and they themselves raised from the grave of oblivion, and brought to plead their aged honours in open presence : than which, what can be a sharper reproof to these degenerate days of ours ? How would it have joyed brave Talbot (the terror of the French) to think that after he had lain two hundred years in his tomb, he should triumph again on the stage, and have his bones new embalmed with the tears of ten thousand spectators at least (at several times) who, in the tragedian that represents his person, imagine they behold him fresh bleeding. I will defend it against any cullion,[1] or club-fisted usurer of them all, there is no immortality can be given a man on earth like unto plays. What talk I to them of immortality, that are the only underminers of honour, and do envy any man that is not sprung up by base brokery like themselves ? They care not if all the ancient houses were rooted out, so that, like the Burgomasters of the Low-countries, they might share the government amongst them, as States, and be quartermasters of our monarchy. All arts to them are vanity ; and if you tell them what a glorious thing it is to have Henry the Fifth represented on the stage leading the French King prisoner, and forcing both him and the Dolphin to swear fealty ; " aye, but " (will they say) " what do we get by it ? " Respecting neither the right of fame that is due to true nobility deceased, nor what hopes of eternity are to be proposed to adventurous minds, to encourage them forward, but only their execrable lucre and filthy unquenchable avarice. They know when they are dead, they shall not be brought upon the stage for any goodness, but in a merriment of the Usurer and the Devil, or buying arms of the Herald, who gives them the lion without tongue, tail or talons because his master, whom he must serve, is a townsman, and a man of peace, and must not keep any quarrelling beasts to annoy his honest neighbours.

[1] Rascal

XIV. THE PLAYGOER

JOHN MARSTON. The Scourge of Villainy, 1599; *Vol. III, page* 107 *in the Bodley Head Quartos.*

Luscus, what's played to-day? faith now I know
I set thy lips abroach, from whence doth flow
Naught but pure Juliet and Romeo.
Say, who acts best? Drusus, or Roscio?
Now I have him, that ne'er of ought did speak
But when of plays or players he did treat.
H'ath made a commonplace book out of plays,
And speaks in print, at least whate'er he says
Is warranted by Curtain [1] plaudities,
If e'er you heard him courting Lesbia's eyes;
Say (courteous Sir), speaks he not movingly
From out some new pathetic Tragedy?
He writes, he rails, he jests, he courts, what not,
And all from out his huge long scraped stock
Of well penn'd plays.

XV. A BOY ACTOR

BEN JONSON. Epigrams, 1616. *Pavy was one of the boy actors of the Children of the Chapel Royal; he died about 1603. The boy companies were exclusively patronized by the élite, and the dramatists who wrote for them were for the most part gentlemen of some standing.*

AN EPITAPH ON SALATHIEL PAVY, A CHILD OF QUEEN ELIZABETH'S CHAPEL

Weep with me, all you that read
   This little story;
And know, for whom a tear you shed
   Death's self is sorry.
'Twas a child that so did thrive
   In grace and feature,
As Heaven and Nature seemed to strive
   Which owned the creature.

---

[1] A small theatre in Shoreditch where Shakespeare's Company played 1597-99.

Years he numbered scarce thirteen
　　When Fates turned cruel,
Yet three full zodiacs had he been
　　The stage's jewel;
And did act, what now we moan,
　　Old men so duly,
As, sooth, the Parcæ [1] thought him one,
　　He played so truly.
So, by error to his fate
　　They all consented;
But viewing him since, alas, too late!
　　They have repented;
And have sought to give new birth,
　　In baths to steep him;
But being so much too good for earth,
　　Heaven vows to keep him.

XVI. PUBLIUS, WHO LOVED BEAR-BAITING

Sir John Davies. Epigrams, c. 1593; *Vol. II, page* 40 *in Grosart's edition.*

In Publium

Publius, a student at the common law,
Oft leaves his books, and for his recreation,
To Paris Garden doth himself withdraw;
Where he is ravished with such delectation,
As down among the bears and dogs he goes;
Where, whilst he skipping cries, "to head, to head",
His satin doublet and his velvet hose
Are all with spittle from above bespread:
When he is like his father's country hall,
Stinking with dogs and muted all with hawkes;
And rightly too on him this filth doth fall,
Which for such filthy sports his books forsakes;

[1] The Fates.

Leaving old Ployden, Dyer, Brooke [1] alone,
To see old Harry Hunkes and Sacarson.[2]

XVII. AN EXECUTION

A true relation of all such things as passed at the Execution of
M. Garnet, 3rd May, 1606 ; *page* 405. *Father Garnet was executed for
complicity in the Gunpowder Plot. At his trial he set up the famous
plea of equivocation, to which the Porter in* Macbeth *refers.*

On the third day of May, Garnet, according to his judgment, was executed upon a scaffold set up for that purpose at the west end of Paul's Church. At his arise up the scaffold, he stood much amazed, fear and guiltiness appearing in his face. The Deans of Paul's and Winchester being present, very gravely and christianly exhorted him to a true and lively faith to Godward, a free and plain acknowledgment to the world of his offence, and if any further treason lay in his knowledge, to unburden his conscience, and show a sorrow and detestation of it. But Garnet, impatient of persuasions and ill pleased to be exhorted by them, desired them not to trouble him : he came prepared and was resolved. Then the Recorder of London (who was by His Majesty appointed to be there) asked Garnet if he had anything to say unto the people before he died. It was no time to dissemble and now his treasons were too manifest to be dissembled ; therefore if he would, the world should witness what at last he censured of himself, and of his fact. It should be free to him to speak what he listed. But Garnet, unwilling to take the offer, said, his voice was low, his strength gone, the people could not hear him, though he spake to them ; but to those about him on the scaffold, he said the intention was wicked, and the fact would have been cruel, and from his soul he should have abhorred it, had it effected. But, he said, he only had a general knowledge of it by M. Catesby, which in that he disclosed not, nor used means to prevent it, herein he had offended. What he knew in particulars

---

[1] Writers of Law text-books.
[2] The famous bears of the Bear Gardens.

LONDON LIFE

was in confession, as he said. But the Recorder wished him to be remembered that the King's Majesty had under his handwriting these four points amongst others :—

1. That Greenway told him of this, not as a fault, but as a thing which he had intelligence of, and told it him by way of consultation.
2. That Catesby and Greenway came together to him to be resolved.
3. That M. Telmond and he had conference of the particulars of the Powder Treason in Essex long after.
4. Greenway had asked him who should be the Protector, but Garnet said, that was to be referred till the blow was past.

"These prove your privity besides confession, and these are extant under your hand." Garnet answered, whatsoever was under his hand was true. And for that he disclosed not to His Majesty the things he knew, he confessed himself justly condemned; and for this did ask forgiveness of His Majesty. Hereupon the Recorder led him to the scaffold to make his confession public.

Then Garnet said, "Good countrymen, I am come hither this blessed day of the Invention of the Holy Cross, to end all my crosses in this life; the cause of my suffering is not unknown to you. I confess I have offended the King, and am sorry for it so far as I was guilty, which was in concealing it, and for that I ask pardon of His Majesty. The treason intended against the King and State was bloody. Myself should have detested it had it taken effect. And I am heartily sorry that any Catholics ever had so cruel a design." Then turning himself from the people to them about him, he made an apology for Mistress Anne Vaux, saying, "There is such an honourable gentlewoman who hath been much wronged in report, for it is suspected and said that I should be married to her, or worse. But I protest the contrary. She is a virtuous gentlewoman, and for me a perfect pure virgin." For the Pope's Briefs, Sir Edmund Baynam's going over seas and the matter of the

Powder Treason, he referred himself to his arraignment, and his confessions: "for whatsoever is under my hand in any of my confessions", said he, "is true."

Then addressing himself to execution, he kneeled at the ladder foot, and asked if he might have time to pray, and how long. It was answered he should limit himself; none should interrupt him. It appeared he could not constantly or devoutly pray; fear of death, or hope of pardon even then so distracted him: for oft in those prayers he would break off, turn, and look about him and answer to what he overheard while he seemed to be praying. When he stood up, the Recorder finding in his behaviour as it were an expectation of a pardon, wished him not to deceive himself, nor beguile his own soul; he was come to die, and must die, requiring him not to equivocate with his last breath; if he knew anything that might be danger to the King or State, he should now utter it. Garnet said, "It is no time now to equivocate"; how it was lawful and when, he had showed his mind elsewhere. But saith he, "I do not now equivocate, and more than I have confessed I do not know."

At his ascending up the ladder, he desired to have warning before he was turned off; but it was told him he must look for no other turn but death. Being upon the gibbet, he used these words, "I commend me to all good Catholics, and I pray God preserve His Majesty, the Queen, and all their posterity, and my Lords of the Privy Council, to whom I remember my humble duty, and I am sorry that I did dissemble with them, but I did not think they had had such proof against me till it was showed me; but when it was proved, I held it more honour for me at that time to confess, than before to have accused. And for my brother Greenway, I would the truth were known, for the false reports that are, make him more faulty than he is. I should not have charged him but that I thought he had been safe. I pray God the Catholics may not fare the worse for my sake, and I exhort them all to take heed they enter not into any treasons, rebellions, or insurrections against the

King "; and with this, ended speaking and fell to praying; and crossing himself, said, "*In nomine Patris et Filii et Spiritus Sancti*",[1] and prayed, "*Maria mater gratiæ, Maria mater misericordiæ, Tu me a malo protege et hora mortis suscipe.*"[2] Then, "*In manus tuas Domine, commendo spiritum meum*";[3] then, "*Per crucis hoc signum,*" (crossing himself) "*fugiat procul omne malignum. Infige Crucem tuam in corde meo Domine.*[4] Let me always remember the Cross", and so returned again to *Maria mater gratiæ*, and then was turned off, and was hung till he was dead.

XVIII. A BALLAD

THOMAS DELONEY. The Lamentation of Mr. Page's Wife, 1590; *page 482 in Mann's edition of Deloney. This ballad, typical of many on current events, is better than most. Ulalia, daughter of Mr. Glandfield of Tavistock, had fallen in love with George Strangwidge, his manager: but when her parents left the neighbourhood and moved to Plymouth, it seemed more convenient that she should marry some one nearer at hand. She was therefore forced to wed Mr. Page, a wealthy old widower, which she found so loathsome that she caused her husband to be strangled in bed by her servant and Strangwidge's man. All four were hanged. The murder evoked much horror and drew attention to the scandal of forced marriage. Two other ballads were written on the subject, and a pamphlet. In 1599 Ben Jonson and Dekker dramatized the event in a play, which is unfortunately lost.*

The Lamentation of Mr. Page's Wife
Of Plymouth, who, being forced to wed him, consented to his
Murder, for the love of G. Strangwidge: for
which they suffered at Barnstable
in Devonshire.

The tune is *Fortune My Foe, &c.*

Unhappy she whom Fortune hath forlorn
Despis'd of grace that proffered grace did scorn,

[1] "In the name of the Father and of the Son and of the Holy Spirit."
[2] "Mary, mother of grace, Mary, mother of pity, protect me from evil and sustain me in the hour of death."
[3] "Into Thy hands, O Lord, I commend my spirit."
[4] "By this sign of the cross all evil fly far from me. Fix Thy Cross in my heart, O Lord."

My lawless love hath luckless wrought my woe,
My discontent content did overthrow.

My loathed life too late I do lament,
My woeful deeds in heart I do repent:
A wife I was that wilful went awry,
And for that fault am here prepared to die.

In blooming years my father's greedy mind,
Against my will, a match for me did find:
Great wealth there was, yea, gold and silver store,
But yet my heart had chosen one before.

Mine eyes disliked my father's liking quite,
My heart did loathe my parent's fond delight:
My childish mind and fancy told to me,
That with his age my youth could not agree.

On knees I prayed they would not me constrain;
With tears I cried their purpose to refrain;
With sighs and sobs I did them often move,
I might not wed whereas I could not love.

But all in vain my speeches still I spent:
My mother's will my wishes did prevent,
Though wealthy Page possessed the outward part,
George Strangwidge still was lodged in my heart.

I wedded was, and wrapped all in woe;
Great discontent within my heart did grow;
I loathed to live, yet lived in deadly strife,
Because perforce I was made Page's wife.

My closen eyes could not his sight abide;
My tender youth did loathe his aged side:
Scant could I taste the meat whereon he fed;
My legs did loathe to lodge within his bed.

Cause knew I none I should despise him so,
That such disdain within my heart should grow,
Save only this, that fancy did me move,
And told me still, George Strangwidge was my love.

Lo! here began my downfall and decay.
In mind I mused to make him straight away:
I that became his discontented wife,
Contented was he should be rid of life.

Methinks the heavens cry vengeance for my fact,
Methinks the world condemns my monstrous act,
Methinks within my conscience tells me true,
That for that deed hell fire is my due.

My pensive soul doth sorrow for my sin,
For which offence my soul doth bleed within;
But mercy, Lord! for mercy still I cry:
Save thou my soul, and let my body die.

Well could I wish, that Page enjoyed his life,
So that he had some other to his wife:
But never could I wish, of low or high,
A longer life than see sweet Strangwidge die.

O woe is me! that had no greater grace
To stay till he had run out Nature's race.
My deeds I rue, but I do repent
That to the same my Strangwidge gave consent.

You parents fond, that greedy-minded be,
And seek to graff upon the golden tree,
Consider well and rightful judges be,
And give you doom 'twixt parents' love and me.

I was their child, and bound for to obey,
Yet not to love where I no love could lay.
I married was to muck and endless strife;
But faith before had made me Strangwidge' wife.

O wretched world! who cankered rust doth bind,
And cursed men who bear a greedy mind;
And hapless I, whom parents did force so
To end my days in sorrow, shame and woe.

You Denshire dames, and courteous Cornwall knights,
That here are come to visit woeful wights,
Regard my grief, and mark my woeful end,
But to your children be a better friend.

And thou, my dear, that for my fault must die,
Be not afraid the sting of death to try:
Like as we lived and loved together true,
So both at once we'll bid the world adieu.

Ulalia, thy friend, doth take her last farewell,
Whose soul with thee in heaven shall ever dwell.
Sweet Saviour Christ! do Thou my soul receive:
The world I do with all my heart forgive.

And parents now, whose greedy minds do show
Your hearts' desire and inward heavy woe,
Mourn you no more, for now my heart doth tell,
Ere day be done my soul shall be full well.

And Plymouth proud, I bid thee now farewell.
Take heed, you wives, let not your hands rebel;
And farewell, life, wherein such sorrow shows,
And welcome, death, that doth my corpse enclose

And now, sweet Lord! forgive me my misdeeds.
Repentance cries for soul that inward bleeds:
My soul and body I commend to Thee,
That with Thy blood from death redeemed me.

Lord! bless our Queen with long and happy life,
And send true peace betwixt each man and wife;
And give all parents wisdom to foresee,
The match is marred where minds do not agree.

T. D.

SECTION SIX

COUNTRY LIFE

I. INNOVATIONS

WILLIAM HARRISON. A Description of England; *page* 118 *in Furnivall's* Elizabethan England. *Harrison was an Essex parson, and his account of the new houses can be verified by a visit to the villages in the Dunmow-Thaxted neighbourhood, where many of the old houses, built of timber and lath round a solid brick chimney, still remain almost untouched.*

There are old men yet dwelling in the village where I remain, which have noted three things to be marvellously altered in England within their sound remembrance, and other three things too too much increased. One is the multitude of chimneys lately erected; whereas in their young days there were not above two or three, if so many, in most uplandish [1] towns of the realm (the religious houses and manor places of their lords always excepted, and peradventure some great personages), but each one made his fire against a reredos [2] in the hall, where he dined and dressed his meat.

The second is the great (although not general) amendment of lodging; for, said they, our fathers, yea and we ourselves also, have lain full oft upon straw pallets, on rough mats covered only with a sheet, under coverlets made of dagswain or hop-harlots (I use their own terms), and a good round log under their heads instead of a bolster or pillow. If it were so that our fathers, or the good man of the house, had within seven years after his marriage purchased a

---

[1] Up-country. [2] Screen.

mattress or flock bed, and thereto a stack of chaff to rest his head upon, he thought himself to be as well lodged as the lord of the town, that peradventure lay seldom in a bed of down or whole feathers, so well were they content, and with such base kind of furniture; which also is not very much amended as yet in some parts of Bedfordshire, and elsewhere, farther off from our southern parts. Pillows, said they, were thought meet only for women in childbed. As for servants, if they had any sheet above them, it was well, for seldom had they any under their bodies to keep them from the pricking straws that ran oft through the canvas of the pallet and rased their hardened hides.

The third thing they tell of is the exchange of vessel, as of treen [1] platters into pewter, and wooden spoons into silver or tin. For so common were all sorts of treen stuff in old time, that a man should hardly find four pieces of pewter (of which one was peradventure a salt) in a good farmer's house, and yet for all this frugality (if it may so be justly called) they were scarce able to live and pay their rents at their days without selling of a cow, or a horse, or more, although they paid but four pounds at the uttermost by the year. Such also was their poverty, that if some one odd farmer or husbandman had been at the alehouse, a thing greatly used in those days, amongst six or seven of his neighbours, and there, in a bravery, to show what store he had, did cast down his purse and therein a noble [2] or six shillings in silver, unto them (for few such men then cared for gold, because it was not so ready payment, and they were oft enforced to give a penny for the exchange of an angel),[3] it was very likely that all the rest could not lay down so much against it; whereas in my time, although peradventure four pounds of old rent be improved to forty, fifty, or a hundred pounds, yet will the farmer, as another palm or date tree, think his gains very small toward the end of his term if he have not six or seven years' rent lying by him, therewith to purchase a new lease, beside a fair garnish of pewter on his cupboard, with so much more in odd

---

[1] Wooden.   [2] 6s. 8d.   [3] 10s.

vessels going about the house, three or four feather beds, so many coverlids and carpets of tapestry, a silver salt, a bowl for wine (if not a whole nest), and a dozen of spoons to furnish up the suit. This also he takes to be his own clear, for what stock of money soever he gathereth and layeth up in all his years, it is often seen that the landlord will take such order with him for the same when he reneweth his lease, which is commonly eight or six years before the old be expired (sith it is now grown almost to a custom that if he come not to his lord so long before, another shall step in for a reversion, and so defeat him outright), that it shall never trouble him more than the hair of his beard when the barber hath washed and shaved it from his chin.

II. OF GARDENS

FRANCIS BACON. Essays. *This essay is a description of the mood in which Bacon designed the Gray's Inn gardens.*

For gardens (speaking of those which are indeed princelike, as we have done of buildings), the contents ought not well to be under thirty acres of ground, and to be divided into three parts : a green in the entrance ; a heath or desert in the going forth ; and the main garden in the midst ; besides alleys on both sides. And I like well that four acres of ground be assigned to the green ; six to the heath ; four and four to either side ; and twelve to the main garden. The green hath two pleasures : the one, because nothing is more pleasant to the eye than green grass kept finely shorn ; the other, because it will give you a fair alley in the midst, by which you may go in front upon a stately hedge, which is to enclose the garden. But because the alley will be long, and in great heat of the year or day, you ought not to buy the shade in the garden by going in the sun through the green, therefore you are, of either side the green, to plant a covert alley, upon carpenter's work, about twelve foot in height, by which you may go in shade into the garden. As for the making of knots or figures with divers-coloured earths, that they may lie under the windows of the house on that side which the garden stands, they be but toys: you may see as good sights many times in tarts. The garden is best to be square; encompassed on all the four sides with a stately arched hedge. The arches to be upon pillars of carpenter's work, of some ten foot high and six foot broad; and the spaces between of the same dimension with the breadth of the arch. Over the arches let there be an entire hedge, of some four foot high, framed also upon carpenter's work; and upon the upper hedge, over every arch, a little turret, with a belly, enough to receive a cage of birds; and over every space between the arches some other little figure, with broad plates of round coloured glass, gilt, for the sun to play upon. But this hedge I intend to be raised upon a bank, not steep but gently slope of some six foot, set all with flowers. Also I understand that this square of the garden should not be the whole breadth of the ground, but to leave, on either side, ground enough for diversity of side alleys; unto which the two covert alleys of the green may deliver you. But there must be no alleys with hedges at either end of this great enclosure; not at the hither end, for letting your prospect upon this fair hedge from the green; nor at the farther end, for letting your prospect from the hedge, through the arches, upon the heath.

For the ordering of the ground within the great hedge, I leave it to variety of device; advising, nevertheless, that whatsoever form you cast it into first, it be not too busy or full of work. Wherein I, for my part, do not like images cut out in juniper or other garden stuff: they be for children. Little low hedges, round, like welts, with some pretty pyramids, I like well; and in some places, fair columns upon frames of carpenter's work. I would also have the alleys spacious and fair. You may have closer alleys upon the side grounds, but none in the main garden. I wish also, in the very middle, a fair mount, with three ascents, and alleys, enough for four to walk abreast; which I would have to be perfect circles, without any bulwarks or embossments; and the whole mount to be thirty foot high; and some fine banqueting house, with some chimneys neatly cast, and without too much glass.

For fountains, they are a great beauty and refreshment; but pools mar all, and make the garden unwholesome and full of flies and frogs. Fountains I intend to be of two natures: the one, that sprinkleth or spouteth water; the other, a fair receipt of water, of some thirty or forty foot square, but without fish, or slime, or mud. For the first, the ornaments of images gilt, or of marble, which are in use, do well: but the main matter is, so to convey the water as it never stay, either in the bowls or in the cistern; that the water be never by rest discoloured, green or red or the like, or gather any mossiness or putrefaction. Besides that, it is to be cleansed every day by the hand. Also some steps up to it, and some fine pavement about it, doth well. As for the other kind of fountain, which we may call a bathing pool, it may admit much curiosity and beauty, wherewith we will not trouble ourselves: as, that the bottom be finely paved, and with images; the sides likewise; and withal embellished with coloured glass, and such things of lustre; encompassed also with fine rails of low statuas. But the main point is the same which we mentioned in the former kind of fountain; which is, that the water be in perpetual motion, fed by a water higher than the pool, and delivered into it by fair spouts, and then discharged away under ground, by some equality of bores, that it stay little. And for fine devices, of arching water without spilling, and making it rise in several forms (of feathers, drinking glasses, canopies and the like), they be pretty things to look on, but nothing to health and sweetness.

For the heath, which was the third part of our plot, I wish it to be framed, as much as may be, to a natural wildness. Trees I would have none in it; but some thickets, made only of sweet-brier and honeysuckle, and some wild vine amongst; and the ground set with violets, strawberries and primroses. For these are sweet, and prosper

COUNTRY LIFE 153

in the shade. And these to be in the heath, here and there, not in any order. I like also little heaps in the nature of mole-hills (such as are in wild heaths), to be set, some with wild thyme, some with pinks, some with germander, that gives a good flower to the eye, some with periwinkle, some with violets, some with strawberries, some with cowslips, some with daisies, some with red roses, some with lilium convallium, some with sweet-williams red, some with bear's foot, and the like low flowers, being withal sweet and sightly. Part of which heaps to be with standards of little bushes pricked upon their top, and part without. The standards to be roses, juniper, holly, berberries (but here and there, because of the smell of their blossom), red currants, gooseberries, rosemary, bays, sweet-briers, and such-like. But these standards to be kept with cutting, that they grow not out of course.

For the side grounds, you are to fill them with variety of alleys, private, to give a full shade, some of them, wheresoever the sun be. You are to frame some of them likewise for shelter, that when the wind blows sharp you may walk as in a gallery. And those alleys must be likewise hedged at both ends, to keep out the wind; and these closer alleys must be ever finely gravelled, and no grass, because of going wet. In many of these alleys likewise, you are to set fruit-trees of all sorts; as well upon the walls as in ranges. And this would be generally observed, that the borders, wherein you plant your fruit-trees, be fair and large, and low, and not steep; and set with fine flowers, but thin and sparingly, lest they deceive the trees. At the end of both the side grounds, I would have a mount of some pretty height, leaving the wall of the enclosure breast high, to look abroad into the fields.

For the main garden, I do not deny but there should be some fair alleys, ranged on both sides with fruit-trees; and some pretty tufts of fruit-trees, and arbours with seats, set in some decent order; but these to be by no means set too thick; but to leave the main garden so as it be not close, but the air open and free. For as for shade, I would have you rest upon the alleys of the side grounds, there to walk, if you be disposed, in the heat of the year or day; but to make account that the main garden is for the more temperate parts of the year; and in the heat of summer, for the morning and the evening, or overcast days.

For aviaries, I like them not, except they be of that largeness as they may be turfed, and have living plants and bushes set in them; that the birds may have more scope and natural nestling, and that no foulness appear in the floor of the aviary. So I have made a platform [1] of a princely garden, partly by precept, partly by drawing, not a model,[2] but some general lines of it; and in this I have spared for no cost. But it is nothing for great princes, that, for the most part, taking advice with workmen, with no less cost set their things together; and sometimes add statuas and such things, for state and magnificence, but nothing to the true pleasure of a garden.

III. SWEET ANKOR IN ARDEN

MICHAEL DRAYTON, Idea's Mirror, 1594; *pages 8 and 24 in Brett's edition.*

AMOUR 13

Clear Ankor, on whose silver-sanded shore
My soul-shrined saint, my fair Idea, lies;
O blessed brook! Whose milk-white swans adore
The crystal stream refined by her eyes;
Where sweet myrrh-breathing Zephyr in the spring
Gently distils his nectar-dropping showers;
Where nightingales in Arden sit and sing
Amongst those dainty dew-empearled flowers.
Say thus, fair brook, when thou shalt see thy queen:
"Lo! here thy shepherd spent his wandering years,
And in this shade, dear nymph, he oft hath been,
And here to thee he sacrificed his tears."
 Fair Arden, thou my Tempe art alone,
 And thou, sweet Ankor, art my Helicon.

---

[1] Sketch.   [2] Detailed plan.

AMOUR 24

Our floods' Queen, Thames, for ships and swans is crowned,
And stately Severn for her shores is praised,
The crystal Trent for fords and fish renowned,
And Avon's fame to Albion's cliffs is raised.
Carlegion Chester vaunts her holy Dee,
York many wonders of her Ouse can tell,
The Peak her Dove whose banks so fertile be,
And Kent will say her Medway doth excel.
Cotswold commends her Isis and her Thame,
Our Northern borders boast of Tweed's fair flood,
Our Western parts extol her Wily's fame,
And old Legea brags of Danish blood :
 Arden's sweet Ankor, let thy glory be
 That fair Idea, she doth live by thee.

IV. THE SCENT OF MOTHER EARTH

WILLIAM BROWNE, Britannia's Pastorals, *Book i, Song 2* ; *vol. i, page 58 in the Muses Library.* *This extract and the next show genuine love and observation of the country ; but the majority of the pastoral poems—such as No. VI in this section—are conventional expressions inspired by a surfeit of town or court life.*

The earth doth yield (which they through pores exhale)
Earth's best of odours, th' aromatical :
Like to that smell which oft our sense descries
Which in a field which long unploughed lies,
Somewhat before the setting of the sun ;
And where the rainbow in the horizon
Doth pitch her tips : or as when in the prime,
The earth being troubled with a drought long time,
The hand of Heaven his spongy clouds doth strain,
And throws into her lap a shower of rain :
She sendeth up (conceived from the sun)
A sweet perfume, an exhalation.
Not all the ointments brought from Delos' Isle,
Nor from the confines of seven-headed Nile,

Nor that brought whence Phœnicians have abodes,
Nor Cyprus' wild vine-flowers, not that of Rhodes,
Nor roses' oil from Naples, Capua.
Saffron confected in Cilicia,
Nor that of quinces, nor of marjoram,
That ever from the isle of Coös came,
Nor these, nor any else, though ne'er so rare,
Could with this place for sweetest smells compare.

V. POOR WAT

WILLIAM SHAKESPEARE, Venus and Adonis, 1593.

But if thou needs wilt hunt, be rul'd by me;
Uncouple at the timorous flying hare,
Or at the fox which lives by subtlety,
Or at the roe which no encounter dare:
   Pursue these fearful creatures o'er the downs,
   And on thy well-breath'd horse keep with thy hounds.

And when thou hast on foot the purblind hare,
Mark the poor wretch, to overshoot his troubles
How he outruns the wind, and with what care
He cranks and crosses with a thousand doubles:
   The many musets through the which he goes
   Are like a labyrinth to amaze his foes.

Sometime he runs among a flock of sheep,
To make the cunning hounds mistake their smell,
And sometime where earth-delving conies keep,
To stop the loud pursuers in their yell,
   And sometime sorteth with a herd of deer;
   Danger deviseth shifts; wit waits on fear:

For there his smell with others being mingled,
The hot scent-snuffing hounds are driven to doubt,
Ceasing their clamour cry till they have singled
With much ado the cold fault cleanly out;
   Then do they spend their mouths: Echo replies,
   As if another chase were in the skies.

By this, poor Wat, far off upon a hill,
Stands on his hinder legs with listening ear,
To hearken if his foes pursue him still :
Anon their loud alarums he doth hear ;
  And now his grief may be compared well
  To one sore sick that hears the passing-bell.

Then shalt thou see the dew-bedabbled wretch
Turn, and return, indenting with the way ;
Each envious briar his weary legs doth scratch,
Each shadow makes him stop, each murmur stay :
  For misery is trodden on by many,
  And being low never reliev'd by any.

VI. THE SIMPLE LIFE

THOMAS CAMPION, Two Books of Airs, *c.* 1614 ; *page* 56 *in the Muses' Library Edition.*

Jack and Joan they think no ill,
But loving live, and merry still ;
Do on their week-days' work, and pray
Devoutly on the holy day :
Skip and trip it on the green,
And help to choose the Summer Queen ;
Lash out, at a country feast,
Their silver penny with the best.

Well can they judge of nappy ale,
And tell at large a winter tale ;
Climb up to the apple loft,
And turn the crabs till they be soft.
Tib is all the father's joy,
And little Tom the mother's boy.
All their pleasure is Content ;
And care, to pay their yearly rent.

Joan can call by name her cows,
And deck her window with green boughs ;

She can wreaths and tutties [1] make,
And trim with plums a bridal cake.
Jack knows what brings gain or loss;
And his long flail can stoutly toss:
Makes the hedge, which others break;
And ever thinks what he doth speak.

Now, you courtly dames and knights,
That study only strange delights;
Though you scorn the homespun gray,
And revel in your rich array:
Though your tongues dissemble deep,
And can your heads from danger keep;
Yet, for all your pomp and train,
Securer lives the silly swain.

VII. COURT LIFE AND COUNTRY LIFE

WILLIAM SHAKESPEARE. As You Like It. *c.* 1599; *Act III, Scene 2. At this period in his life Shakespeare seems not to have been on the side of the pastoralists. Touchstone and Jaques, who both emphatically prefer Court life, sneer at it; and later in the play, William, a very dull yokel, is introduced to show the contrast between the real yokel and the pretty shepherds and shepherdesses.*

CORIN, *the old shepherd, and* TOUCHSTONE, *the clown, come in together.*

CORIN. And how like you this shepherd's life, Master Touchstone?

TOUCHSTONE. Truly, shepherd, in respect of itself, it is a good life; but in respect that it is a shepherd's life, it is naught. In respect that it is solitary, I like it very well; but in respect that it is private, it is a very vile life. Now in respect it is in the fields, it pleaseth me well; but in respect that it is not in the Court, it is tedious. As it is a spare life, look you, it fits my humour well; but as there is no more plenty in it, it goes much against my stomach. Hast any philosophy in thee, shepherd?

[1] Posies.

COUNTRY LIFE

CORIN [*stolidly*]. No more but that I know the more one sickens the worse at ease he is; and that he that wants money, means and content is without three good friends; that the property of rain is to wet and fire to burn; that good pasture makes fat sheep, and that a great cause of the night is lack of the sun; that he that hath learned no wit by nature nor art may complain of good breeding or comes of a very dull kindred.

TOUCHSTONE [*ironically*]. Such a one is a natural philosopher. Wast ever in Court, shepherd?

CORIN. No, truly.

TOUCHSTONE. Then thou art damned.

CORIN. Nay, I hope——

TOUCHSTONE. Truly, thou art damned, like an ill-roasted egg all on one side.

CORIN. For not being at Court? Your reason.

TOUCHSTONE. Why, if thou never was at Court, thou never sawest good manners; if thou never sawest good manners, then thy manners must be wicked; and wickedness is sin, and sin is damnation. Thou art in a parlous state, shepherd.

CORIN. Not a wit, Touchstone; those that are good manners at the Court are as ridiculous in the country as the behaviour of the country is most mockable at the Court. You told me you salute not at the Court, but you kiss your hands: that courtesy would be uncleanly, if courtiers were shepherds.

TOUCHSTONE. Instance, briefly; come, instance.

CORIN. Why, we are still handling our ewes, and their fells, you know, are greasy.

TOUCHSTONE. Why, do not your courtier's hands sweat? and is not the grease of a mutton as wholesome as the sweat of a man? Shallow, shallow. A better instance, I say; come.

CORIN. Besides, our hands are hard.

TOUCHSTONE. Your lips will feel them the sooner. Shallow again. A more sounder instance, come.

CORIN. And they are often tarred over with the surgery

of our sheep; and would you have us kiss tar? The courtier's hands are perfumed with civet.

TOUCHSTONE. Most shallow man! thou worms' meat, in respect of a good piece of flesh indeed! Learn of the wise, and perpend: civet is of a baser birth than tar, the very uncleanly flux of a cat. Mend the instance, shepherd.

CORIN [*dimly realizing that* TOUCHSTONE *is mocking him*]. You have too courtly a wit for me, I'll rest.

TOUCHSTONE. Wilt thou rest damned? God help thee, shallow man! God make incision [1] in thee! thou art raw.

CORIN [*on his dignity*]. Sir, I am a true labourer: I earn that I eat, get that I wear, owe no man hate, envy no man's happiness, glad of other men's good, content with my harm, and the greatest of my pride is to see my ewes graze and my lambs suck.

VIII. ENGLISH INNS

FYNES MORYSON. An Itinerary, 1617; *Vol. IV, page 174 in the Maclehose edition.*

I have heard some Germans complain of the English inns by the highway, as well for dearness as for that they had only roasted meats; but these Germans landing at Gravesend, perhaps were injured by those knaves that flock thither only to deceive strangers, and use Englishmen no better, and after went from thence to London, and were there entertained by some ordinary hosts of strangers, returning home little acquainted with English customs. But if these strangers had known the English tongue, or had had an honest guide in their journeys, and had known to live at Rome after the Roman fashion, which they seldom do (using rather Dutch inns and companions), surely they should have found that the world affords not such inns as England hath, either for good and cheap entertainment after the guests' own pleasure, or for humble attendance on passengers, yea, even in very poor villages, where if Curculio of Plautus should see the thatched houses,

[1] I.e. to let blood.

he would fall into a fainting of his spirits, but if he should smell the variety of meats, his starveling look would be much cheered. For as soon as a passenger comes to an inn, the servants run to him, and one takes his horse and walks him till he be cold, then rubs him and gives him meat, yet I must say that they are not much to be trusted in this last point, without the eye of the master or his servant, to oversee them. Another servant gives the passenger his private chamber, and kindles his fire, the third pulls off his boots and makes them clean. Then the host or hostess visits him, and if he will eat with the host, or at a common table with others, his meal will cost him sixpence, or in some places but fourpence (yet this course is less honourable and not used by gentlemen): but if he will eat in his chamber, he commands what meat he will, according to his appetite, and as much as he thinks fit for him and his company, yea, the kitchen is open to him, to command the meat to be dressed as he best likes, and when he sits at table, the host or hostess will accompany him, or if they have many guests, will at least visit him, taking it for courtesy to be bid sit down. While he eats, if he have company especially, he shall be offered music, which he may freely take or refuse, and if he be solitary, the musicians will give him the good day with music in the morning. It is the custom, and no way disgraceful, to set up part of supper for his breakfast. In the evening, or in the morning after breakfast (for the common sort use not to dine, but ride from breakfast to supper time, yet coming early to the inn for better resting of their horses), he shall have a reckoning in writing, and if it seem unreasonable, the host will satisfy him, either for the due price, or by abating part, especially if the servant deceive him any way, which one of experience will soon find. Having formerly spoken of ordinary expenses by the highway, as well in the particular journal of the first part, as in a chapter of this part, purposely treating thereof, I will now only add, that a gentleman and his man shall spend as much as if he were accompanied with another gentleman and his man, and if gentlemen will in such sort join together to eat at one table, the expenses will be much diminished. Lastly, a man cannot more freely command at home in his own house than he may do in his inn, and at parting, if he give some few pence to the chamberlain and ostler, they wish him a happy journey.

England hath three public feasts of great expense and pompous solemnity, namely the Coronation of the Kings, the Feast of St. George, as well upon his day yearly, as at all times when any Knight of the Order is installed, and the third when Sergeants at the Law are called. The Lord Mayor of the City of London, upon the day when he is sworn and enters his office, keeps a solemn feast with public shows of great magnificence, besides that, he and the Sheriffs of the City daily keep well furnished tables to entertain any gentleman or stranger that will come to them, to the great honour of the City, in this particular passing all other cities of the world known to us.

For the point of drinking, the English at a feast will drink two or three healths in remembrance of special friends, or respected honourable persons, and in our time some gentlemen and commanders from the wars of Netherland brought in the custom of the Germans' large carousing, but this custom is in our time also in good measure left. Likewise in some private gentlemen's houses, and with some captains and soldiers, and with the vulgar sort of citizens and artisans, large and intemperate drinking is used; but in general the greater and better part of the English hold all excess blameworthy, and drunkenness a reproachful vice. Clowns and vulgar men only use large drinking of beer or ale, how much soever it is esteemed excellent drink even among strangers, but gentlemen carouse only in wine, with which many mix sugar, which I never observed in any other place or kingdom to be used for that purpose. And because the taste of the English is thus delighted with sweetness, the wines in taverns (for I speak not of merchants' or gentlemen's cellars) are commonly mixed at the filling thereof, to make them pleasant. And the same delight in sweetness hath made

COUNTRY LIFE 163

the use of corands [1] of Corinth so frequent in all places, and with all persons in England, as the very Greeks that sell them, wonder what we do with such great quantities thereof, and know not how we should spend them, except we use them for dyeing, or to feed hogs.

IX. COUNTRY RECREATIONS

GERVASE MARKHAM. Country Contentments, 1615.

There be many other particular recreations necessary for the knowledge and practice of our husbandman ; as first, shooting in the long-bow, which is both healthful for the body and necessary for the commonwealth ; the first extending the limbs and making them pliant, the other enabling strength fit to preserve and defend his country. And first, for shooting in the longbow, a man must observe these few rules ; first, that he have a good eye to behold and discern his mark, a knowing judgment to understand the distance of ground, to take the true advantage of a side wind and to know in what compass his arrow must fly, and a quick dexterity to give his shaft a strong, sharp and sudden loose. He must, in the action itself, stand fair, comely and upright with his body, his left foot a convenient stride before his right, both his hams stiff, his left arm holding his bow in the midst stretched straight out, and his right arm with his three first fingers and his thumb drawing the string to his right ear, the notch of his arrow resting between his forefinger and long finger of his right hand, and the steel of his arrow below the feathers upon the middle knuckle of his forefinger on his left hand, he shall draw his arrow up close unto the head and deliver it on the instant without hanging on the string. The best bow is either Spanish or English yew, and the worst, of witchen or elm. The best shaft is of birch, sugar-chest, or brazel ; and the best feathers grey or white.

The marks to shoot at three, butts, pricks, or rovers.

[1] Currants.

The butt is a level mark and therefore would have a strong arrow with a very broad feather. The prick is a mark of some compass, yet most certain in the distance, therefore would have nimble, strong arrows with a middle feather, all of one weight; and flying the rover is a mark uncertain, sometimes long, sometimes short, and therefore must have arrows lighter or heavier, according unto the distance of place.

If infirmity in the arm, or back, take from a man the use of the long-bow, he may then with a cross-bow made for gaffle [1] carried upon a string, and the nether end placed in a rest, with arrows made strong, heavy and suitable to the strength of the bow, shoot at all the former marks, and reap the same pleasure he formerly did with his long-bow.

There is another recreation, which however unlawful in the abuse thereof, yet exercised with moderation, is even of physicians themselves held exceeding wholesome, and hath been prescribed for a recreation to great persons, and that is bowling, in which a man shall find great art in choosing out his ground, and preventing the winding, hanging, and many turning advantages of the same, whether it be in open wide places, or in close alleys: and in this sport, the choosing of the bowl is the greatest cunning; your flat bowls being the best for close alleys, your round biased bowls for open grounds of advantage, and your round bowls like a ball, for green swards that are plain and level.

Not inferior to these sports, either for health or action, are the tennis or balloon. The first being a pastime in close or open courts, striking a little round ball to and fro, either with the palms of the hand, or with racket. The other a strong and moving sport, in the open field, with a great ball of a double leather filled with wind, and driven to and fro with the strength of a man's arm, armed in a bracer of wood; either of which actions must be learnt by the eye and practice, not by the ear or reading.

[1] Lever for bending the cross-bow.

X. THE PERFECT ANGLER

GERVASE MARKHAM. Country Contentments, 1615.

Now for the inward qualities of mind: albeit some writers reduce them to twelve heads, which indeed, whosoever enjoyeth cannot choose but be very complete in much perfection, yet I must draw them into many other branches. The first and most especial whereof is, that a skilful angler ought to be a general scholar, and seen in all the liberal sciences, as a grammarian, to know how either to write or discourse of his art in true and fitting terms, either without affectation or rudeness. He should have sweetness of speech, to persuade and entice others to delight in an exercise so much laudable. He should have strength of arguments, to defend and maintain his profession against envy or slander. He should have knowledge in the sun, moon and stars, that by their aspects he may guess the seasonableness or unseasonableness of the weather, the breeding of storms, and from what coasts the winds are ever delivered. He should be a good knower of countries, and well used to highways, that by taking the readiest paths to every lake, brook or river, his journeys may be more certain and less wearisome. He should have knowledge in proportions of all sorts, whether circular, square or diametrical, that when he shall be questioned of his diurnal progresses, he may give a geographical description of the angles and channels of rivers, how they fall from their heads, and what compasses they fetch in their several windings. He must also have the perfect art of numbering, that in the sounding of lakes and rivers, he may know how many foot or inches each severally containeth; and by adding, subtracting, or multiplying the same, he may yield the reason of every river's swift or slow current. He should not be unskilful in music, that whensoever either melancholy, heaviness of his thoughts, or the perturbations of his own fancies stirreth up sadness in him, he may remove the same with some godly hymn or anthem, of which David gives him ample examples.

He must be of a well settled and constant belief, to enjoy the benefit of his expectation ; for then to despair, it were better never to be put in practice : and he must ever think where the waters are pleasant, and anything likely, that there the Creator of all good things hath stored up much of plenty ; and though your satisfaction be not as ready as your wishes, yet you must hope still, that with perseverance, you shall reap the fullness of your harvest with contentment. Then he must be full of love, both to his pleasure and to his neighbour. To his pleasure, which otherwise will be irksome and tedious, and to his neighbour, that he neither give offence in any particular, nor be guilty of any general destruction. Then he must be exceeding patient, and neither vex nor excruciate himself with losses or mischances, as in losing the prey when it is almost in the hand, or by breaking his tools by ignorance or negligence, but with pleased sufferance amend errors, and think mischances instructions to better carefulness.

He must then be full of humble thoughts, not disdaining when occasion commands to kneel, lie down, or wet his feet or fingers as oft as there is any advantage given thereby, unto the gaining the end of his labour. Then must he be strong and valiant, neither to be amazed with storms, nor affrighted with thunder, but hold them according to their natural causes, and the pleasure of the Highest. Neither must he, like the fox which preyeth upon lambs, employ all his labour against the smaller fry ; but like the lion that seizeth elephants, think the greatest fish which swimmeth a reward little enough for the pains which he endureth. Then must he be liberal, and not working only for his own belly, as if it could never be satisfied, but he must with much cheerfulness bestow the fruits of his skill amongst his honest neighbours, who, being partners of his gain, will doubly renown his triumph ; and that is ever a pleasing reward to virtue.

Then must he be prudent, that apprehending the reasons why the fish will not bite, and all other casual impediments which hinder his sport, and knowing the remedies for the

COUNTRY LIFE

same, he may direct his labours to be without troublesomeness.

Then he must have a moderate contention of the mind to be satisfied with indifferent things, and not out of any avaricious greediness, think everything too little, be it never so abundant.

Then must he be of a thankful nature, praising the Author of all goodness and showing a large gratefulness for the least satisfaction.

Then must he be of a perfect memory, quick and prompt to call into his mind all the needful things which are any way in this exercise to be employed, lest by omission or by forgetfulness of any, he frustrate his hopes, and make his labours effectless. Lastly, he must be of a strong constitution of body, able to endure much fasting, and not of a gnawing stomach, observing hours in which, if it be unsatisfied, it troubleth both the mind and body and loseth that delight which maketh the pastime only pleasing.

Thus having showed the inward virtues and qualities which should always accompany a perfect angler, it is very meet now to give unto you certain cautions, which being carefully observed, you shall with more ease obtain the fullness of your desires. First, therefore, when you go to angle, you shall observe that all your tools, lines, or implements, be (as the seaman saith) yare, fit and ready ; for to have them ravelled, ill made or in unreadiness, they are great hindrances unto your pleasure. Then look that your baits be good, sweet, fine and agreeing with the season ; for if they be otherwise unproper in any of their natures, they are useless and you had better have been at home than by the river. Then you must not angle in unseasonable times, for the fish being not inclined to bite, it is a strange enticement that can compel them. Then you must be careful neither by your apparel, motions, or too open standing, to give affright to the fish ; for when they are scared, they fly from you, and seek society in an empty house. Then must you labour in clear and untroubled waters, for when the brooks are anything white, muddy and thick, either through inundations or other trouble, it is impossible to get anything with the angle. Then, to respect the temper of the weather; for extreme wind or extreme cold taketh away all manner of appetite from fish; so doth likewise too violent heat, or rain that is great, heavy and beating, or any storms, snows, hail, or blusterings, especially that which cometh from the east, which of all is the worst. Those which blow from the south are bad; and those which come from the north or west are indifferent. Many other observations there are, but they shall follow in their due places.

XI. EATING AND DRINKING

WILLIAM HARRISON. A Description of England, 1577.

In number of dishes and change of meat the nobility of England (whose cooks are for the most part musical-headed Frenchmen and strangers) do most exceed, sith there is no day in manner that passeth over their heads, wherein they have not only beef, mutton, veal, lamb, kid, pork, coney,[1] capon, pig, or so many of these as the season yieldeth, but also some portion of the red or fallow deer, beside great variety of fish and wild fowl, and thereto sundry other delicates wherein the sweet hand of the seafaring Portugal is not wanting: so that for a man to dine with one of them, and to taste of every dish that standeth before him (which few use to do, but each one feedeth upon that meat him best liketh for the time, the beginning of every dish notwithstanding being reserved unto the greatest personage that sitteth at the table, to whom it is drawn up still by the waiters as order requireth, and from whom it descendeth again even to the lower end, whereby each one may taste thereof), is rather to yield unto a conspiracy with a great deal of meat for the speedy suppression of natural health than the use of a necessary mean to satisfy himself with a competent repast to sustain his body withal. But, as this large feeding is not seen in their guests, no more is it in their

[1] Rabbit.

COUNTRY LIFE 169

own persons ; for, sith they have daily much resort unto their tables (and many times unlooked for), and thereto retain great numbers of servants, it is very requisite and expedient for them to be somewhat plentiful in this behalf. . . .

The gentlemen and merchants keep much about one rate and each of them contenteth himself with four, five, or six dishes, when they have but small resort, or peradventure with one or two, or three at the most, when they have no strangers to accompany them at their tables. And yet their servants have their ordinary diet assigned, besides such as is left at their master's boards, and not appointed to be brought thither the second time, which nevertheless is often seen, generally in venison, lamb, or some especial dish, whereon the merchantman himself liketh to feed when it is cold, or peradventure for sundry causes incident to the feeder is better so than if it were warm or hot. To be short, at such times as the merchants do make their ordinary or voluntary feasts, it is a world to see what great provision is made of all manner of delicate meats, from every quarter of the country, wherein, besides that they are often comparable herein to the nobility of the land, they will seldom regard anything that the butcher usually killeth, but reject the same as not worthy to come in place. In such cases also jellies of all colours, mixed with a variety of the representation of sundry flowers, herbs, trees, forms of beasts, fish, fowls and fruits, and thereunto marchpane [1] wrought with no small curiosity, tarts of divers hues, and sundry denominations, conserves of old fruits, foreign and homebred, suckets,[2] codinacs,[3] marmalades, marchpane, sugar-bread,[4] gingerbread, florentines,[5] wild fowls, venison of all sorts, and sundry outlandish confections, altogether seasoned with sugar (which Pliny calleth *mel ex arundinibus*, a device not common nor greatly used in old time at the table, but only in medicine, although it grew in Arabia, India and Sicilia), do generally bear the sway, besides

[1] Marzipan.   [2] Crystallized plums.   [3] Quince marmalade.
[4] Confectionery.   [5] A kind of game pie.

infinite devices of our own not possible for me to remember. Of the potato, and such venerous roots as are brought out of Spain, Portugal and the Indies to furnish up our banquets, I speak not, wherein our mures [1] of no less force, and to be had about Crosby-Ravenswath, do now begin to have place.

But among all these, the kind of meat which is obtained with most difficulty and cost, is commonly taken for the most delicate, and thereupon each guest will soonest desire to feed. And as all estates do exceed herein, I mean for strangeness and number of costly dishes, so these forget not to use the like excess in wine, insomuch as there is no kind to be had, neither anywhere more store of all sorts than in England, although we have none growing with us but yearly to the proportion of 20,000 or 30,000 ton and upwards, notwithstanding the daily restraints of the same brought over unto us, whereof at great meetings there is not some store to be had. Neither do I mean this of small wines only, as claret, white, red, French, etc., which amount to about fifty-six sorts, according to the number of regions from whence they came, but also of the thirty kinds of Italian, Grecian, Spanish, Canarian, etc., whereof *vernage*, catepument, raspis, muscadell, romnie, bastard lire, osy caprie, clary and malmesey, are not least of all accompted of, because of their strength and valour. For, as I have said in meat, so the stronger the wine is, the more it is desired, by means whereof, in old time, the best was called *theologicum*, because it was had from the clergy and religious men, unto whose houses many of the laity would often send for bottles filled with the same, being sure they would neither drink nor be served of the worst, or such as was any ways mingled or brewed by the vinterer ; nay, the merchant would have thought that his soul should have gone straightway to the Devil if he should have served them with other than the best. Furthermore, when these have had their course which nature yieldeth, sundry sorts of artificial stuff as hippocras and wormwood wine must in like manner

[1] Myrrh.

succeed in their turns, beside stale ale and strong beer, which nevertheless bear the greatest brunt in drinking, and are of so many sorts and ages as it pleaseth the brewer to make them.

XII. ENCLOSURES FOR SHEEP FARMING

THOMAS BASTARD. *Chrestoleros*, 1598; *page* 49 *in Grosart's edition. The real troubles of the agriculturist are seldom mentioned by the better known poets; they were not interested in the economic problems of the country.*

>Sheep have eat up our meadows and our downs,
>Our corn, our wood, whole villages and towns.
>Yea, they have eat up many wealthy men,
>Besides widows and orphan child[e]ren:
>Besides our statutes and our iron laws
>Which they have swallowed down into their maws.
>   Till now I thought the proverb did but jest
>   Which said a black sheep was a biting beast.

SECTION SEVEN

MATTERS OF RELIGION

I. THE CHURCH OF ENGLAND

WILLIAM HARRISON. A Description of England, 1577; *page 77 in* Furnivall. *Harrison, who was inclined to Puritanism, is describing the practices in the Essex churches which he knew best. Elsewhere the more elaborate ceremonial still survived.*

As for our churches themselves, bells and times of morning and evening prayer remain as in times past, saving that all images, shrines, tabernacles, rood-lofts, and monuments of idolatry are removed, taken down, and defaced, only the stories in glass windows excepted, which, for want of sufficient store of new stuff, and by reason of extreme charge that should grow by the alteration of the same into white panes throughout the realm, are not altogether abolished in most places at once, but by little and little suffered to decay, that white glass may be provided and set up in their rooms. Finally, whereas there was wont to be a great partition between the choir and the body of the church, now it is either very small or none at all, and (to say the truth) altogether needless, sith the minister saith his service commonly in the body of the church, with his face toward the people, in a little tabernacle of wainscot provided for the purpose, by which means the ignorant do not only learn divers of the Psalms and usual prayers by heart, but also such as can read, do pray together with him, so that the whole congregation at one instant pour out their petitions unto the living God for the whole estate of His Church in most earnest and fervent manner. Our holy and festival days are very well reduced also unto a less number; for whereas (not long since) we had under the Pope four score and fifteen called festival, and thirty *profesti*, beside the Sundays, they are all brought unto seven and twenty, and, with them, the superfluous numbers of idle wakes, guilds, fraternities, church-ales,[1] help-ales and soul-ales, called also dirge-ales, with the heathenish rioting at bride-ales, are well diminished and laid aside. And no great matter were it if the feasts of all our apostles, evangelists and martyrs, with that of all saints, were brought to the holy days that follow upon Christmas, Easter, and Whitsuntide, and those of the Virgin Mary, with the rest, utterly removed from the Calendars, as neither necessary nor commendable in a reformed church.

II. SIMONY

JOHN WEEVER. Epigrams in the Oldest Cut and Newest Fashion, 1599; *page* 70 *in McKerrow's edition.*

AD MATHONEM

Matho, I'm told that many do think much,
Because I call you Pillar of the Church:
Matho, you bought a Deanery at best rate,
And two Church-livings now impropriate,
And sold to Guidus a rich Parsonage;
(For divers causes) gave a Vicarage:
And now hath got three livings at one lurch ₁
Art thou not then a pillar [2] of the Church?

III. THE CHARACTER OF A CHURCH PAPIST

JOHN EARLE. Microsmography, 1628; No. 10 *in Irwin's edition.*

A Church Papist is one that parts his religion betwixt his conscience and his purse, and comes to church not to serve

[1] Different kinds of occasion for merrymaking. The church ale was the equivalent of the modern bazaar or "sale of work", only ale was the commodity sold for the benefit of church expenses.
[2] With a pun on pill = rob.

God, but the King. The face of the law makes him wear the mask of the Gospel, which he uses not as a means to save his soul, but charges.[1] He loves Popery well, but is loth to lose by it ; and though he be somewhat scared with the bulls of Rome, yet they are far off, and he is struck with more terror at the apparitor.[2] Once a month he presents himself at the church, to keep off the churchwarden, and brings in his body to save his bail. He kneels with the congregation, but prays by himself, and asks God forgiveness for coming thither. If he be forced to stay out a sermon, he pulls his hat over his eyes, and frowns out the hour ; and when he comes home, thinks to make amends for this fault by abusing the preacher. His main policy is to shift off the communion, for which he is never unfurnished of a quarrel, and will be sure to be out of charity at Easter ; and indeed he lies not, for he has a quarrel to the sacrament. He would make a bad martyr and good traveller, for his conscience is so large he could never wander out of it ; and in Constantinople would be circumcised with a reservation. His wife is more zealous and therefore more costly, and he bates her in tires,[3] what she stands him in religion. But we leave him hatching plots against the State, and expecting Spinola.

IV. THE SPANISH INQUISITION

Strange and wonderful things happened to Richard Hasleton, born at Braintree in Essex, in his ten years' travels in many foreign countries, 1595 ; Vol. VIII, page 374 in Arber's English Garner.

Then were the Officers of the Inquisition sent for by the Captain, which came the second day after our coming there [*to Palma*], and at their coming, they offered me the *pax*, which I refused to touch. Whereupon they reviled me, and called me Lutheran, and taking me presently out of the galley, carried me on shore to Majorca, and finding the

---

[1] Expense—i.e. he comes to church to save the fine for absence.

[2] The officer responsible for bringing offenders before the Ecclesiastical Courts.

[3] Bates her in tires: cuts off her dress allowance.

MATTERS OF RELIGION

Inquisitor walking in the market-place they presented me to him, saying, "Here is the prisoner." He immediately commanded me to prison; whither they carried me, and put a pair of shackles on my heels; where I remained two days.

Then was I brought forth into a church, where the Inquisitor sat usually in judgment: who, being ready set, commanded me to kneel down and to do homage to certain images which were before me. I told him, I would not do that which I knew to be contrary to the commandments of Almighty God; neither had I been brought up in the Roman law, neither would I submit myself to it. He asked me why I would not. I answered, that whereas in England, where I was born and brought up, the Gospel was truly preached, and maintained by a most gracious Princess, therefore I would not now commit idolatry, which is utterly condemned by the Word of God. Then he charged me to utter the truth, otherwise I should abide the smart.

Then was a stool set, and he commanded me to sit down before him; and offered me the cross, bidding me reverently to lay my hand upon it, and urged me instantly to do it: which moved me so much, that I did spit in the Inquisitor's face.

So, for that time, we had no more reasoning. For the Inquisitor did ring a little bell to call the keeper, and he carried me to ward again.

And the third day, I was brought forth again to the place aforesaid. Then the Inquisitor asked me what I had seen in the churches of England. I answered that I had seen nothing in the Church of England but the Word of God truly preached. Then he demanded how I had received the Sacraments. I replied that I had received them according to the institution of Christ; that is, I received the bread in remembrance that Christ in the flesh died upon the cross for the redemption of man. "How," said he, "hast thou received the wine?" Whereto I replied and said, that I received the wine in remembrance that Christ shed His blood to wash away our sins. He said it was in their manner. I said, "No." Then he charged me to speak the truth, or I should die for it. I told him, "I did speak the truth; and would speak the truth; for," said I, "it is better for me to die guiltless than guilty." Then did he, with great vehemency, charge me again to speak the truth; and sware by the Catholic Church of Rome, that if I did not, I should die in fire. Then I said, "If I died in the faith which I had confessed, I should die guiltless"; and told him he had made a vain oath. And so I willed him to use no circumstance to dissuade me from the truth: "for you cannot prevail. Though I be now in your hands, where you have power over my body, yet have you no power over my soul." I told him he made a long matter far from the truth. For which, he said I should die. Then he bade me say what I could to save myself. Where I replied as followeth: Touching the manner of the receiving of Sacraments, where he said it was like to theirs; "you," said I, "when you receive the bread, say it is the very body of Christ, and likewise you affirm the wine to be His very Blood," which I denied; saying it was impossible for a mortal man to eat the material body of Christ, or to drink His Blood. Then he said I had blasphemed the Catholic Church. I answered that I had said nothing against the true Catholic Church; but altogether against the false Church. He asked how I could prove it; saying if I could not prove it, I should die a most cruel death.

Note, by the way, that when any man is in durance for religion he is called to answer before no open assembly, but only in the presence of the Inquisitor, the Secretary and the Solicitor, whom they term the Broker. The cause is, as I take it, because they doubt that very many of their own people would confess the Gospel, if they did but see and understand their absurd dealing.

Again to the matter. Because it was so secret, they urged me to speak the more. Then he inquired whether I had been confessed. I said, "Yes." He demanded, "To whom?" I said, "To God." He asked me if I had ever

MATTERS OF RELIGION

confessed to any friar. I said, "No, for I do utterly defy them. For how can he forgive me my sins, which is himself a sinner, as all other men are?" "Yes," said he, "he which confesseth himself to a friar, who is a Father, may have remission of his sins by his mediation." "Which," I said, "I would never believe." Wherefore seeing they could seduce me by no means, to yield to their abominable idolatry, the Secretary cried, "Away with him!" The Inquisitor and he frowned very angrily on me for the answers which I had given, and said they would make me tell another tale. So, at the ringing of a little bell, the keeper came and carried me to ward again. At my first examination, when the keeper should lead me away, the Inquisitor did bless me with the Cross, but never after.

Two days after, was I brought again, and set upon a stool before the Inquisitor. He bade me ask *misericordium*. I told him, "I would crave mercy of Jesus Christ who died for my sins. Other *misericordium* would I crave none!" Then he commanded me to kneel before the altar. I said, "I would, but not to pray to any image ; for your altar is adorned with many painted images which were fashioned by the hands of sinful men ; which have mouths, and speak not ; ears, and hear not ; noses, and smell not ; hands, and handle not ; feet have they, and walk not—which God doth not allow at His altar, for He hath utterly condemned them by His Word." Then he said, I had been wrongly taught. "For", said he, "whosoever shall see these figures in earth, may the better remember Him in heaven Whose likeness it doth represent, Who would be a Mediator to God for us." But I replied, that all images were an abomination to the Lord, for He hath condemned them in express words by His own mouth, saying, "Thou shalt not make thyself any graven image, &c." "Yes," said he, "but we have need of a Mediator to make intercession for us, for we are unworthy to pray to God ourselves, because we are vile sinners." I said, there was no Mediator but Jesus Christ. Where, after many absurd reasons and vain persuasions, he took a pause.

Then I asked him why he kept me so long in prison, which never committed offence to them, knowing very well that I had been captive in Algiers nearly five years space, saying, that when God, by His merciful providence had, through many great dangers, set me in a Christian country, and delivered me from the cruelty of the Turk, when I thought to find such favour as one Christian oweth to another, I found them now more cruel than the Turks, not knowing any cause why. "The cause", said he, "is because the King hath wars with the Queen of England." For at that instant, there was their army prepared ready to go to England. Whereupon they would divers times give me reproachful words, saying that I should hear shortly of their arrival in England, with innumerable vain brags, which I omit for brevity. Then did I demand, "If there were not peace between the King and the Queen's Majesty, whether they would keep me still?" "Yea," said he, "unless thou wilt submit thyself to the faith of the Romish Church." So he commanded me away. I asked wherefore he sent for me, and to send me away, not alleging any matter against me. He said I should have no other matter alleged but that which I had spoken with mine own mouth. Then I demanded why they would have the Romish Church to have the supremacy? Whereto he would make no answer. Then I asked if they took me to be a Christian? "Yes," said he, "in some respects; but you are out of the faith of the true Church." Then the keeper took me to prison again.

And after for the space of three weeks I was brought forth to answer three several times every week. At which times they did sometimes threaten me with death, somewhile with punishment; and many times they attempted to seduce me with fair words and promises of great preferment; but when they saw nothing would draw me from the truth, they called me "shameless Lutheran", saying many times, "See, he is of the very blood of Luther! He hath his very countenance!" with many other frivolous speeches.

After all this, he commanded to put me in the dungeon within the Castle, five fathoms under ground; giving me, once a day, a little bread and water. There remained I one whole year, lying on the bare ground, seeing neither sun nor moon; no, not hearing man, woman nor child speak, but only the keeper which brought my small victual.

V. THE ENGLISH COLLEGE AT ROME

ANTHONY MUNDAY. *The English Roman Life*, 1582; *Vol. XII, pages 29 and 37 in the Bodley Head Quartos. The English College at Rome, where Englishmen received a theological training, was the chief centre of the Catholic plots against the State. It was under the special patronage of the Pope, and thence many of the Jesuit missionaries set out. Munday's connection with the College was thoroughly discreditable. He went to Rome to serve his own ends; on his return to England he became a Government spy and helped to identify and arrest the Jesuits as they came over.*

The English College is a house both large and fair, standing in the way to the Pope's Palace, not far from the Castle Sante Angello. In the College the scholars are divided by certain number into every chamber, as in some four, in some six, or so many as the Rector thinketh convenient, as well for the health of the scholars, as the troubling not much room. Every man hath his bed proper to himself, which is two little trestles, with four or five boards laid along over them, and thereon a quilted mattress, as we call it in England, which every morning after they are risen, they fold up their sheets handsomely, laying them in the midst of the bed, and so roll it up to one end, covering it with the quilt, that is their coverlet all the night time.

First in the morning, he that is the porter of the College ringeth a bell; at the sound whereof every student ariseth and turneth up his bed as I have said before. Not long after, the bell ringeth again, when as every one presently kneeling on his knees, prayeth for the space of half an hour; at which time, the bell being tolled again, they arise and bestow a certain time in study, every one having his desk, table and chair to himself very orderly, and all the time of study, silence is used of every one in the chamber, not one offering molestation in speech to another. The time of study expired, the bell calleth them from their chambers down into the *Refectorium*, where every one taketh a glass of wine and a quarter of a manchet,[1] and so he maketh his *collatione*. Soon after, the bell is knolled again, when as the students, two and two together, walk to the Roman College, which is the place of school or instruction, where every one goeth to his ordinary lecture, some to Divinity, some to Physic, some to Logic, and some to Rhetoric. There they remain the lecture time, which being done, they return home to the College again, where they spend the time till dinner, in walking and talking up and down the gardens.

And an order there is appointed by the Rector and the Jesuits, and obeyed by all the students, that whosoever doth not in the morning turn up his bed handsomely, or is not on his knees at prayer time, or heareth not Mass before he go to school, or after he comes home, but forgetteth it, or else if he go forth and put not the peg at his name in the table;[2] for there is a table hangeth by the door, which hath a long box adjoining to it, wherein lieth a great company of wooden pegs, and against the name of every scholar written in the table (which is observed by order of the alphabet) there is a hole made, wherein, such as have occasion to go abroad, must duly put a peg, to give knowledge who is abroad and who remaineth within, beside divers other orders they have for slight matters, the neglecting thereof is public penance at dinner time, when as all the students are placed at the tables, such as have so transgressed goeth up into the pulpit (which standeth there because one readeth all the dinner time) and there he sayeth: "Because I have not fulfilled this or that (whatsoever order it be that he hath broken), I am adjured such a penance"; either to kneel in the midst

[1] Biscuit.   [2] Notice board.

MATTERS OF RELIGION

of the hall on his bare knees, and there to say his beads over, or to say certain *Pater nosters* and *Ave Marias*, or to stand upright and have a dish of pottage before him on the ground and so to bring up every spoonful to his mouth; or to lose either one or two or three of his dishes appointed for his dinner; or to stand there all the dinner time and eat no meat; and divers other, which according as it is, either afterward he hath his dinner or supper, or else goes without it. And all these penances I have been forced to do, for that I was always apt to break one order or other. . . .

As for their fare, trust me it is very fine and delicate, for every man hath his own trencher, his manchet, knife, spoon and fork laid by it, and then a fair white napkin covering it, with his glass and pot of wine set by him. And the first mess, or "antepast" (as they call it) that is brought to the table, is some fine meat to urge them to have an appetite, as sometime the Spanish anchovies, and sometime stewed prunes and raisins of the sun together, having such fine tart syrup made to them, as I promise you a weak stomach would very well digest them. The second is a certain mess of pottage of that country manner, no meat sod in them, but are made of divers things, whose proper names I do not remember, but me thought they were both good and wholesome. The third is boiled meat, as kid, mutton, chicken and such-like; every man a pretty modicum of each thing. The fourth is roasted meat of the daintiest provision that they can get, and sometimes stewed and baked meat, according as pleaseth master cook to order it. The first and last is sometime cheese, sometime preserved conceits, sometime figs, almonds and raisins, a lemon and sugar, a pomegranate, or some such sweet gear; for they know that Englishmen loveth sweet meats.

And all the dinner while, one of the scholars, according as they take it by weekly turn, readeth; first a chapter of their Bible and then in their *Martirologium*, he readeth the martyrdom of some of the Saints, as Saint Francis, Saint

Martin, Saint Longinus, that thrust the spear into Christ's side, Saint Agatha, Saint Barbara, Saint Cecilia, and divers others; among whom they have imprinted the martyrdom of Doctor Story, the two Nortons, John Felton and others calling them by the name of Saints, who were here executed at Tyburn for high treason.

The dinner done, they recreate themselves for the space of an hour, and then the bell calleth them to their chambers, where they stay a while, studying on their lectures given them in the forenoon; anon the bell summoneth them to school again, where they stay not past an hour, but they return home again and so soon as they be come in they go into the *Refectorium*, and there every one hath his glass of wine and a quarter of a manchet again, according as they had in the morning.

Then they depart to their chambers, from whence at convenient time they are called to exercise of disputation: the divines to a Jesuit appointed for them, and every study to a several Jesuit, where they continue the space of an hour, and afterward till supper time they are at their recreation.

After supper, if it be in winter time, they go with the Jesuits, and sit about a great fire, talking, and in all their talk they strive who shall speak worst of her Majesty, of some of her Council, of some Bishop here, or such-like; so that the Jesuits themselves will often take up their hands and bless themselves, to hear what abominable tales they will tell them. After they have talked a good while, the bell calleth them to their chambers, the porter going from chamber to chamber and lighteth a lamp in every one, so when the scholars come, they alight their lamps, lay down their beds, and go sit at their desks and study a little, till the bell rings, when every one falls on his knees to prayers. Then one of the priests in the chamber, as in every chamber there is some, beginneth the Latin Litany, all the scholars in the chamber answering him, and so they spend the time till the bell rings again, which is for every one to go to bed.

VI. A SEMINARY PRIEST

THOMAS DEKKER. The Double PP., 1606; *Vol. II, page* 175 *in Grosart's edition. This is the popular view of the Jesuits; written shortly after the Gunpowder Plot.*

A PRIEST SEMINANT, OR THE POPE'S HUSBANDMAN

A papist seminant [1] springs from the brood
Of th' arrogant Jesuit, and sows
Sedition in men's hearts, drains from their blood
All pure allegiance, and where gentry grows
Most pliant to be wrought, his charms he throws.
He deals with willows rather than with oaks,
Bending with words the subject, not with strokes.
A fencer, yet a coward; for he teaches
Others to kill their sovereigns, yet he dares not
Venture upon a king himself; he preaches
Close in your ear; to cleave a state, he cares not
To make his head the wedge; and therefore spares not
His own blood more to shed; proud of this doom,
A Tyburn traitor is a saint in Rome.

VII. THE DANGERS OF THE PURITAN MOVEMENT

RICHARD HOOKER, Of the Laws of Ecclesiastical Polity, 1594; *vol. i, page* 140 *in the Everyman edition. At this time the Puritans were regarded with great suspicion because of the extravagant claims made by the more violent zealots. They wished to reorganize society in a new " discipline " formed according to the Mosaic Law, to which they would have compelled Queen and nobility to become subject. Twenty years later (see page* 185), *the Puritan was believed to be a hypocrite but not much worse. Hooker wrote to convince the Puritans that the State Polity of the Church of England was in accordance with the Scriptures.*

[Having narrated some of the excesses committed by the Puritans with the authority of Scripture, Hooker continues:]

Therefore sith the world hath had in these men so fresh experience, how dangerous such active errors are, it must

[1] From a seminary college.

not offend you though touching the sequel of your present mispersuasions much more be doubted, than your own intent and purposes do haply aim at. And yet your words are already somewhat, when ye affirm that your Pastors, Doctors, Elders, and Deacons ought to be in this Church of England, " whether her Majesty and our state will or no " ; when for the animating of your confederates ye publish the musters which ye have made of your own bands, and proclaim them to amount I know to how many thousands ; when ye threaten, that sith neither your suits to the parliament, nor supplications to our convocation-house, neither your defences by writing nor challenges of disputation in behalf of that cause are able to prevail, we must blame ourselves, if to bring in discipline some such means hereafter be used as shall cause all our hearts to ache. " That things doubtful are to be construed in the better part," is a principle not safe to be followed in matters concerning the public state of a commonweal. But howsoever these, and the like speeches, be accounted as arrows idly shot at random, without either eye had to any mark, or regard to their lighting-place ; hath your longing desire for the practice of your discipline brought the matter already unto this demurrer against you, whether the people and their godly pastors that way affected ought not to make separation from the rest, and to begin the exercise of discipline without the license of civil powers, which license they have sought for, and are not heard ? Upon which question as ye have now divided yourselves, the warier sort of you taking the one part, and the forwarder in zeal the other ; so in case these earnest ones should prevail, what other sequel can any wise men imagine but this, that having first resolved that attempts for discipline without superiors are lawful, it will follow in the next place to be disputed what may be attempted against superiors which will not have the sceptre of that discipline to rule over them ? Yea, even by you which have stayed yourselves from running headlong with the other sort, somewhat notwithstanding there hath been done without the leave or liking of your lawful superiors,

MATTERS OF RELIGION 185

for the exercise of a part of your discipline amongst the clergy thereto addicted. And lest examination of the principal parties therein should bring those things to light, which might hinder and let your proceedings; behold, for a bar against that impediment, one opinion ye have newly added unto the rest even upon this occasion, an opinion to exempt you from taking oaths which may turn to the molestation of your brethren in that cause. The next neighbour opinion whereunto when occasion requireth may follow, for dispensation with oaths already taken, if they afterwards be found to import a necessity of detecting aught which may bring such good men into trouble or damage whatsoever the case may be. O merciful God, what man's wit is there able to sound the depth of those dangerous evils, whereinto our weak and impotent nature is inclinable to sink itself, rather than to show an acknowledgement of error in that which once we have unadvisedly taken upon us to defend, against the stream as it were of a contrary public resolution!

VIII. THE PURITAN AT BARTHOLOMEW FAIR

BEN JONSON. Bartholomew Fair, 1614; *Act III, Scene* 1. *The Puritans were charged chiefly with hypocrisy and gluttony by their enemies. This play was written twenty years after the preceding extract.*

At Bartholomew Fair, Smithfield. LEATHERHEAD *and* TRASH *stand behind their stalls;* KNOCKEM *and* BUSY, *two Puritans, enter.*

KNOCKEM. Sir, I will take your counsel, and cut my hair, and leave vapours; I see that tobacco, and bottle-ale, and pig, and wit, and very Ursla herself, is all vanity.

BUSY. Only pig was not comprehended in my admonition, the rest were; for long hair, it is an ensign of pride, a banner; and the world is full of those banners, very full of banners. And bottle-ale is a drink of Satan's, a diet-drink of Satan's, devised to puff us up, and make us swell in this latter age of vanity; as the smoke of tobacco, to keep us in mist and error; but the fleshly woman, which you call Ursla, is above all to be avoided, having the marks upon her of the three enemies of man : the world, as being in the fair; the devil, as being in the fire; and the flesh, as being yourself.

[MRS. PURECRAFT *joins them.*]

PURECRAFT. Brother Zeal-of-the-land, what shall we do? my daughter Win-the-fight is fallen into her fit of longing again.

BUSY. For more pig! there is no more, is there?

PURECRAFT. To see some sights in the Fair.

BUSY. Sister, let her fly the impurity of the place swiftly, lest she partake of the pitch thereof. Thou art the seat of the beast, O Smithfield, and I will leave thee! Idolatry peepeth out on every side of thee. [*He goes forward.*]

KNOCKEM. An excellent right hypocrite! Now his belly is full, he falls a-railing and kicking, the jade. A very good vapour! I'll in and joy Ursla with telling how her pig works; two and a half he eat to his share; and he has drunk a pailful. He eats with his eyes, as well as his teeth. [*He goes out.*]

LEATHERHEAD. What do you lack, gentlemen? what is't you buy? rattles, drums, babies [1]——

BUSY. Peace, with thy apocryphal wares, thou profane publican; thy bells, thy dragons, and thy Toby's dogs. Thy hobby-horse is an idol, a very idol, a fierce and rank idol; and thou the Nebuchadnezzar, the proud Nebuchadnezzar of the Fair, that settest it up, for children to fall down to and worship.

LEATHERHEAD. Cry you mercy, sir; will you buy a fiddle to fill up your noise?

[LITTLEWIT *and his wife enter.*]

LITTLEWIT. Look, Win, do, look a' God's name, and save your longing. Here be fine sights.

[1] Dolls.

MATTERS OF RELIGION

PURECRAFT. Ay, child, so you hate them, as our brother Zeal does, you may look on them.

LEATHERHEAD. Or what do you say to a drum, sir?

BUSY. It is the broken belly of the beast, and thy bellows there are his lungs, and these pipes are his throat, those feathers are of his tail, and thy rattles the gnashing of his teeth.

TRASH. And what's my gingerbread, I pray you?

BUSY. The provender that pricks him up. Hence with thy basket of popery, thy nest of images, and whole legend of gingerwork.

LEATHERHEAD. Sir, if you be not quiet the quicklier, I'll have you clapped fairly by the heels for disturbing the Fair.

BUSY. The sin of the Fair provokes me, I cannot be silent.

PURECRAFT. Good brother Zeal!

LEATHERHEAD. Sir, I'll make you silent, believe it.

LITTLEWIT [to LEATHERHEAD]. I'd give a shilling you could i' faith, friend.

LEATHERHEAD. Sir, give me your shilling, I'll give you my shop, if I do not; and I'll leave it in pawn with you in the meantime.

LITTLEWIT. A match, i' faith; but do it quickly, then.

[LEATHERHEAD *goes out.*]

BUSY [to MRS. PURECRAFT]. Hinder me not, woman. I was moved in spirit, to be here this day, in this Fair, this wicked and foul Fair; and fitter may it be called a Foul than a Fair; to protest against the abuses of it, the foul abuses of it, in regard of the afflicted saints, that are troubled, very much troubled, exceedingly troubled with the opening of the merchandise of Babylon again, and the peeping of popery upon the stalls here, here, in the high places. See you now Goldylocks, the purple strumpet there, in her yellow gown and green sleeves? the profane pipes, the tinkling timbrels, a shop of relics!

LITTLEWIT [*as* BUSY *tries to seize the wares*]. Pray you, forbear; I am put in trust with them.

BUSY. And this idolatrous grove of images, this flasket of idols, which I will pull down—— [*He overthrows the gingerbread basket.*]
TRASH. O my ware, my ware! God bless it!
BUSY. In my zeal, and glory to be thus exercised.

[LEATHERHEAD *returns with* BRISTLE, HAGGISE, *and other Officers.*]

LEATHERHEAD. Here he is, pray you hold on his zeal; we cannot sell a whistle for him in tune. Stop his noise first.
BUSY. Thou canst not; 'tis a sanctified noise. I will make a loud and most strong noise, till I have daunted the profane enemy. And for this cause——
LEATHERHEAD. Sir, here's no man afraid of you, or your cause. You shall swear it in the stocks, sir.
BUSY. I will thrust myself into the stocks, upon the pikes of the land.

[*They seize him.*]

LEATHERHEAD. Carry him away.
PURECRAFT. What do you mean, wicked men?
BUSY. Let them alone, I fear them not.

[*Officers carry* BUSY *away.*]

IX. HORROR OF HELL FIRE

The Repentance of Robert Greene, 1592; *Vol. VI, page 10 in the Bodley Head Quartos. Greene wrote his* Repentance *as he was dying in the late summer of* 1592. *Apart from the repetition of orthodox and pious sentiments, a genuine horror of hell fire is the most noticeable religious emotion in Elizabethan literature.*

Living thus a long time, God (who suffereth sinners to heap coals of fire upon their own heads, and to be fed fat with sin against the day of vengeance) suffered me to go forward in my loose life. Many warnings I had to draw me from my detestable kind of life, and divers crosses to contrary my actions, but all in vain; for though I were sundry times afflicted with many foul and grievous dis-

MATTERS OF RELIGION

eases, and thereby scourged with the rod of God's wrath, yet when by the great labour and friendship of sundry honest persons they had (though to their great charges) sought and procured my recovery, I did with the dog *Redire in vomitum*, I went with the sow again to wallow in the mire, and fell to my former follies as frankly as if I had not tasted any iota of want, or never been scourged for them. *Consuetudo peccandi tollit sensum peccati*; my daily custom in sin had clean taken away the feeling of my sin; for I was so given to these vices aforesaid, that I counted them rather venial escapes and faults of nature than any great and grievous offences; neither did I care for death, but held it only as the end of life. For coming one day into Aldersgate Street to a wellwiller's house of mine, he, with other of his friends, persuaded me to leave my bad course of life, which at length would bring me to utter destruction, whereupon I scoffingly made them this answer: "Tush, what better is he that dies in his bed than he that ends his life at Tyburn: all owe God a death: if I may have my desire while I live, I am satisfied; let me shift after death as I may." My friends hearing these words, greatly grieved at my graceless resolution, made this reply: "If you fear not death in this world, nor the pains of the body in this life, yet doubt the second death and the loss of your soul, which, without hearty repentance, must rest in hell fire for ever and ever."

"Hell," quoth I, "what talk you of hell to me? I know if I once come there I shall have the company of better men than myself; I shall also meet with some mad knaves in that place and so long as I shall not sit there alone, my care is the less. But you are mad folks," quoth I, "for if I feared the Judges of the Bench no more than I dread the Judgments of God, I would, before I slept, dive into one churl's bag or other and make merry with the shells I found in them so long as they would last." And though some in this company were friars of mine own fraternity to whom I spake the words, yet they were so amazed at my profane speeches that they wished themselves forth of my company. Whereby appeareth that my continual delight was in sin, and that I made myself drunk with the dregs of mischief. But being departed thence unto my lodging, and now grown to the full, I was checked by the mighty hand of God : for sickness (the messenger of death) attacked me, and told me my time was but short, and that I had not long to live : whereupon I was vexed in mind and grew very heavy. As thus I sat solemnly thinking of my end, and feeling myself was sicker and sicker, I fell into a great passion, and was wonderfully perplexed, yet no way discovered my agony, but sat still calling to mind the lewdness of my former life : at what time, suddenly taking *The Book of Resolution* in my hand, I light upon a chapter therein, which discovered unto me the miserable state of the reprobate, what Hell was, what the worm of Conscience was, what torments there was appointed for the damned souls, what unspeakable miseries, what unquenchable flames, what intolerable agonies, what incomprehensible griefs : that there was nothing but fear, horror, vexation of mind, deprivation from the sight and favour of God, weeping and gnashing of teeth, and that all those tortures were not termined or dated within any compass of years, but everlasting, world without end ; concluding all in this of the Psalms : *Ab inferis nulla est redemptio.*[1]

X. HORROR OF HELL FIRE

THOMAS DEKKER. Dekker His Dream, 1620 ; *Vol. III, page* 41 *in Grosart's edition.*

How then, it may be asked, did my weak sight
Pierce these thick walls of horror, where no light
Ever shed beam ? why on that sorcerous coast
Where hags and witches dwell was not I lost ?
My spirit had balls of wild fire in his head
For eyes, methought, and I by them was led:
For all these coalpits, faddomed deep as hell,
Still burn, yet are the flames invisible.

[1] "There is no release from hell."

MATTERS OF RELIGION

This fire is none of that which God lent man,
When driven by sin out, he from Paradise ran,
Bitten with cold, beaten with frosts and snow,
And in mere pity did that warmth bestow,
Teaching him how to kindle it at first,
And then with food combustible have it nursed:
No, this red gloomy furnace is a firing,
Devouring, yet not wasting, nor self tiring.
   Arithmetic cannot in figures set
An age of numbered years to swell so great
As to fill up that time when these shall die,
Being NEVER, for it burns eternally,
From the world's first foundation, to th' confounding:
Were deluges on deluges abounding,
Not all that rain, able to drown the world,
Reach'd it to heaven, nor thousand oceans hurled
On top of all those waters, can ever slake
Or quench the least drop of this brimstone lake.
For, which most dreadful is, the flames cease never
To torture souls, and yet no light seen ever.
It is a burning which doth brightness lack,
The coals being infinite hot, and infinite black.
Yet through my horse of Hell galloped amain,
Now plunged in boiling lakes, then up again,
Leaping into vast caves, where heat never comes;
For sharper cold than winter's breath benumbs
The air so stiff it freezeth all to ice
And clouds of snow, whose flakes are harder thrice
Than those quadrangled hailstones, which in thunder
Kill teams and ploughmen, and rive oaks in sunder.

XI. "THE SPIRITS CALLED THE FAIRY"

KING JAMES I. Dæmonology, 1597; *Vol. IX, page 73 in the Bodley Head Quartos. King James' Dæmonology was based partly on his wide reading in books on spiritualism, partly on his own experiences in the Scottish witch trials of 1591–2. The book is written in the form of a dialogue wherein Epistemon the understanding scholar*

(= *James*) *expounds the various devices of the Devil to Philomathes the eager pupil. A more pleasing view of fairies can be found in* A Midsummer Night's Dream.

The description of the fourth kind of spirits called the Fairy: What is possible therein and what is but illusions. How far this dialogue entreats of all these things and to what end.

PHILOMATHES. Now I pray you come on to that fourth kind of spirits.

EPISTEMON. That fourth kind of spirits, which by the Gentiles was called Diana and her wandering court, and amongst us was called the Fairy, (as I told you) or our good neighbours, was one of the sorts of illusions that was rifest in the time of Papistry : for although it was holden odious to prophesy by the devil, yet whom these kind of spirits carried away and informed, they were thought to be sonsiest and of best life. To speak of the many vain trattles founded upon that illusion : how there was a King and Queen of Fairy, of such a jolly court and train as they had ; how they had a teynd and duty, as it were, of all goods ; how they naturally rode and went, ate and drank, and did all other actions like natural men and women : I think it liker Virgil's *Campi Elysii,* nor anything that ought to be believed by Christians, except in general, that as I spake sundry times before, the devil illuded the senses of sundry simple creatures in making them believe that they saw and heard such things as were nothing so indeed.

PHILOMATHES. But how can it be then that sundry witches have gone to death with that confession, that they have been transported with the fairy to such a hill, which opening they went in, and there saw a fair Queen, who being now lighter, gave them a stone that had sundry virtues, which at sundry times hath been produced in judgment ?

EPISTEMON. I say that, even as I said before of that imaginary ravishing of the spirit forth of the body. For may not the devil object to their phantasy, their senses being dulled and, as it were, asleep, such hills and houses

MATTERS OF RELIGION

within them, such glistering courts and trains, and whatsoever such-like wherewith he pleased to delude them, and in the meantime, their bodies being senseless, to convey in their hand any stone or such-like thing, which he makes them to imagine to have received in such a place?

XII. A WISE WOMAN

HENRY CHETTLE. Kind-Heart's Dream, 1592; *Vol. IV, page 62 in the Bodley Head Quartos.*

It happened within these few years about Hampshire, there wandered a walking Mort,[1] that went about the country selling of tape; she had a good voice, and would sing sometime to serve the turn; she would often be a leech, another time a fortune-teller. In this last occupation we will now take her, for therefore was she taken, having first overtaken an honest simple farmer and his wife in this manner. On a summer's evening, by the edge of the forest, she chanced to meet the forenamed farmer's wife, to whom, when she had offered some of her tape, she began quickly with her to fall in talk, and at the first, staring her in the face, assures her she shall have such fortune as never had any of her kin, and if her husband were no more unlucky than she, they should be possessed of so infinite a sum of hidden treasure as no man in England had ever seen the like. The plain woman, tickled with her soothing, entreated her to go home, which she at first making somewhat strange, was at last content. There had she such cheer as farmers' houses afford, who fare not with the meanest. Shortly the good man comes in, to whom his wife relates her rare fortune and what a wise woman she had met with. Though the man were very simple, yet made he some question what learning she had, and how she came by knowledge of such things.

"O sir," said she, "my father was the cunningest juggler in all the country, my mother a gipsy, and I have more cunning than any of them both."

[1] The cant phrase for a beggar-woman.

"Where lies the treasure thou talkest on?" said the farmer.

"Within this three miles," quoth she.

"I wonder thou thyself gettest it not," said the man, "but livest, as it seems, in so poor estate."

"My poverty", answered this cozener, "is my chiefest pride: for such as we cannot ourselves be rich, though we make others rich. Beside, hidden treasure is by spirits possessed and they keep it only for them to whom it is destined. And more," said she, "if I have a several room to myself, hanged round about with white linen, with other instruments, I will by morning tell ye whether it be destined to you."

The goodman and wife giving credit to her words, fetched forth their finest sheets and garnished a chamber as she appointed; seven candles she must have lighted, and an angel [1] she would have laid in every candlestick. Thus furnished, she locks herself into the room, and appoints them two only to watch, without making any of their servants privy. Where, using sundry mumbling fallacies, at last she called the man unto her, whom she saddled and bridled, and having seven times rid him about the room, caused him to arise and call his wife, for to her belonged the treasure. Both man and wife being come, in very sober manner she told them that they alone must attend in that place, whilst she forced the spirits to release the treasure and lay it in some convenient place for them to fetch, but in any wise they must not reveal about what she went, neither touch bread nor drink till her return. So, taking up the seven angels, away she went, laughing to herself how she had left them waiting.

All night sat the man and his wife attending her coming, but she was wise enough. Morning came, the servants mused what their master and dame meant, that were wont with the lark to be the earliest risers, yet sith they heard them talk, they attempted not to disturb them. Noon drawing on, the farmer feeling by the chimes in his

[1] Worth 10s.

belly 'twas time to dine, was by his wife counselled to stay till the wise woman's return; which he patiently intending, on a sudden the scent of the ploughswains' meat so pierced his senses, that had all India been the meed of his abstinence, eat he will, or die he must. His wife, more money wise, intended rather to starve than lose the treasure, till about evening one of their neighbours brought them news of a woman cozener that by a Justice was sent to Winchester for many lewd pranks. The man would needs see if it were the same, and coming thither, found it to be no other; where, thinking at least to have good words, she impudently derided him, especially before the Bench, who asked her what reason she had to bridle and saddle him. "Faith," said she, "only to see how like an ass he looked."

XIII. EVIL SPIRITS AVAUNT

EDMUND SPENSER, Epithalamium, 1595.

Let no lamenting cries, nor doleful tears,
Be heard all night within nor yet without:
Ne let false whispers, breeding hidden fears,
Break gentle sleep with misconceived doubt.
Let no deluding dreams, nor dreadful sights
Make sudden sad affrights;
Ne let house fires, nor lightning's helpless harms,
Ne let the Puck, nor other evil sprites,
Ne let mischievous witches with their charms,
Ne let hobgoblins, names whose sense we see not,
Fray us with things that be not.
Let not the screech owl nor the stork be heard:
Nor the night raven that still deadly yells,
Nor damned ghost call'd up with mighty spells
Nor grisly vultures make us once afeared:
Ne let th' unpleasant choir of frogs still croaking
Make us to wish their choking.
Let none of these their dreary accents sing;
Nor let the woods them answer, nor their echo ring.

SECTION EIGHT

MEN OF LETTERS

I. A DEFENCE OF THE ENGLISH TONGUE

RICHARD MULCASTER. Elementary, 1582; *page* 260 *in Campagnec's edition. At this date* (1582), *the learned were still prone to regard the English tongue, compared with the Latin, as little better than a convenient local dialect, incapable of producing a serious literature. Lyly's* Euphues (1579), *Sidney's* Arcadia (c. 1580) *in prose, Spenser's* Shepherd's Calendar (1579) *in verse, were deliberate attempts to show that English could be written in a high style.*

There be two special considerations which keep the Latin and other learned tongues, though chiefly the Latin, in great countenance among us ; the one thereof is the knowledge which is registered in them, the other is the conference which the learned of Europe do commonly use by them, both in speaking and writing. Which two considerations being fully answered, that we seek them from profit and keep them for that conference, whatsoever else may be done in our tongue, either to serve private uses, or the beautifying of our speech, I do not see, but it may well be admitted, even though in the end it displaced the Latin, as the Latin did others, and furnished itself by the Latin learning. For is it not indeed a marvellous bondage to become servants to one tongue for learning sake, the most of our time, with loss of most time, whereas we may have the very same treasure in our own tongue with the gain of most time ? Our own bearing the joyful title of our liberty and freedom, the Latin tongue remembering us of our thraldom and bondage ? I love Rome, but London better ;

I favour Italy, but England more; I honour the Latin, but I worship the English. I wish all were in ours, which they had from others, neither offer I them wrong which did the like to others, and by their own precedent do let us understand how boldly we may venture, notwithstanding the opinion of some such of our people, as desire rather to please themselves with a foreign tongue wherewith they are acquainted, than to profit their country in their natural language, where their acquaintance should be. It is no objection to say, will ye rob those tongues of their honour which have honoured you, or which if they had not been to make you learned, you had not been to strip them from learning. For I honour them still, and that so much as who so doth most, even in wishing mine own tongue partaker of their honour. For if I had them not in great admiration because I know their value, I would not think it to be any honour for my country tongue to resemble their grace. I confess their furniture, and wish it were in ours, which was taken from other to furnish out them. For the tongues which we study were not the first getters, though by learned travel they prove good keepers, and yet ready to return and discharge their trust when it shall be demanded, in such a sort as it was committed for term of years, and not for inheritance. And therefore no disgrace where they did receive with condition to deliver, if they do deliver when they are desired. But a dishonour to that tongue which hath a delivery both devised and tendered, and will not receive it. From which dishonour, I would England were free, and that learning received which is ready to be delivered. I confess their good fortune which had so great a forestart before other tongues, as they be most welcome wheresoever they set foot, and alway in wonder above any other for their rare worthiness, which have all men's opinions concerning other speeches in such a captivate prejudice of their own excellence as none is thought any, but when it is like to them, and yet the most like to be marvellously behind.

II. THE PATRON AND THE POET

The Return from Parnassus, Part I, 1600 ; *Act I, Scene* 1. *Literary men did not make much profit from their writings before the eighteenth century. At this time a professional writer sold his manuscript outright to a printer and tried to make up by dedicating his book to a wealthy patron who was expected to recompense his admirer in cash. Some ingenious writers had different names printed in different copies of their book and so collected from more than one patron.*

PATRON. How now, fellow ? Have you anything to say to me ?

INGENIOSO. Pardon, sir, the presumption of a poor scholar, whose humble devoted ears being familiar with the commendations that unpartial fame bestoweth upon your worship, reporting what a free-hearted Maecenas you are unto poor artists, that other favourers of learning in comparison of your worship are unworthy to untie your worship's pursestrings, that it hath been your ancient desire to get witty subjects for your liberality, that you could never endure the seven liberal sciences to carry their fardles on their backs like footmen, but have animated their poor dying pens, and put life to their decayed purses ; hereupon I, unfurnished of all things but learning, cast myself down at your worship's toes, resolving that liberality sojourneth here with you, or else it hath left our untoward country. Take in good part, I beseech you, your own eternity, my pains, wherein in the ages to come, men shall read your praises and give a shrewd guess at your virtues.

PATRON [*reading in the epistle dedicatory this sentence,* " Desolate eloquence and forlorn poetry, your most humble suppliants *in forma pauperum,*[1] lay prostrate at your dainty feet and adore your excellence, &c."] I do in some sort like this sentence, for in my days I have been a great favourer of scholars, but surely of late the *utensilia* of potions and purges have been very costly unto me. For my own part, I had not cared for dying, but when I am dead, I know not what will become of scholars ; hitherto I have besprinkled them prettily with the drops of my bounty.

[1] " In the guise of poor men."

INGENIOSO. Oh, your worship may be bold with yourself! No other tongue will be so niggard as to call those drops which indeed are plenteous showers, that so often have refreshed thirsty brains and sunburnt wits; and might it now please the cloud of your bounty to break, it never found a dryer soil to work upon, or a ground that will yield a more pleasant requital.

PATRON. Indeed these lines are pretty, and in time thou may'st do well. I have not leisure as yet to read over this book, yet, howsoever, I do accept of thy duty, and will do something if occasion serve; in the meantime, hold, take a reward. [*He gives him two groats.*] I tell thee Homer had scarce so much bestowed upon him in all his lifetime; indeed, our continuance is enough for a scholar, and the sunshine of our favour yields good heat of itself; howsoever, I am somewhat prodigal in that way, in joining gifts to my countenance; yet it is fit that all such young men as you are, should know that all duty is far inferior to our deserts, that in great humility do vouchsafe to read your labours. Well, my physic works; I cannot stay to take a full sight of your pamphlet; hereafter I will look on it, and at my better leisure, and in my good discretion, favour you accordingly.

III. THE POET AT WORK

THOMAS DEKKER. Satiromastix or the Untrussing of the Humorous Poet, 1601. *In this passage Dekker is mocking Jonson, who had portrayed himself as Horace in his Poetaster a few weeks before.*

HORACE *is discovered sitting in his study, with a lighted candle beside him, and his books lying about in confusion. He is in the throes of composition.*

HORACE [*writing*]:
"To thee whose foreheads wells with roses,
Whose most haunted bower,
Gives life and scent to every flower,
Whose most adorèd name encloses

Things abstruse, deep, and divine,
Whose yellow tresses shine,
Bright as Eoan fire.
Oh me, thy priest, inspire!
For I to thee and thine immortal name,
[*As his inspiration flags.*] In—in—in golden tunes,
For I to thee and thine immortal name—
In—sacred raptures flowing, flowing, swimming, swimming.
In sacred raptures swimming,
Immortal name, game, dame, tame, lame, lame, lame,
Pux, hath, shame, proclaim, oh——
In sacred raptures flowing, will proclaim, not——
Oh me, thy priest, inspire!
For I to thee and thine immortal name,
In flowing numbers filled with spright and flame."
Good, good! "In flowing numbers filled with spright and flame."

IV. LITERARY SOCIETY IN DUBLIN

LODOVICK BRYSKETT. A Discourse of Civil Life, 1606. *Bryskett describes the origin of his book.*

Yet there is a gentleman in this company whom I have had often a purpose to entreat, that as his leisure might serve him, he would vouchsafe to spend some time with me to instruct me in some hard points which I cannot of myself understand; knowing him to be not only perfect in the Greek tongue, but also very well read in philosophy, both moral and natural. Nevertheless, such is my bashfulness, as I never yet durst open my mouth to disclose this my desire unto him, though I have not wanted some heartening thereunto from himself. For of love and kindness to me, he encouraged me long sithence to follow the reading of the Greek tongue, and offered me his help to make me understand it. But now that so good an opportunity is offered unto me, to satisfy in some sort my desire, I think I should commit a great fault, not to myself alone, but to all this company, if I should not enter my request thus far, as to move him to spend this time which we have now destined to familiar discourse and conversation, in declaring unto us the great benefits which men obtain by the knowledge of Moral Philosophy, and in making us to know what the same is, what be the parts thereof, whereby virtues are to be distinguished from vices ; and finally that he will be pleased to run over in such order as he shall think good, such and so many principles and rules thereof, as shall serve not only for my better instruction, but also for the contentment and satisfaction of you all. For I nothing doubt but that every one of you will be glad to hear so profitable a discourse and think the time very well spent wherein so excellent a knowledge shall be revealed unto you, from which every one may be assured to gather some fruit as well as myself.

"Therefore," said I, turning myself to M. Spenser, "it is you, sir, to whom it pertaineth to show yourself courteous now unto us all and to make us all beholding unto you for the pleasure and profit which we shall gather from your speeches, if you shall vouchsafe to open unto us the goodly cabinet, in which this excellent treasure of virtues lieth locked up from the vulgar sort. And thereof in the behalf of all, as for myself, I do most earnestly entreat you not to say us nay."

Unto which words of mine, every man applauding, most with like words of request and the rest with gesture and countenances expressing as much, M. Spenser answered in this manner.

"Though it may seem hard for me to refuse the request made by you all, whom every one alone I should for many respects be willing to gratify, yet as the case standeth, I doubt not but with the consent of the most part of you, I shall be excused at this time of this task which would be laid upon me, for sure I am, that it is not unknown unto you, that I have already undertaken a work tending to the same effect, which is in heroical verse under the title of a ' Faery Queen ' to represent all the moral virtues, assigning to every virtue a Knight to be the patron and defender of the same, in whose actions and feats of arms and chivalry and the operations of that virtue whereof he is the protector, are to be expressed, and the vices and unruly appetites that oppose themselves against the same, to be beaten down and overcome. Which work, as I have already well entered into, if God shall please to spare my life that I may finish it according to my mind, your wish, M. Bryskett, will be in some sort accomplished, though perhaps not so effectually as you could desire. And the same may very well serve for my excuse, if at this time I crave to be forborne in this your request, since any discourse that I might make thus on the sudden in such a subject would be but simple, and little to your satisfactions. For it would require good advisement and premeditation for any man to undertake the declaration of these points that you have proposed, containing in effect the ethic part of Moral Philosophy. Whereof, since I have taken in hand to discourse at large in my poem before spoken, I hope the expectation of that work may serve to free me at this time from speaking in that matter, notwithstanding your motion and all your entreaties. But I will tell you how I think by himself he may very well excuse my speech, and yet satisfy all you in this matter. I have seen (as he knoweth) a translation made by himself out of the Italian tongue of a dialogue comprehending all the ethic part of Moral Philosophy, written by one of those three he formerly mentioned, and that is by Giraldi, under the title of *A Dialogue of Civil Life*. If it please him to bring us forth that translation to be here read among us, or otherwise to deliver to us, as his memory may serve him, the contents of the same, he shall, I warrant you, satisfy you all at the full, and himself will have no cause but to think the time well spent in reviewing his labours, especially in the company of so many his friends, who may thereby reap much profit and the translation happily fare the better by some mending it may receive in the perusing, as all writings else may do by the often examination of the same. Neither let it trouble him that I so turn over to him again the task he would have put me to ; for it falleth out fit for him to verify the principal of all this apology, even now made for himself ; because thereby it will appear that he hath not withdrawn himself from service of the state to live idle or wholly private to himself, but hath spent some time in doing that which may greatly benefit others, and have served not a little to the bettering of his own mind and increasing his knowledge, though he for modesty pretend much ignorance, and plead want in wealth, much like some rich beggars, who either of custom, or for covetousness, go to beg of others those things whereof they have no want at home."

With this answer of M. Spenser's, it seemed that all the company were well satisfied, for after some few speeches whereby they had showed an extreme longing after his work of *The Faery Queen*, whereof some parcels had been by some of them seen, they all began to press me to produce my translation mentioned by M. Spenser that it might be perused among them ; or else that I should, as near as I could, deliver unto them the contents of the same, supposing that my memory would not much fail me in a thing so studied and advisedly set down in writing as a translation must be.

V. THE MERMAID TAVERN

Mr. Francis Beaumont's letter to Ben Jonson : written before he and Mr. Fletcher came to London with two of the precedent comedies, then not finished, which deferred their merry meetings at the " Mermaid," c. 1608. This famous poem, here quoted in full, describes the meetings of Jonson's literary set at the " Mermaid." Literary men knew each other personally and they criticized new work in the tavern and not in the review columns of the weeklies. Towards the end of the period, Jonson's literary set almost monopolized poetry. The Mermaid Tavern was in Bread Street, Cheapside.

The sun (which doth the greatest comfort bring
To absent friends, because the selfsame thing
They know, they see, however absent) is
Here our best haymaker (forgive me this !

It is our country's style). In this warm shine
I lie, and dream of your full Mermaid wine.
Oh, we have water mix'd with claret lees,
Drink apt to bring in drier heresies
Than beer, good only for the sonnet's strain,
With fustian metaphors to stuff the brain;
So mix'd, that, given to the thirstiest one,
'Twill not prove alms, unless he have the stone:
I think with one draught man's invention fades,
Two cups had quite spoil'd Homer's *Iliades*.
'Tis liquor that will find out Sutcliff's wit,
Lie where he will, and make him write worse yet.
Fill'd with such moisture, in most grievous qualms,
Did Robert Wisdom write his singing psalms;
And so must I do this; and yet I think
It is a potion sent us down to drink,
By special Providence, keeps us from fights,
Makes us not laugh when we make legs to knights.
'Tis this that keeps our minds fit for our states,
A medicine to obey our magistrates;
For we do live more free than you, no hate,
No envy at one another's happy state,
Moves us; we are all equal; every whit
Of land that God gives men here is their wit,
If we consider fully; for our best
And gravest man will with his main house jest,
Scarce please you; we want subtility to do
The city tricks, lie, hate and flatter too;
Here are none that can bear a painted show,
Strike when you wink, and then lament the blow;
Who, like mills set the right way for to grind,
Can make their gains alike with every wind; '
Only some fellows, with the subtlest pate
Amongst us, may perchance equivocate
At selling of a horse, and that's the most.
Methinks the little wit I had is lost
Since I saw you; for wit is like a rest
Held up at tennis, which men do the best

MEN OF LETTERS

With the best gamesters. What things have we seen
Done at the Mermaid! Heard words that have been
So nimble, and so full of subtle flame,
As if that every one from whence they came
Had meant to put his whole wit in a jest
And had resolved to live a fool the rest
Of his dull life; then when there hath been thrown
Wit able enough to justify the town
For three days past; wit that might warrant be
For the whole City to talk foolishly
Till that were cancell'd; and when that was gone,
We left an air behind us, which alone
Was able to make the two next companies
Right witty; though but downright fools, mere wise,
When I remember this, and see that now
The country gentlemen begin to allow
My wit for dry-bobs, then I needs must cry,
I see my days of ballading grow nigh;
I can already riddle, and can sing
Catches, sell bargains, and I fear shall bring
Myself to speak the hardest words I find,
Over as oft as any, with one wind,
That takes no medicines. But one thought of thee
Makes me remember all these things to be
The wit of our young men, fellows that show
No part of good, yet utter all they know;
Who, like trees of the garden, have growing souls,
Only strong Destiny, which all controls,
I hope hath left a better fate in store
For me thy friend, than to live ever poor,
Banish'd unto this home: Fate once again
Bring me to thee, who canst make smooth and plain
The way of knowledge for me, and then I,
Who have no good but in thy company,
Protest it will my greatest comfort be
To acknowledge all I have to flow from thee.
Ben, when these scenes are perfect, we'll taste wine:
I'll drink thy Muse's health, thou shalt quaff mine.

VI. A POT POET

JOHN EARLE. Microcosmography, 1628; No. 28 *in Irwin's edition. For a specimen of the pot poet's work see page* 143.

A POT POET
is the dregs of wit, yet mingled with good drink may have some relish. His inspirations are more real than others, for they do but feign a god, but he has his by him. His verse runs like the tap, and his invention, as the barrel, ebbs and flows at the mercy of the spiggot. In thin drink he aspires not above a ballad, but a cup of sack inflames him, and sets his Muse and nose a-fire together. The Press is his mint, and stamps him now and then a sixpence or two in reward of the baser coin his pamphlet. His works would scarce sell for three half-pence, though they are given oft for three shillings, but for the pretty title that allures the country gentleman; for which the printer maintains him in ale a fortnight. His verses are like his clothes miserable centoes and patches, yet their pace is not altogether so hobbling as an almanac's. The death of a great man or the burning of a house furnish him with an argument, and the nine Muses are out straight in mourning gowns, and Melpomene cries, "fire! fire!" He is a man now much employed in commendations of our navy, and a bitter inveigher against the Spaniard. His frequentest works go out in single sheets, and are chanted from market to market to a vile tune and a worse throat; whilst the poor country wench melts like her butter to hear them. And these are the stories of some men of Tyburn, or a strange monster out of Germany; or, sitting in a bawdy-house, he writes God's judgments. He drops away at last in some obscure painted cloth, to which himself made the verses, and his life, like a can too full, spills upon the bench. He leaves twenty shillings on the score, which my hostess loses.

VII. TO MY BOOKSELLER

BEN JONSON. Epigrams, 1616.

Thou that mak'st gain thy end, and wisely well,
Call'st a book good or bad, as it doth sell,
Use mine so too ; I give thee leave ; but crave
For the luck's sake, it thus much favour have,
To lie upon thy stall till it be sought ;
Not offered, as it made suit to be bought ;
Nor have my title-leaf on posts or walls,
Or in cleft-sticks, advanced to make calls
For termers, or some clerk-like serving-man,
Who scarce can spell th' hard names ; whose knight less can.
If, without these vile arts, it will not sell,
Send it to Bucklersbury,[1] there 'twill well.

VIII. THE CHARACTER OF BEN JONSON

WILLIAM DRUMMOND of Hawthornden. *Conversations with Ben Jonson*, 1619 ; *Vol. I, page 151 in Herford and Simpson's edition of Jonson's works. Ben Jonson visited Drummond when he made his journey on foot to Scotland in 1618–19. His " Conversations " were recorded by Drummond, who added this character of his guest.*

He is a great lover and praiser of himself ; a condemner and scorner of others ; given rather to lose a friend than a jest ; jealous of every word and action of those about him (especially after drink, which is one of the elements in which he liveth) ; a dissembler of ill parts which reign in him, a bragger of some good that he wanteth ; thinketh nothing well but what either he himself or some of his friends and countrymen hath said or done. He is passionately kind and angry ; careless either to gain or keep ; vindictive, but, if he be well answered, at himself. For any religion, as being versed in both.

Interpreteth best sayings and deeds often to the worst. Oppressed with fantasy, which hath ever mastered his

[1] For the use of the grocer.

reason, a general disease in many poets. His inventions are smooth and easy, but above all, he excelleth in a translation.

IX. GABRIEL HARVEY ON ROBERT GREENE

GABRIEL HARVEY. Four Letters, 1592; *Vol. II, page 19 in the Bodley Head Quartos. Harvey had very rashly attacked Greene and his circle in print. Greene answered so abusively that Harvey proposed to go to law, but Greene died before any action could be taken and the quarrel was continued by Nashe. Harvey foolishly and maliciously published this letter after Greene's death. This account of his enemy's life, though cruel, was true enough, as can be seen from Greene's own* Repentance. *See page* 188.

I was altogether unacquainted with the man, and never once saluted him by name : but who in London hath not heard of his dissolute and licentious living ; his fond disguising of a Master of Art with ruffianly hair, unseemly apparel and more unseemly company ; his vainglorious and thrasonical braving ; his piperly extemporizing and tarletonizing ; [1] his apish counterfeiting of every ridiculous and absurd toy ; his fine cozening of jugglers, and finer juggling with cozeners ; his villainous cogging [2] and foisting ; his monstrous swearing and horrible forswearing ; his impious profaning of sacred texts ; his other scandalous and blasphemous raving ; his riotous and outrageous surfeiting ; his continual shifting of lodgings ; his plausible mustering and banqueting of roisterly acquaintance at his first coming ; his beggarly departing in every hostess's debt ; his infamous resorting to the Bankside, Shoreditch, Southwark, and other filthy haunts ; his obscure lurking in basest corners ; his pawning of his sword, cloak and what not, when money came short ; his impudent pamphletting, fantastical interluding and desperate libelling, when other cozening shifts failed ; his employing of Ball (surnamed, Cutting Ball) till he was intercepted at Tyburn, to levy a crew of his trustiest companions to guard him in danger of

[1] Jest mongering, like Tarleton, the famous clown.
[2] Cheating.

arrests; his keeping of the foresaid Ball's sister, a sorry ragged quean, of whom he had his base son, Infortunatus Greene; his forsaking of his own wife, too honest for such a husband; particulars are infinite; his condemning of superiors, deriding of other, and defying of all good order.

Compare base fellows and noble men together, and what in a manner wanted he of the ruffianly and variable nature of Catiline, or Antony, but the honourable fortunes of Catiline, and Antony? They that have seen much more than I have heard (for so I am credibly informed) can relate strange and almost incredible comedies of his monstrous disposition, wherewith I am not to infect the air or defile this paper. There be enough, and enough such histories, both dead and living; though youth be not corrupted, or age accloyed with this legendary. Truly I have been ashamed to hear some ascertained reports of his most woeful and rascal estate; how the wretched fellow, or shall I say the prince of beggars, laid all to gage for some few shillings, and was attended by lice, and would pitifully beg a penny pot of Malmesy; and could not get any of his old acquaintance to comfort, or visit him in his extremity, but Mistress Appleby, and the mother of Infortunatus. Alas, even his fellow writer, a proper young man, if advised in time, that was a principal guest at that fatal banquet of pickle herring, (I spare his name, and in some respects wish him well) came never more at him, but either would not, or happily could not, perform the duty of an affectionate and faithful friend. The poor cordwainer's [1] wife was his only nurse, and the mother of Infortunatus, his sole companion; but when Mistress Appleby came, as much to expostulate injuries with her, as to visit him. God help good fellows, when they cannot help themselves. Slender relief in the predicament of privations, and feigned habits. Miserable man, that must perish, or be succoured by counterfeit or impotent supplies.

I once bemoaned the decayed and blasted estate of M. Gascoigne, who wanted not some commendable parts of

[1] Shoemaker.

conceit and endeavour, but unhappy M. Gascoigne, how lordly happy, in comparison of most unhappy M. Greene ! He never envied me so much as I pitied him from my heart, especially when his hostess Isam, with tears in her eyes and sighs from a deeper fountain (for she loved him dearly) told me of his lamentable begging of a penny pot of Malmesy, and sir reverence, how lowsy he and the mother of Infortunatus were (I would her surgeon found her no worse than lowsy) and how he was fain, poor soul, to borrow her husband's shirt whiles his own was a-washing, and how his doublet and hose and sword were sold for three shillings ; and beside the charges of his winding sheet, which was four shillings, and the charges of his burial yesterday in the new churchyard near Bedlam, which was six shillings and fourpence, how deeply he was indebted to her poor husband, as appeared by his own bond of ten pounds, which the good woman kindly showed me, and beseeched me to read the writing beneath, which was a letter to his abandoned wife, in the behalf of his gentle host, not so short as persuasible in the beginning and pitiful in the ending.

"Doll, I charge thee by the love of our youth and by my soul's rest, that thou wilt see this man paid ; for if he and his wife had not succoured me, I had died in the streets. —ROBERT GREENE."

X. JONSON ON SHAKESPEARE

BEN JONSON. Discoveries, *pub.* 1640; *Vol. V, page* 28 *in the Bodley Head Quartos.*

I remember the players have often mentioned it as an honour to Shakespeare, that in his writing (whatsoever he penn'd) he never blotted out line. My answer hath been, would he had blotted a thousand ! which they thought a malevolent speech. I had not told posterity this, but for their ignorance, who choose that circumstance to commend their friend by, wherein he most faulted. And to justify mine own candour, for I lov'd the man, and do honour his memory, on this side Idolatry, as much as any. He was, indeed, honest, and of an open and free nature; had an excellent fantasy, brave notions and gentle expressions, wherein he flowed with that facility, that sometime it was necessary he should be stopp'd: *Sufflaminandus erat*,[1] as Augustus said of Haterius. His wit was in his own power; would the rule of it had been so too. Many times he fell into those things could not escape laughter, as when he said in the person of Caesar, one speaking to him, "Caesar, thou dost me wrong." He replied, "Caesar did never wrong, but with just cause"; and such-like, which were ridiculous. But he redeemed his vices with his virtues. There was ever more in him to be praised, than to be pardoned.

XI. THE OLD POET REMEMBERS HIS YOUTH

MICHAEL DRAYTON, Elegies upon Sundry Occasions, 16; *page* 108 *in Brett's edition*.

My dearly loved friend, how oft have we
In winter evenings, meaning to be free,
To some well chosen place used to retire;
And there with moderate meat, and wine, and fire,
Have passed the hours contentedly with chat;
Now talk of this, and then discours'd of that,
Spoke our own verses 'twixt ourselves, if not
Other men's lines, which we by chance had got,
Or some stage pieces famous long before,
Of which your happy memory had store;
And I remember you much pleased were
Of those who lived long ago to hear,
As well as of those, of these latter times,
Who have enriched our language with their rhymes,
And in succession, how still up they grew,
Which is the subject that I now pursue;
For, from my table,[2] you must know that I
Was still inclined to noble poesy,
When that once *Pueriles* I had read,
And newly had my *Cato* construed,

[1] "He had to be checked." [2] Exercise book.

In my small self I greatly marvell'd then,
Amongst all other, what strange kind of men
These poets were ; and pleased with the name,
To my mild tutor merrily I came,
(For I was then a proper goodly page,
Much like a pigmy, scarce ten years of age)
Clasping my slender arms about his thigh,
" O my dear master ! Cannot you," quoth I,
" Make me a poet ? do it if you can
And you shall see, I'll quickly be a man."
Who me thus answered smiling, " Boy," quoth he,
" If you'll not play the wag, but I may see
You ply your learning, I will shortly read
Some poets to you." Phoebus be my speed,
To't hard went I ; when shortly he began
And first read to me honest Mantuan,
Then Virgil's *Eclogues*, being enter'd thus,
Methought I straight had mounted Pegasus
And in his full career could make him stop,
And bound upon Parnassus' bi-cliffed top.
I scorned your ballad then, though it were done
And had for " Finis " William Elderton.
But soft, in sporting with this childish jest,
I from my subject have too long digressed,
Then to the matter that we have in hand
Jove and Apollo for the Muses stand.

XII. THE POETS' ELYSIUM

THOMAS DEKKER. A Knight's Conjuring, 1607.

One field there is among all the rest, set round about with willows ; it is called the Field of Mourning, and in this, upon banks of flowers that are withered away, even with the scorching sighs of those that sit upon them, are a band of malcontents ; they look for all the world like the mad folks in Bedlam, and desire like them to be alone, and these are forlorn lovers. . . .

Beyond all these places is there a grove which stands by

itself like an island; for a stream which makes music in the running clasps it round about like a hope girdle of crystal. Laurels grew so thick on all the banks of it that lightning itself, if it came thither, hath no power to pass through them. It seems, without, a desolate and unfrequented wood (for those within are retired unto themselves), but from them came forth such harmonious sounds that birds build nests only in the trees there to teach tunes to their young ones prettily. This is called the Grove of Bay Trees, and to this consort room resort none but the children of Phœbus —poets and musicians; the one creates the ditty and gives it the life or number, the other lends it voice and makes it speak music. When these happy spirits sit asunder their bodies are like so many stars; and when they join together in so many troops, they show like so many heavenly constellations. Full of pleasant bowers and quaint arbours is all this walk. In one of which old Chaucer, reverend for priority, blyth in cheer, buxom in his speech, and benign in his haviour, is circled round with all the makers or poets of his time, their hands leaning on one another's shoulders, and their eyes fixed seriously upon his, whilst their ears are all tied to his tongue by the golden chain of his numbers; for here, like Evander's mother, they spake all in verse; no Attic eloquence is so sweet; their language is so pleasing to the gods that they utter their oracles in no other.

Grave Spenser was no sooner entered into this chapel of Apollo but these elder fathers of the divine fury gave him a laurel and sung his welcome. Chaucer called him his son and placed him at his right hand. All of them, at a sign given by the whole choir of Muses that brought him hither, closing up their lips in silence, and tuning all their ears for attention to hear him sing out the rest of his Fairy Queen's praises.

In another compartment sat learned Watson, industrious Kyd, ingenious Atchlow, and though he had been a player, ennobled out of their pens and yet because he had been their lover a register to the Muses, inimitable Bentley; these were likewise carousing to one another at the holy well, some of them singing peans to Apollo, some of them hymns to the rest of the gods, whilst Marlowe, Greene and Peele had got under the shade of a large vine, laughing to see that Nashe, that was but newly come to their college, still haunted with the sharp and satirical vein that followed him here on earth; for Nashe inveighed bitterly as he was wont to do against dry-fisted patrons, accusing them of his untimely death, because if they had given his Muse that cherishment which she most worthily deserved he had fed to his dying day on fat capons, burnt sack and sugar, and not so desperately have ventured his life and shortened his days by keeping company with pickle herrings. The rest asked him what news in the world; he told them that barbarism was now grown to be an epidemical disease, and more common than the toothache. Being demanded how poets and players agreed now, "Troth," says he, "as physicians and patients agree; for the patient loves the doctor no longer than till he gets his health, and the player loves the poet so long as the sickness lies in the twopenny gallery when no more will come into it. Nay," says he, "into so low a misery, if not contempt, is the sacred art of poesy fallen that though a writer, who is worthy to sit at the table of the sun, waste his brains to earn applause from the more worthy spirits, yet when he has done his best he works but like Ocnus that makes ropes in hell; for as he twists an ass stands by and bites them in sunder, and that ass is no other than the audience with hard hands."

He had no sooner spoken this, but in comes Chettle, sweating and blowing by reason of his fatness; to welcome whom, because he was of old acquaintance, all rose up and fell presently on their knees to drink health to all lovers of Helicon; in doing which they made such a noise that all this conjuring which is past (being but a dream) I suddenly started up and am now awake.

SECTION NINE

MOODS AND MANNERS

I. THE ITALIANATE

ROGER ASCHAM. The Schoolmaster, 1570; *p.132 in Mayor's edition. Moralists deplored the evil results which followed a visit to Italy, and the follies of the travelled gentleman are constantly satirized by dramatists. But statesmen took a wider view of the advantages of travel. See Bacon's essay* On Travel, *and page* 84.

But I am afraid that over many of our travellers into Italy do not eschew the way to Circes' Court, but go, and ride, and run, and fly thither; they make great haste to come to her; they make great suit to serve her; yea, I could point out some with my finger that never had gone out of England but only to serve Circes, in Italy. Vanity and vice, and any licence to ill living in England was counted stale and rude unto them. And so, being mules and horses before they went, returned very swine and asses home again; yet everywhere very foxes with subtle and busy heads, and, where they may, very wolves, with cruel, malicious hearts. A marvellous monster, which for filthiness of living, for dullness to learning himself, for wiliness in dealing with others, for malice in hurting without cause, should carry at once in one body, the belly of a swine, the head of an ass, the brain of a fox, the womb of a wolf. If you think we judge amiss, and write too sore against you, hear what the Italian sayeth of the Englishman, what the master reporteth of the scholar, who uttereth plainly what is taught by him, and what is learned by you, saying, *Englese Italianato, e un diabolo incarnato*,[1] that is to say, you remain men in shape and fashion but become devils in life and condition. This is not the opinion of one, for some private spite, but the judgment of all, in a common proverb, which riseth of that learning and those manners which you gather in Italy; a good schoolhouse of wholesome doctrine and worthy masters of commendable scholars, where the master had rather defame himself for his teaching, than not shame his scholar for his learning! A good nature of the master and fair conditions of the scholars! And now choose you, you Italian Englishmen, whether you will be angry with us for calling you monsters, or with the Italians, for calling you devils, or else with your own selves that take so much pains, and go so far, to make yourselves both. If some yet do not well understand what is an Englishman Italianated, I will plainly tell him. He that by living, and travelling in Italy, bringeth home into England out of Italy the religion, the learning, the policy, the experience, the manners of Italy. That is to say, for religion, Papistry or worse. For learning, less commonly than they carried out with them; for policy, a factious heart, a discoursing head, a mind to meddle in all men's matters; for experience, plenty of new mischiefs never known in England before; for manners, variety of vanities and change of filthy living. These be the enchantments of Circes, brought out of Italy, to mar men's manners in England; much, by example of ill life, but more by precepts of fond books, of late translated out of Italian into English, sold in every shop in London, commended by honest titles the sooner to corrupt honest manners; dedicated over boldly to virtuous and honourable personages, the easier to beguile simple and innocent wits. It is pity that those, which have authority and charge to allow and disallow books to be printed, be no more circumspect herein than they are. Ten sermons at Paul's Cross do not so much good for moving men to true doctrine, as one of those books do harm, with enticing men to ill living. Yea, I say further,

[1] "An Englishman Italianate is a devil incarnate."

those books tend not so much to corrupt honest living, as they do to subvert true religion. More papists be made by your merry books of Italy than by your earnest books of Louvain. And because our great physicians do wink at the matter and make no count of this sore, I, though not admitted one of their fellowship, yet having been many years a prentice to God's true Religion, and trust to continue a poor journeyman therein all days of my life, for the duty I owe, and love I bear, both to true doctrine and honest living, though I have no authority to amend the sore myself, yet I will declare my good will, to discover the sore to others.

II. APING THE GREAT

BEN JONSON. Epigrams, 1616.

ON DON SURLY

Don Surly, to aspire the glorious name
Of a great man, and to be thought the same,
Makes serious use of all great trade he knows,
He speaks to men with a rhinocerote's nose,
Which he thinks great; and so reads verses too;
And that is done as he saw great men do.
He has tympanies [1] of business in his face,
And can forget men's names with a great grace.
He will both argue, and discourse in oaths,
Both which are great; and laugh at ill-made clothes,
That's greater yet; to cry his own up neat.
He doth at meals, alone, his pheasant eat,
Which is main greatness, and at his still board,
He drinks to no man; that's, too, like a lord.
He keeps another's wife, which is a spice
Of solemn greatness; and he dares at dice
Blaspheme God greatly, or some poor hind beat,
That breathes in his dog's way, and this is great.

[1] Swellings.

Nay, more, for greatness' sake, he will be one
May hear my epigrams, but like of none.
Surly, use other arts, these only can
Style thee a most great fool, but no great man.

III. HOW TO BECOME A GENTLEMAN

BEN JONSON. Every Man Out of his Humour, 1599; *Act I, Scene 1.*

SOGLIARDO, *who would be a gentleman, consults* CARLO BUFFONE.

SOGLIARDO. Now look you, Carlo : this is my humour now ! I have land and money, my friends left me well, and I will be a gentleman whatsoever it cost me.

CARLO. A most gentlemanlike resolution.

SOGLIARDO. Tut ! an I take an humour of a thing once, I am like your tailor's needle, I go through : but, for my name, signior, how think you ? will it not serve for a gentleman's name, when the "signior" is put to it, ha ?

CARLO. Let me hear ; how is it ?

SOGLIARDO. Signior Insulso Sogliardo : methinks it sounds well.

CARLO. Oh, excellent ! tut ! an all fitted to your name, you might very well stand for a gentleman : I know many Sogliardos gentlemen.

SOGLIARDO. Why, and for my wealth I might be a Justice of Peace.

CARLO. Ay, and a constable for your wit.

SOGLIARDO. All this is my lordship you see here, and those farms you came by.

CARLO. Good steps to gentility too, marry ; but, Sogliardo, if you affect to be a gentleman indeed, you must observe all the rare qualities, humours, and compliments of a gentleman.

SOGLIARDO. I know it, signior, and if you please to instruct, I am not too good to learn, I'll assure you.

CARLO. Enough, sir—I'll make admirable use in the

projection of my medicine upon this lump of copper here.
[*Aside.*] I'll bethink me for you, sir.

SOGLIARDO. Signior, I will both pay you, and pray you, and thank you, and think on you.

MACILANTE [*who stands apart observing these two*]. 'Sblood,
why should such a prickeared hind as this
Be rich, ha ? a fool ! such a transparent gull
That may be seen through ! wherefore should he have land,
Houses and lordships ? Oh, I could eat my entrails,
And sink my soul into the earth with sorrow.

CARLO. First, to be an accomplished gentleman, that is, a gentleman of the time, you must give over housekeeping in the country, and live altogether in the City amongst gallants ; where, at your first appearance, 'twere good you turned four or five hundred acres of your best land into two or three trunks of apparel—you may do it without going to a conjurer, and be sure you mix yourself still with such as flourish in the spring of the fashion, and are least popular ; study their carriage and behaviour in all ; learn to play at primero and passage, and ever (when you lose) have two or three peculiar oaths to swear by, that no man else swears : but, above all, protest in your play, and affirm, "upon your credit as you are a true gentleman", at every cast ; you may do it with a safe conscience, I warrant you.

SOGLIARDO. O admirable rare ! he cannot choose but be a gentleman that has these excellent gifts : more, more, I beseech you.

CARLO. You must endeavour to feed cleanly at your ordinary, sit melancholy, and pick your teeth when you cannot speak : and when you come to plays, be humorous, look with a good starched face, and ruffle your brow like a new boot, laugh at nothing but your own jests, or else as the noblemen laugh. That's a special grace, you will observe.

SOGLIARDO. I warrant you, sir.

CARLO. Ay, and sit on the stage and flout, provided you have a good suit.

SOGLIARDO. Oh, I'll have a suit only for that, sir.
CARLO. You must talk much of your kindred and allies.
SOGLIARDO. Lies! No, signior, I shall not need to do so. I have kindred in the City to talk of : I have a niece is a merchant's wife ; and a nephew, my brother Sordido's son, of the Inns of Court.
CARLO. Oh, but you must pretend alliance with courtiers and great persons: and ever when you are to dine or sup in any strange presence, hire a fellow with a great chain (though it be copper, it's no matter) to bring you letters, feigned from such a nobleman, or such a knight, or such a lady. "To their worshipful, right rare, and nobly qualified friend and kinsman, Signior Insulso Sogliardo " : give yourself style enough. And there, while you intend circumstances of news, or inquiry of their health, or so, one of your familiars, whom you must carry about you still, breaks it up, as 'twere in a jest, and reads it publicly at the table : at which you must seem to take as unpardonable offence as if he had torn your mistress's colours, or breathed upon her picture, and pursue it with that hot grace, as if you would advance a challenge upon it presently.
SOGLIARDO. Stay, I do not like that humour of challenge, it may be accepted ; but I'll tell you what's my humour now, I will do this : I will take occasion of sending one of my suits to the tailor's, to have the pocket repaired, or so ; and there such a letter as you talk of, broke open and all, shall be left : oh, the tailor will presently give out what I am, upon the reading of it, worth twenty of your gallants.
CARLO. But then you must put on an extreme face of discontentment at your man's negligence.
SOGLIARDO. Oh, so I will, and beat him too : I'll have a man for the purpose.
MACILANTE. You may ; you have land and crowns : O partial fate!
CARLO. Mass, well remembered, you must keep your men gallant at the first, fine pied liveries laid with good gold

lace : there's no loss in it ; they may rip it off and pawn it, when they lack victuals.

SOGLIARDO. By 'r Lady, that is chargeable, signior, 'twill bring a man in debt.

CARLO. Debt! why, that's the more for your credit, sir: it's an excellent policy to owe much in these days, if you note it.

SOGLIARDO. As how, good signior ? I would fain be a politician.

CARLO. Oh ! look where you are indebted any great sum, your creditor observes you with no less regard, than if he were bound to you for some huge benefit, and will quake to give you the least cause of offence, lest he lose his money. I assure you in these times, no man has his servant more obsequious and pliant, than gentlemen their creditors : to whom, if at any time you pay but a moiety, or a fourth part, it comes more acceptably than if you gave them a new-year's gift.

SOGLIARDO. I perceive you, sir : I will take up, and bring myself in credit, sure.

CARLO. Marry this, always beware you commerce not with bankrupts, or poor needy Ludgathians : they are imprudent creatures, turbulent spirits, they care not what violent tragedies they stir, nor how they play fast and loose with a poor gentleman's fortunes, to get their own. Marry, these rich fellows, that have the world, or the better part of it, sleeping in their counting-houses, they are ten times more placable, they ; either fear, hope, or modesty restrains them from offering any outrages : but this is nothing to your followers, you shall not run a penny more in arrearage for them, an you list, yourself.

SOGLIARDO. No ! how should I keep 'em then ?

CARLO. Keep 'em ! 'sblood, let them keep themselves, they are no sheep, are they ? What ! you shall come in houses, where plate, apparel, jewels, and divers other pretty commodities lie negligently scattered, and I would have those Mercuries follow me, I trow should remember they had not their fingers for nothing.

SOGLIARDO. That's not so good methinks.

CARLO. Why, after you have kept them a fortnight, or so, and showed them enough to the world, you may turn them away, and keep no more but a boy, it's enough.

SOGLIARDO. Nay, my humour is not for boys, I'll keep men, an I keep any; and I'll give coats, that's my humour: but I lack a cullisen.[1]

CARLO. Why now you ride to the City, you may buy one; I'll bring you where you shall have your choice for money.

SOGLIARDO. Can you, sir?

CARLO. Oh, ay: you shall have one take measure of you, and make you a coat of arms to fit you, of what fashion you will.

SOGLIARDO. By word of mouth, I thank you, signior: I'll be once a little prodigal in a humour, i' faith, and have a most prodigious coat.

IV. THE GULL

SIR JOHN DAVIES. Epigrams, c. 1593; *Vol. II, page 8 in Grosart's edition.*

OF A GULL

Oft in my laughing rimes, I name a Gull:
But this new term will many questions breed;
Therefore at first I will express at full,
Who is a true and perfect Gull indeed:
A Gull is he who fears a velvet gown,
And, when a wench is brave, dares not speak to her;
A Gull is he which traverseth the town
And is for marriage known a common woer;
A Gull is he which while he proudly wears
A silver-hilted rapier by his side,
Indures the lies and knocks about the ears,
Whilst in his sheath his sleeping sword doth bide;

[1] Badge.

A Gull is he which wears good handsome clothes,
And stands, in presence, stroking up his hair,
And fills up his unperfect speech with oaths,
But speaks not one wise word throughout the year:
But to define a Gull in terms precise—
A Gull is he which seems, and is not wise.

V. THE MELANCHOLIC HUMOUR

WILLIAM SHAKESPEARE. Hamlet, *c.* 1601; *Act III, Scene* 1.
The "melancholie humour", which took many forms, was analysed in great detail by Burton in The Anatomy of Melancholy, 1621. *With many it was a pose, but a genuine strain of disillusion and bitterness is noticeable in the literature of the first quarter of the seventeenth century. Hamlet's melancholy can be paralleled in many places, but it sums up most the chief causes of the prevailing bitterness.*

To be, or not to be, that is the question:
Whether 'tis nobler in the mind, to suffer
The slings and arrows of outrageous fortune;
Or to take up arms against a sea of troubles,
And by opposing end them? To die: to sleep;
No more; and, by a sleep, to say we end
The heart-ache, and the thousand natural shocks
That flesh is heir to, 'tis a consummation
Devoutly to be wish'd. To die, to sleep;
To sleep: perchance to dream: ay, there's the rub;
For in that sleep of death what dreams may come
When we have shuffled off this mortal coil
Must give us pause. There's the respect,
That makes calamity of so long life;
For who would bear the whips and scorns of time,
The oppressor's wrong, the proud man's contumely.
The pangs of despis'd love, the law's delay,
The insolence of office, and the spurns
That patient merit of the unworthy takes,
When he himself might his quietus make
With a bare bodkin? Who would fardels bear,
To grunt and sweat under a weary life,
But that the dread of something after death,

The undiscover'd country from whose bourn
No traveller returns, puzzles the will
And makes us rather bear those ills we have
Than fly to others that we know not of?
Thus conscience does make cowards of us all;
And thus the native hue of resolution
Is sicklied o'er with the pale cast of thought,
And enterprises of great pitch and moment
With this regard their currents turn awry,
And lose the name of action.

VI. THE DANCER

JOHN MARSTON. The Scourge of Villainy, 1599; *Vol. XIII, page* 105 *in the Bodley Head Quartos.*

Room for a capering mouth, whose lips ne'er stir
But in discoursing of the graceful slur.
Who ever heard spruce skipping Curio
E'er prate of aught but of the whirl on toe,
The turn above ground, Robrus' sprawling kicks,
Fabius' caper, Harry's tossing tricks?
Did ever any ear e'er hear him speak
Unless his tongue of cross-points did entreat?
His teeth do caper whilst he eats his meat,
His heels do caper whilst he takes his seat;
His very soul, his intellectual
Is nothing but a mincing capreal.
He dreams of toe-turns, each gallant he doth meet
He fronts him with a traverse in the street.
Praise but Orchestra, and the skipping art,
You shall command him, faith you have his heart
Even cap'ring in your fist. A hall, a hall!
Room for the spheres, the orbs celestial
Will dance Kempe's jig: they'll revel with neat jumps;
A worthy poet hath put on their pumps.
O wit's quick traverse, but *sance ceo's* slow;
Good faith 'tis hard for nimble Curio.

VII. DRESS

WILLIAM HARRISON. A Description of England, 1577; *page* 108 *in* Furnival.

For my part, I can tell better how to inveigh against the enormity than describe any certainty of our attire ; since such is our mutability, that to-day there is none to the Spanish guise, to-morrow the French toys are most fine and delectable, ere long no such apparel as that which is after the high Almain [1] fashion, by and by the Turkish manner is generally best liked of, otherwise the Morisco [2] gowns, the Barbarian fleeces, the mandilion [3] worn to Colley Weston ward,[4] and the short French breeches make such a comely vesture that, except it were a dog in a doublet, you shall not see any so disguised as are my countrymen of England. And as these fashions are diverse, so likewise it is a world to see the costliness and the curiosity, the excess and the vanity, the pomp and the bravery, the change and the variety, and finally the fickleness and the folly, that is in all degrees, insomuch that nothing is more constant in England than inconsistency of attire. Oh, how much cost is bestowed nowadays upon our bodies, and how little upon our souls ! How many suits of apparel hath the one, and how little furniture hath the other ! How long time is asked in decking up of the first, and how little space left wherein to feed the latter ! How curious, how nice also, are a number of men and women, and how hardly can the tailor please them in making it fit for their bodies ! How many times must it be sent back again to him that made it ! What chafing, what fretting, what reproachful language, doth the poor workman bear away ! [5] And many times when he doth nothing to it at all, yet when it is brought home again it is very fit and handsome ; then must we put it on, then must the long seams of our hose be set by a plumb-line, then we puff, then we blow, and finally sweat

[1] High German.   [2] Moorish.
[3] Soldier's cloak.   [4] Hitched over the shoulder.
[5] Cf. *The Taming of the Shrew*.

16

till we drop, that our clothes may stand well upon us. I will say nothing of our heads, which sometimes are polled,[1] sometimes curled, or suffered to grow at length like woman's locks, many times cut off, above or under the ears, round as by a wooden dish. Neither will I meddle with our variety of beards, of which some are shaven from the chin like those of Turks, not a few cut short like to the beard of Marquess Otto, some made round like a rubbing brush, others with a pique de vant [2] (O fine fashion !), or now and then suffered to grow long, the barbers being grown to be so cunning in this behalf as the tailors. And therefore if a man have a lean and straight face, a Marquess Otto's cut will make it broad and large ; if it be platter-like, a long slender beard will make it seem the narrower ; if he be weasel-becked,[3] then much hair left on the cheeks will make the owner look big like a bowdled hen,[4] and as grim as a goose, if Cornelis of Chelmsford say true. Many old men do wear no beards at all. Some lusty courtiers also and gentlemen of courage do wear rings of gold, stones or pearl in their ears, whereby they imagine the workmanship of God not to be a little amended. But herein they rather disgrace than adorn their persons, as by their niceness in apparel, for which I say most nations do not unjustly deride us, as also for that we do seem to imitate all nations round about us, wherein we be like to the polypus or chameleon. . . . In women also it is most to be lamented that they do now far exceed the lightness of our men (who nevertheless are transformed from the cap even to the very shoe), and such staring attire as in time past was supposed meet for none but light housewives only, is now become a habit for chaste and sober matrons. What should I say of their doublets with pendant codpieces,[5] of the breast full of jags and cuts, and sleeves of sundry colours ? Their galligascons [6] to bear out their bums and make them their attire to fit plum round (as they term it) about them. Their fardingals,[7] and diversely

[1] Close cut.
[2] Calf's tail.
[3] With a face like a weasel.
[4] With feathers ruffled.
[5] The opening in the hose.
[6] Breeches.
[7] Petticoats.

coloured nether stocks [1] of silk, jersey,[2] and such-like, whereby their bodies are rather deformed than commended? I have met with some of these trulls [3] in London so disguised that it hath passed my skill to discern whether they were men or women.

VIII. FOLLIES AND FASHIONS

JOHN LANE. Tom Tell-Troth's Message, 1600; *page* 120 *in the New Shakespeare Society's reprint.*

Ambitious thoughts, hearts haughty, minds aspiring,
Proud looks, fond gaits, and what not undiscreet,
As servants wait, men's body still atiring
With far fetched gewgaws for young children meet:
    Wherewith whilst they themselves do daily deck,
    Bravado-wise, they scorn to brook the check.

Some covet winged sleeves like Mercury,
Others, round hose much like to Fortune's wheel
(Noting thereby their own unconstancy),
Some wear short cloaks, some cloaks that reach their heel.
    These apish tricks used in their daily weeds,[4]
    Betray fantastic thoughts, fond words, foul deeds.

Bold Bettris braves and brags it in her wires,
And busked [5] she must be, or not bust at all,
Their riggish [6] heads must be adorned with tires,
With periwigs, or with a golden caul.[7]
    Tut, tut, 'tis nothing in th' Exchange to change
    Monthly, as doth the moon, their fashions strange.

It seems, strange birds in England now are bred,
And that rare fowls in England build their nest,
When Englishmen with plumes adorn their head,
As with a cock's comb or a peacock's crest.
    These painted plumes, men in their caps do wear,
    And women in their hands do trickly bear.

---

[1] Stockings.   [2] Worsted.   [3] Loose women.
[4] Clothes.   [5] Corsetted.   [6] Wanton.   [7] Hair-net.

Perhaps some women being foul, do use
Fowl's feathers to shroud their deformity.
Others perchance these plumes do rather choose,
From weather and wind to shield their physnomy.
    But whilst both men and women use these feathers,
    They are deem'd light as feathers, wind and weathers.

Some dames are pump'd, because they live in pomp,
That with Herodias they might nimbly dance,
Some in their pantophels[1] too stately stomp,
And most in corked shoes do nicely prance.
    But here I doubtful stand, whether to blame
    The shoemakers, or them that wear the same. . . .

A painter lately with his pencil drew
The picture of a Frenchman and Italian,
With whom he placed the Spaniard, Turk and Jew;
But by himself he sat the Englishman.
    Before these laughing, went Democritus,
    Behind these weeping, went Heraclitus.

All these in comely vestures were attired,
According to the custom of their land,
The Englishman excepted, who desired
With other feathers, like a jay to stand.
    Thus, whilst he seeketh foreign bravery,
    He is accused of unconstancy.

Some call him ape, because he imitates:
Some fool, because he fancies every bauble;
Some liken him to fishes caught with baits,
Some to the wind, because he is unstable.
    Then blame him not, although 'gainst Englishmen,
    This Englishman writ with his plaintive pen.

[1] Slippers.

IX. THESE DEGENERATE DAYS

BARNABE RICHE. Riche his Farewell to the Military Profession, 1581 ; *page 10 in the Shakespeare Society reprint.*

To become a courtier, there is as little gains to be gotten ; for liberality, who was wont to be a principal officer as well in the Court as in the country, by whose means well doing could never go unrewarded, is turned Jack out to Office, and others appointed to have the custody of him, to hold him short, that he range no more abroad, so that no man can speak with him ; and they say the poor gentleman is so fleeced from time to time by those that be his keepers, that he hath nothing to give that is good but it falls to their shares.

To become a student in the law, there are such a number of them already, that he thinks it is not possible that one of them should honestly thrive by another ; and some will say that one lawyer and one goshawk were enough in one shire. But of my conscience, there are more lawyers in some one shire in England, with attorneys, solicitors, or as they are termed, brokers of causes, or pettifoggers, than there are goshawks in all Norway.

To become a merchant, traffic is so dead by means of these foreign broils, that unless a man would be a thief to his country, to steal out prohibited wares, there were small gains to be gotten.

To become a farmer, lands be so racked at such a rate that a man should but toil all the days of his life to pay his landlord's rent.

But what occupation, or handy craft might a man then follow to make himself rich, when every science depends upon new-fangled fashions ? For he that to-day is accompted for the finest workman, within one month some new found fellow comes out with some new found fashion, and then he bears the prize, and the first accompted but a bungler ; and within another month after, the second shall be served with the same sauce, and thus there is no artificer that can hold his credit long.

Such is the miserable condition of this our present time. This is the course of the world, but especially here in England, where there is no man thought to be wise but he that is wealthy; where no man is thought to speak truth but such as can lie, flatter and dissemble; where there is no advice allowed for good but such as tendeth more for gain than for glory; and what pinching for a penny that should be spent in our country's defence! How prodigal for a pound to be spent upon vanities and idle devices! What small recompense to soldiers, that fight with foes for their country's quiet! How liberal to lawyers that set friends at defiance, and disquiet a whole commonwealth! What fawning upon him whom fortune doth advance! What frowning upon him whom she hath brought low! What little care of the poor, and such as be in want! What feasting of the rich and such as be wealthy! What sumptuous houses built by men of mean estate! What little hospitality kept from high and low degree!

X. THESE DEGENERATE DAYS

BEN JONSON. Discoveries, 1640; *Vol. V, page 15 in the Bodley Head Quartos.*

The time was, when men would learn and study good things, not envy those that had them. Then men were had in price for learning; now, letters only make men vile. He is upbraidingly called a poet, as if it were a most contemptible nickname. But the professors, indeed, have made the learning cheap. Railing and tinkling rhymers, whose writings the vulgar more greedily read, as being taken with the scurrility and petulancy of such wits. He shall not have a reader now unless he jeer and lie. It is the food of men's natures; the diet of the times! Gallants cannot sleep else. The writer must lie, and the gentle reader rests happy to hear the worthiest works misinterpreted, the clearest actions obscured, the innocentest life traduced. And in such a licence of lying, a field so fruitful of slanders, how can there be matter wanting to his laugh-

ter? Hence comes the Epidemical Infection. For how
can they escape the contagion of the writings, whom the
virulency of the calumnies hath not stay'd off from reading?

XI. THE NEEDY BORE

JOHN DONNE. Satires, *c.* 1594; *from the fourth Satire.*

Well; I may now receive, and die. My sin
Indeed is great, but yet I have been in
A purgatory, such as fear'd hell is
A recreation and scant map of this.
My mind, nor with pride's itch, nor yet hath been
Poison'd with love to see, or to be seen.
I had no suit there, nor new suit to show,
Yet went to Court; but as Glaze which did go
To Mass in jest, catch'd, was fain to disburse
The hundred marks, which is the statute's curse,
Before he 'scaped; so't pleased my destiny—
Guilty of my sin in going—to think me
As prone to all ill, and of good as forget-
Full, as proud, lustful, and as much in debt,
As vain, as witless, and as false as they
Which dwell in Court, for once going that way.
Therefore I suffer'd this; towards me did run
A thing more strange, than on Nile's slime the sun
E'er bred, or all which into Noah's ark came;
A thing which would have posed Adam to name;
Stranger than seven antiquaries' studies,
Than Afric's monsters, Guiana's rarities;
Stranger than strangers; one, who for a Dane,
In the Danes' massacre had sure been slain,
If he had lived then; and without help dies,
When next the 'prentices 'gainst strangers rise;
One, whom the watch, at noon, lets scarce go by;
One, to whom th' examining justice sure would cry,
"Sir, by your priesthood, tell me what you are."
His clothes were strange, though coarse and black, though
    bare;

Sleeveless his jerkin was, and it had been
Velvet, but 'twas now—so much ground was seen—
Become tufftaffety; and our children shall
See it plain rash awhile, then naught at all.
The thing hath travell'd, and, faith, speaks all tongues,
And only knoweth what to all states belongs.
Made of th' accents and best phrase of all these,
He speaks one language. If strange meats displease,
Art can deceive, or hunger force my taste,
But pedants' motley tongue, soldiers' bombast,
Mountebanks' drug-tongue, nor the terms of law
Are strong enough preparatives, to draw
Me to bear this, yet I must be content
With his tongue, in his tongue, called compliment;
In which he can win widows, and pay scores,
Make men speak treason, cozen subtlest whores,
Outflatter favourites, or outlie either
Jovius, or Surius, or both together.
He names me, and comes to me; I whisper, "God!
How have I sinn'd, that Thy wrath's furious rod,
This fellow, chooseth me?" He saith, "Sir,
I love your judgment; whom do you prefer,
For the best linguist?" And I sillily
Said, that I thought Calepine's dictionary . . .

He, like to a high-stretched lute-string, squeak'd, "Oh, sir,
'Tis sweet to talk of kings." "At Westminster,"
Said I, "the man that keeps the Abbey tombs,
And for his price doth with whoever comes
Of all our Harrys and our Edwards talk,
From king to king, and all their kin can walk.
Your ears shall hear naught but kings; your eyes meet
Kings only; the way to it is King's Street."
He smack'd and cried, "He's base, mechanic, coarse,
So are all your Englishmen in their discourse.
Are not your Frenchmen neat? Mine, as you see,
I have but one, sir, look—he follows me."

"Certes they're neatly clothed. I of this mind am,
Your only wearing is your grogaram."
"Not so, sir, I have more." Under this pitch
He would not fly; I chafed him. But as itch
Scratched into smart, and as blunt iron, ground
Into an edge, hurts worse; so. I, fool, found
Crossing hurt me. To fit my sullenness,
He to another key his style doth dress,
And asks, "What news?" I tell him of new plays.
He takes my hand, and as a still which stays
A semi-breve, 'twixt each drop, he niggardly,
As loth to enrich me, so tells many a lie,
More than ten Holinsheds, or Halls, or Stows,[1]
Of trivial household trash. He knows; he knows
When the Queen frowned, or smiled, and he knows what
A subtle statesman may gather of that;
He knows who loves whom; and who by poison
Hastes to an office's reversion;
He knows who hath sold his land, and now doth beg,
A licence, old iron, boots, shoes, and egg-
Shells to transport; shortly boys shall not play
At span-counter,[2] or blow-point,[3] but shall pay
Toll to some courtier; and wiser than all us,
He knows what lady is not painted. Thus
He with home meats cloys me. I belch, spew, spit,
Look pale, and sickly, like a patient, yet
He thrusts on more; and as he'd undertook
To say Gallo-Belgicus without book,
Speaks of all states and deeds that have been since
The Spaniards came, to the loss of Amiens.
Like a big wife, at sight of loathèd meat,
Ready to travail, so I sigh and sweat
To hear this Macaron talk. In vain; for yet,
Either my humour, or his own to fit,
He, like a privileged spy, whom nothing can
Discredit, libels now 'gainst each great man.

[1] Three famous chroniclers. [2] Shove-halfpenny.
[3] Push-pin.

He names a price for every office paid;
He saith our wars thrive ill, because delay'd;
That offices are entail'd, and that there are
Perpetuities of them, lasting as far
As the Last Day; and that great officers
Do with the pirates share, and Dunkirkers . . .

                Therefore to my power
Toughly and stubbornly I bear this cross; but th' hour
Of mercy now was come; he tries to bring
Me to pay a fine to 'scape his torturing,
And says, "Sir, can you spare me——"—I said, "Willingly."
"Nay, sir, can you spare me a crown?" Thankfully I
Gave it, as ransom; but as fiddlers, still,
Though they be paid to be gone, yet needs will
Thrust one more jig upon you; so did he
With his long complimental thanks vex me.
But he is gone, thanks to his needy want,
And the prerogative of my crown; scant
His thanks were ended, when I—which did see
All the Court fill'd with more strange things than he—
Ran from thence with such, or more haste than one
Who fears more actions doth haste from prison.

THE ENVOI

WILLIAM SHAKESPEARE. Hamlet, c. 1601; *Act II, Scene 2.*

What a piece of work is a man! how noble in reason! how infinite in faculty! in form and moving how express and admirable! in action how like an angel! in apprehension how like a God! the beauty of the world! the paragon of animals!

INDEX

actors, 67, 138
alchemy, 76
angling, 165
Ankor, 154-5
apothecaries, 120
archery, 128, 163
aviaries, 154

barbers, 88, 121
ballads, 143
ballad singers, 126
Bartholomew Fair, 128, 185
bearbaiting, 139
beards, 226
Beaumont, 203
beds, 148
Bobadill, 107
Book of Resolution, 190
books, advertising, 207
bow, 163
bowls, 164
Burbage, 67

Carey, 11-13, 13-15
Carr, R., Earl of Somerset, 16, 19-23
Cecil, 33, 42
Chamberlain, 57
" Characters," 36, 87, 173, 206
Chaucer, 213
Chettle, 214
chimneys, 148
Church of England, 173
Church papist, 173, 231
College at Rome, 179-82
Comedy of Errors, 74

commodities, 108
Corin, 158
Coryat, 84, 90
Corydon and Phyllida, 6
Counters, The, 126
coursing, 156
country life, 157, 158, 160, 203
court life, 158, 159
cross-bow, 164
Curtain Theatre, 138

dancing, 224
daughters, education of, 81
degeneracy of the times, 229, 230
debts, payment of French, 42
degree, 30
dress, 16, 18, 88, 215, 227
Drayton, 211
drinking, 162, 169-71
drunkenness, 130
Duke Humphrey, 116

eating, 168-70
Elizabeth, Princess, 23-8, 28
Elizabeth, Queen, 1, 5, 11, 34
Elvetham, royal visit to, 3-8
English language, 191
Epithalamium, 195
Essex, Countess of, 19
evil spirits, 195
Eyre, Simon, 94

factory, 92
Falstaff, 45
Faery Queen, 203
fairies, 191, 195

foist, 117-19
food, 7
fountains, 152

Garnet, 140
gentlemen, 218
Gorboduc, 134
Gracious Street, 127
Gray's Inn, 93, 150
Greene, 208, 214
Grenville, 37-42
gulls, 222

Hakluyt, 105, 111
hare, 156
Harington, 15
Harvey, 208
Henry the Fifth, 137
hell-fire, 189, 190
herrings, 99
Hertford, Ld., 5

inns, 160
Inns of Court, 36, 73, 139, 229
inquisition, 174-79
Italianate English, 215

James, King, 14, 15-18, 25, 34
Jews, 90
Jonson, 199, 205, 207, 210

Kempe, 67
knight of post, 116

Latin grammar lesson, 64, 75
London, alarms in, 57
luxury, increase of, 148

Machiavel, 32
Marlowe, 214
melancholy, 212, 223
Mermaid Tavern, 203
moneylenders, 108
music, 62

Nashe, 214
nip, 117-19
noblemen, 34

Overbury, murder of, 18

Page, Mr., 143
parsons, 61
patronage, 198
Paul's Walk, 115
Pavey, 138
people, 29
Plautus, 135
plague, 131-2
playgoers, 133, 138
plays, 132-3, 134-6, 136-7
poets, 198, 199, 206, 208, 210, 211, 230
priests, 140, 183
private tutor, 75
pronunciation, 62
pupils, 74
puritans, 76, 183, 185

quack healers, 119

recruiting, 45, 50
Revenge, 37-42
Romeo, 138

sailors, 101
scholars, 53, 55
school, 64
schoolmasters, 61, 64
seditions, causes of, 52, 53
Shakespeare, 210
sheep, 171
shoemakers, 94
Sidney, 8, 10, 11, 134
simony, 173
soldiers, 50, 80
Spenser, 200, 213
Stella, 8
students, 71, 179-82
Surly, 217

INDEX

tennis, 164
Terence, 135
tobacco, 107
toothache, 120, 121–4
Touchstone, 158
train-bands, 50
travellers, 84, 87, 88

unemployment, 53, 55
University behaviour, 71

Virginia, 103–5, 105–6

watch, 124
Westminster, 232
windows, 172
wines, 129, 170
Winwood, 42
wise woman, 193
wooden vessels, 149

PARLIN MEMORIAL LIBRARY
EVERETT, MASS.

Printed in the United
124852LV00004B/1